CW00410788

Othello

ARDEN EARLY MODERN DRAMA GUIDES

Series Editors:

Andrew Hiscock
University of Wales, Bangor, UK and Lisa Hopkins,
Sheffield Hallam University, UK

Arden Early Modern Drama Guides offer practical and accessible introductions to the critical and performative contexts of key Elizabethan and Jacobean plays. Each guide introduces the text's critical and performance history but also provides students with an invaluable insight into the landscape of current scholarly research through a keynote essay on the state of the art and newly commissioned essays of fresh research from different critical perspectives.

A Midsummer Night's Dream edited by Regina Buccola

Doctor Faustus edited by Sarah Munson Deats

King Lear edited by Andrew Hiscock and Lisa Hopkins

1 Henry IV edited by Stephen Longstaffe

'Tis Pity She's a Whore edited by Lisa Hopkins

Women Beware Women edited by Andrew Hiscock

Volpone edited by Matthew Steggle

The Duchess of Malfi edited by Christina Luckyj

The Alchemist edited by Erin Julian and Helen Ostovich

The Jew of Malta edited by Robert A. Logan

Macbeth edited by John Drakakis and Dale Townshend

Richard III edited by Annaliese Connolly

Twelfth Night edited by Alison Findlay and
Liz Oakley-Brown

The Tempest edited by Alden T. Vaughan and
Virginia Mason Vaughan

Further titles in preparation

Othello

A Critical Reader

Robert C. Evans

Bloomsbury Arden Shakespeare
An imprint of Bloomsbury Publishing Plc

B L O O M S B U R Y
LONDON • NEW DELHI • NEW YORK • SYDNEY

Bloomsbury Arden Shakespeare

An imprint of Bloomsbury Publishing Plc

Imprint previously known as Arden Shakespeare

50 Bedford Square	1385 Broadway
London	New York
WC1B 3DP	NY 10018
UK	USA

www.bloomsbury.com

BLOOMSBURY, THE ARDEN SHAKESPEARE and the Diana logo are trademarks of Bloomsbury Publishing Plc

First published 2015

© Robert C. Evans and contributors

Robert C. Evans has asserted his right under the Copyright, Designs and Patents Act, 1988, to be identified as author of this work.

All rights reserved. No part of this publication may be reproduced or transmitted in any form or by any means, electronic or mechanical, including photocopying, recording, or any information storage or retrieval system, without prior permission in writing from the publishers.

No responsibility for loss caused to any individual or organization acting on or refraining from action as a result of the material in this publication can be accepted by Bloomsbury or the author.

British Library Cataloguing-in-Publication Data
A catalogue record for this book is available from the British Library.

ISBN: HB: 978-1-4725-2037-1
PB: 978-1-4725-2036-4
ePDF: 978-1-4725-2039-5
ePub: 978-1-4725-2038-8

Library of Congress Cataloging-in-Publication Data
A catalog record for this book is available from the Library of Congress.

Typeset by Fakenham Prepress Solutions, Fakenham, Norfolk NR21 8NN

To Alvin Kernan,
encouraging teacher and generous mentor

CONTENTS

SERIES
INTRODUCTION

The drama of Shakespeare and his contemporaries has remained at the very heart of English curricula internationally and the pedagogic needs surrounding this body of literature have grown increasingly complex as more sophisticated resources become available to scholars, tutors and students. This series aims to offer a clear picture of the critical and performative contexts of a range of chosen texts. In addition, each volume furnishes readers with invaluable insights into the landscape of current scholarly research as well as including new pieces of research by leading critics.

This series is designed to respond to the clearly identified needs of scholars, tutors and students for volumes which will bridge the gap between accounts of previous critical developments and performance history and an acquaintance with new research initiatives related to the chosen plays. Thus, our ambition is to offer innovative and challenging guides that will provide practical, accessible and thought-provoking analyses of early modern drama. Each volume is organized according to a progressive reading strategy involving introductory discussion, critical review and cutting-edge scholarly debate. It has been an enormous pleasure to work with so many dedicated scholars of early modern drama and we are sure that this series will encourage you to read 400-year-old playtexts with fresh eyes.

Andrew Hiscock and Lisa Hopkins

ACKNOWLEDGEMENTS

I wish to thank the contributors for their diligence, dedication, expertise and good humour, but I especially wish to thank the General Editors for their kind encouragement and steady guidance, and particularly for their patience when unexpected delays arose. Finally, all of us are indebted to Nick Fawcett for his careful copyediting. Thanks are also due to Kelley Jeans for her help with the proofreading. And I can never sufficiently express my grattitude to the members of a special seminar (funded by the A. W. Mellon Foundation) who brought the play to life in ways I will never forget. Those were exemplary students in every respect.

I am grateful to Auburn University at Montgomery for providing research leave when, in perhaps the busiest year of my life, I needed it more than ever. Darren Harris-Fain (my department chair) Michael Burger (my dean), and Joe King, our provost, deserve special thanks.

My best students and closest colleagues have been invaluable sources of stimulation, but I owe most thanks, as always, to my wife, Ruth. Three goofy dogs – all of whom appeared, at various times, out of nowhere – have given us more joy and laughter than I can possibly say.

NOTES ON CONTRIBUTORS

Christopher Baker is Professor of English at Armstrong State University and a past president of the South Central Renaissance Conference. He is author of *Religion in the Age of Shakespeare*, editor of *Absolutism and the Scientific Revolution, 1600–1720: A Biographical Dictionary*, and an assistant editor of the forthcoming MLA Variorum edition of *Cymbeline*. His essays have appeared in *Milton Studies*, *Ben Jonson Journal*, *Comparative Drama*, *Studia Neophilologica*, *John Donne Journal*, *Journal of Modern Literature* and elsewhere.

Robert C. Evans is I. B. Young Professor of English at Auburn University at Montgomery. External awards include fellowships from the American Council of Learned Societies, the American Philosophical Society, the National Endowment for the Humanities, the UCLA Center for Medieval and Renaissance Studies, and the Folger, Huntington and Newberry Libraries. He is the author or editor of more than thirty books and of numerous essays.

Raphael Falco is a Professor of English at the University of Maryland, Baltimore County and held the 2012–13 Lipitz Professorship of the Arts, Humanities, and Social Sciences. He received his BA and MA from Columbia University and his PhD from New York University. His books include *Conceived Presences* (University of Massachusetts Press, 1994), *Charismatic Authority in Early Modern English Tragedy* (Johns Hopkins, 2000), and *Charisma and Myth* (Continuum/Bloomsbury, 2010).

Imtiaz Habib is a Professor of English at Old Dominion University, where he has been a Burgess Scholar and a Hixon Research Fellow. He is the author of several books and numerous articles on Shakespeare and on early modern English literature, culture and politics, including especially discourses of race.

Richard Harp is Chair of the English department at the University of Nevada, Las Vegas, and founding co-editor of the *Ben Jonson Journal* (Edinburgh University Press), which will publish a special issue in 2016 discussing the work of Jonson and Shakespeare. In addition to publications on Renaissance literature he has also published on modern Irish literature and on composition.

Lisa Hopkins is Professor of English at Sheffield Hallam University and co-editor of *Shakespeare*, the journal of the British Shakespeare Association, and of the Arden Early Modern Drama Guides. Her most recent publications include *Renaissance Drama on the Edge* (Ashgate, 2014), *Magical Transformation on the Early Modern Stage*, co-edited with Helen Ostovich (Ashgate, 2014), and *Essex: The Cultural Impact of an Elizabethan Courtier*, co-edited with Annaliese Connolly (Manchester University Press, 2013).

Steven Hrdlicka is a graduate student at the University of Nevada, Las Vegas, and expects to receive his PhD in 2016. His major academic fields are Medieval and Renaissance literature and rhetoric and composition. This is his first publication.

Alison V. Scott is a senior lecturer in English Literature at the University of Queensland in Australia where she teaches Shakespeare and early modern literature. Her publications include *Selfish Gifts: The Politics of Exchange and English Courtly Literature, 1580–1628* (Fairleigh Dickinson University Press, 2006) and *Literature and the Idea of Luxury in Early Modern England* (2015).

Matthew Steggle is Professor of English at Sheffield Hallam University. He has written three monographs on aspects of early modern drama; he was a Contributing Editor to *The Cambridge Works of Ben Jonson* (2012); and he has edited *Measure for Measure* for the *Norton Shakespeare*, 3rd edition (forthcoming 2016). He is co-editor of the ejournal *Early Modern Literary Studies*.

TIMELINE

1564: Birth of William Shakespeare in Stratford-upon-Avon.

1565: *Hecatommithi*, by the Italian writer Giraldi Cinthio, is published. It contains a novella that is the principal source of Shakespeare's *Othello*.

1567: *Certaine Tragicall Discourses of Bandello*, translated by Geoffrey Felton, is published. Discourse IV is a possible source of Shakespeare's *Othello*.

1570–3: Turkish forces take Cyprus from Venice, despite suffering a significant defeat at sea by a navy resourced by Western European forces in the Battle of Lepanto (1571).

1584: A French translation of Cinthio's novella appears; Shakespeare may have read it.

1592: A charter is issued that gives 53 London merchants a monopoly on English trade with Venice and Turkey. Shakespeare writes *Titus Andronicus*, which features a 'coal-black' and 'thick-lipp'd' villain (Aaron).

1599: Sir Lewis Lewkenor's *The Commonwealth and Government of Venice* is published. It influences both *Othello* and *The Merchant of Venice* (1596–7). The latter play features a 'tawny' Moor.

1600: An ambassador of the King of Barbary arrives in London. Some scholars believe that this North African Moor may have been one possible model for Shakespeare's Othello. In November, John Pory publishes an English translation of John Leo's *A Geographical Historie of Africa*, which is believed to have influenced Shakespeare's *Othello*. In late December, a charter gives 83 London merchants a monopoly on trade with Venice and Turkey.

1601: Philemon Holland's English translation of Pliny's *Historie of the World* appears and is a source for many details in Shakespeare's *Othello*. Efforts are made to expel 'negroes and blackamoors' from England.

Late 1601–autumn 1604: Possible period of composition of Shakespeare's *Othello*. Recent scholars tend to favour 1603–4.

1602: Efforts are made to return (to Barbary) a number of Moors serving on English ships.

1603: In March, Queen Elizabeth I dies. King James VI of Scotland becomes King James I of England. Richard Knolles's *Generall Historie of the Turkes* is published, from which Shakespeare may have borrowed details for his play.

1603–18: Shakespeare's *Othello* may possibly have been acted at the Globe, a public theatre, before its first recorded performance in late 1604 at the royal court. After 1604, it continued to be acted both at the open-air Globe and at the indoor Blackfriars theatres.

1604: The play receives its first recorded performance on 1 November at the royal banqueting house before King James.

1616: Shakespeare dies.

1618–42: *Othello* continues to be acted at the open-air Globe playhouse and at the indoor Blackfriars theatre until theatres in general are closed because of the Civil Wars.

1621: On 6 October, *The Tragedie of Othello, the moore of Venice* is registered on the Stationer's Register for possible publication.

1622: A quarto (pamphlet-sized) edition of the play appears and is attributed to William Shakespeare.

1623: The play appears in a longer, revised edition as part of the First Folio of Shakespeare's plays. This edition includes over a hundred and fifty more lines than the 1622 quarto. However, it also contains fewer stage directions than the quarto.

1630: A second quarto edition is published, based on the First Folio printing but including details from the first quarto edition.

1660–9: With the Restoration of the monarchy after the Civil Wars and Interregnum, theatres are reopened and *Othello* is one of many old plays revived and restaged. Performances occur during this period at The Cockpit, Drury Lane, and Bridges Street theatres. Nicholas Burt plays Othello; Iago is played by Walter Clunn and then Michael Mohun.

Circa 1674–82: The play is staged at the Drury Lane theatre with Charles Hart as Othello and Michael Mohun as Iago.

1682–1709: Thomas Betterton stars as Othello at Drury Lane, with Samuel Sandford as Iago until 1702.

1710–27: Barton Booth stars as Othello at Drury Lane.

1720–51: James Quin plays the title role at Lincoln's Inn Fields, with Colley Cibber as Iago.

1734–77: Charles Maclin plays Iago, with James Quin as Othello at the Haymarket theatre.

1745–6: David Garrick plays Othello for three performances at Drury Lane.

1747–75: Spranger Barry plays Othello at Drury Lane, with a variety of Iagos and with Susanna Cibber as Desdemona.

1771–94: Robert Bensley stars as Iago at Covent Garden.

1780–5: John Henderson stars as Iago at Covent Garden.

1785–1805: J. P. Kemble plays the title role at Drury Lane, with Sarah Siddons as Desdemona.

1803: 'Variorum' editions of Shakespeare's works begin to appear in the nineteenth century. Drawing upon a rich editorial tradition already established in the eighteenth century, they are designed to be detailed and scholarly.

1814–33: Edmund Kean plays Othello at Drury Lane, with various Iagos.

1816–51: W. C. Macready plays the title role, with various Iagos and Desdemonas at Covent Garden.

1826–71: Edwin Forrest plays Othello at the Bowery in New York.

1837–72: Samuel Phelps plays Othello at the Haymarket and at Sadler's Wells.

1860–73: Edwin Booth plays Othello at two different theatres in New York.

1886: A *New Variorum* edition of *Othello* is published, with numerous scholarly annotations.

1886–1921: Frank Benson plays Othello in Stratford-upon-Avon.

1889: Giuseppe Verdi's operatic version, *Otello*, appears.

1898: Ellen Terry plays Desdemona to Frank Cooper's Othello in Fulham.

1902–99: *Othello* is regularly staged in such prominent locations as London, New York, Stratford-upon-Avon,

Birmingham and Johannesburg, featuring a variety of actors and actresses.

1930: Paul Robeson, a black American actor, plays Othello in London, with Peggy Ashcroft as Desdemona.

1938: Ralph Richardson stars as Othello, with Laurence Olivier as Iago, in a production directed by Tyrone Guthrie at London's Old Vic.

1943: The black actor Paul Robeson plays Othello in an immensely popular New York production.

1952: Orson Welles directs and stars in a film of the play.

1956: Richard Burton and John Neville alternate the roles of Othello and Iago at the Old Vic.

1964: Laurence Olivier plays Othello at the Old Vic, with Frank Finlay and Maggie Smith as Desdemona. This version is released as a film in 1965.

1980–90: Major international productions are staged practically every single year during this decade, featuring such notable Othellos as Paul Scofield, Anthony Hopkins (in a television production for the BBC), James Earl Jones, Ben Kingsley, John Kani and Willard White. Notable Iagos include Bob Hoskins, Christopher Plummer and Ian McKellen.

1990: *Othello: An Annotated Bibliography* (compiled by Margaret Lael Mikesell and Virginia Mason Vaughan) appears, covering fifty years of scholarship on the play.

1995: The first major film of the play with a black Othello (Laurence Fishburne) appears, with Kenneth Branagh as Iago.

2001: A television adaptation appears, starring Eamonn Walker and Christopher Eccleston.

Introduction

Robert C. Evans

Othello has always been seen as one of Shakespeare's most important plays. It was the subject of more comments in the 1600s than any other Shakespearean tragedy, and today it can seem especially 'relevant'. Long considered one of his major tragic dramas (along with *Hamlet*, *King Lear* and *Macbeth*), it has come to seem increasingly significant in the past few decades because of its treatment of such timely issues as race, gender, homoeroticism and domestic relations. In the centuries since its first performances, it has generated intense reactions from audiences, readers and critics of all sorts, and the intensity of interest in the play has never, perhaps, been greater than it is today. Not all critics have completely admired *Othello*, but most readers and playgoers have found the work exceptionally powerful, the latter sometimes reacting in highly emotional ways. It is the one play by Shakespeare that has been most often adapted and transformed by other writers.[1]

Of the four 'great' tragedies, *Othello* is usually seen as the least political and even the least philosophical but also as the most domestic and personal. Othello, after all, is not a royal personage (unlike the lead characters in the other tragedies just mentioned). He was not even born in Venice but is instead an outsider, a hired hand, a highly competent and respected mercenary. Although the play's first act suggests that battles and martial heroism may prove to be the work's major themes, instead the focus quickly shifts to the private relationship between Othello and Desdemona. In this emphasis on a married couple, the 'great' tragedy that *Othello* most resembles is *Macbeth*. Yet *Othello* also, of course, features a particularly corrupt and cynical villain (Iago), who in many ways resembles Edmund from *King Lear*. Surely the presence of Iago is one reason this play has long been so successful, especially onstage. Iago's evil is both galling and appalling. He has always aroused particularly strong reactions in the theatre, and some actors consider Iago, not Othello, the play's best role.

Most scholarly discussions of *Othello* usually begin by trying to establish its date of composition. Suggestions have ranged from late 1601 to late 1604 and various other dates in between. Most recent editors favour later rather than earlier dates, but there is no real consensus. We do know that the play was performed at the royal court in November 1604, although it may have been performed before then in a public theatre (probably the Globe). Questions of dating are not of mere academic interest, because a date of composition can suggest the kinds of audiences, issues and cultural conditions Shakespeare may have had in mind as he wrote the work. Scholars are on much firmer ground when they discuss the various sources that either did or may have influenced the writing of the work. The main source, indisputably, was a sixteenth-century Italian novella by Giraldi Cinthio, which Shakespeare probably knew from the original text or possibly through translation. Knowing that Cinthio was Shakespeare's chief source gives us some real insight into his creative process, allowing us especially to see how his treatment of the same basic story differs from that of his main source. According to some students of the play, Shakespeare, unlike Cinthio, exalts and spiritualizes the love between Othello and Desdemona. Others argue that Othello is simultaneously both more and less credulous than he is in Cinthio's version and that this difference works to Shakespeare's advantage. Still other scholars note that Shakespeare gave much greater emphasis to some characters (especially Desdemona, Iago, Emilia, Bianca and Cassio) than Cinthio did and that Shakespeare also added several characters not in his Italian source (such as Roderigo and Brabantio). In general, the tendency in recent scholarship has been to stress, rather than underplay, the importance of Cinthio's novella as a source for Shakespeare's drama.

Scholars have also, necessarily, been much concerned with relations between the two surviving texts of *Othello* – the first a small 'quarto' pamphlet (1622), the second the text included in the massive 'first folio' of Shakespeare's works (1623). Various editors believe that both the quarto *and* the folio texts are flawed. In any case, word choices in the two versions sometimes differ in significant ways. Editors must choose which text to take as primary and/or how to combine them. It has sometimes been variously argued (1) that the 1622 quarto represented a copy, by a scribe, of Shakespeare's working manuscript; (2) that the 1623 folio version was based on a copy, by a scribe, of Shakespeare's own revision; and therefore (3) that the folio version is closer to Shakespeare's final intention than is the quarto. Some editors therefore use the quarto version as the basic text but include any changes made in the folio. The folio *Othello* is more than a hundred and fifty lines longer than the quarto and features more than a thousand differences in wording. Some commentators have argued that Shakespeare himself revised the play and that he used the revision as an opportunity to enhance the roles of both Desdemona and Emilia in the drama's final act.

Although it is by definition a 'tragedy', *Othello* has also been discussed in terms of various other genres or subgenres – that is, other particular *kinds* of literature. Many commentators see it as a sort of 'domestic' tragedy, emphasizing conflict within a home or family, especially between a married couple. Yet it has been suggested that although Othello seems an admirable hero at the start of the play, by the end he seems a figure from domestic comedy – jealous, betrayed by his wife, and the target of Iago's contempt. The whole play, in this sense, changes genres – beginning by seeming a happy comedy featuring a loving couple who defeat an irate father, but then making a generic move towards a kind of violent farce. Othello, according to this view, loses much of his earlier dignity and mainly becomes Iago's plaything. The play thus comes to resemble certain domestic tragedies of the time, such as *Arden of Faversham* and *A Warning for Fair Women*. In fact, Iago emerges as by far the most interesting figure of the play from the perspective of 'genre studies'. Scholars routinely compare him to the crafty, witty 'Vice' figures of traditional morality plays. Such characters often delighted in their clever evil, and Shakespeare had already created an especially memorable example of this kind of self-conscious schemer in the main character of his history play titled *Richard III*. Iago, like Richard, is so deliberately and self-consciously evil that he becomes the focus of our stunned fascination.

Of course, whatever specific kind (or kinds) of drama *Othello* is, its events are played out in an especially interesting setting. Venice in Shakespeare's day was particularly famous because of its republican form of government, its status as one of the world's leading commercial centres (an idea already reflected in the title of Shakespeare's earlier play *The Merchant of Venice*), and its symbolism as an outpost of Christianity in a part of the globe increasingly controlled by Islam. Venice was considered both a highly civilized city and a place famous for its allegedly loose sexual morals. Iago plays on this reputation as he tries to stoke Othello's jealousy and undermine Othello's trust in Desdemona. Othello, despite his many accomplishments and his enormous value to Venice as a military commander, is in many ways both a literal and figurative outsider. Iago preys on 'the Moor's' insecurities as a non-Venetian, insinuating repeatedly that Othello cannot trust Venetians in general and Venetian women (especially his wife) in particular. Ironically, of course, it is really *Iago* (himself a Venetian) whom Othello cannot and should not trust, but it is finally Iago whom Othello trusts the most. Othello lives just long enough to realize how thoroughly he has been deceived *by* Iago *about* Desdemona. The woman he ultimately considers the most disgusting example of Venetian hypocrisy is in fact the very best example of Venetian virtue.

Race has been an even more important topic of critical discussion than Venice. Usually, when alone or with Roderigo, Iago repeatedly refers to Othello as 'the Moor' and expresses racist contempt for Othello's dark skin and 'thick lips'. Is his racism widely shared in Venice? Is Venice a fundamentally racist city? Is Othello even black? These are issues that have been much discussed, especially in the last fifty years. Various experts have argued that Othello's skin colour is very black indeed. Others have maintained that Elizabethans used the word 'Moor' to refer both to Arabs and to 'blacks'. Some students of the play have argued that Brabantio, Iago and, eventually, even Othello himself assume that race-mixing is unnatural. For many readers, theatregoers, film viewers and academics, the issue of race now seems crucial. Yet Othello's dark skin, many believe, would have mattered very much not only to the characters in the play but also to Shakespeare's Elizabethan contemporaries.

Most readers and scholars assume that Venice is a thoroughly racist society, although some commentators have noted that the very earliest responses to *Othello* ignored the issue of race. Indeed, a case can be made that the play's only thoroughly racist characters are its obvious villain (Iago), his less-than-brilliant side-kick (Roderigo), and Desdemona's offended father, who apparently treats Othello well only up until the point when he realizes that 'the Moor' has married his daughter without permission. Brabantio's racist rhetoric in the play's first trial scene fails to persuade anyone, and indeed despite his colour Othello is valued and commended by almost everyone in the play *except* Iago, Roderigo, Brabantio and, eventually, Emilia. Perhaps one point of the play is that the Venetians' real, underlying racism surfaces when they no longer have any reason to hide it, although this would not explain the fact that almost no one except Emilia condemns Othello in racist terms as the play closes and as Desdemona lies murdered on her bed. In any case, race and racism are

crucial issues in practically any recent discussion of the play,
and they have long been crucial in staged performances,
particularly in racist societies. Whether the play itself is racist
or is instead an exposure and implied excoriation of racism
have also been much-debated issues.

Othello, the character at the heart of these controversies,
has been discussed in various ways. Is he noble? A 'noble
savage'? A credulous fool? An ultimately good man who, in
his own estimation, loved sincerely but irrationally? Various
critics, beginning with Thomas Rymer in the late 1600s,
have questioned whether Othello's motives seem credible,
but the play's many defenders have explained his motivations
in numerous plausible ways. To some, Othello seems very
complex (both strong and weak, both confident and insecure).
It has also been argued, for instance, that he usually decides
well when he trusts his instincts but decides badly when he
reasons excessively. Additionally, he has been seen by others
as a fundamentally noble human being who debases himself
by giving into his passions. Some critics even think he falls
much lower, morally, than any other great Shakespearean hero
(although it is hard to argue that he is worse than Macbeth).
Alternatively, he is sometimes perceived not as jealous by
nature but as particularly unfortunate in his choice of Iago, his
long-time officer, as his chief friend and confidant. By the end
of the play, however, Othello has arguably recovered much of
the grandeur he had lost in the intervening scenes. Scholars
have sometimes seen Iago and Desdemona as relatively static
characters (one purely evil; the other wholly good), while
they have often described Othello as the character who is
most morally complex and who genuinely changes during
the course of the play. He strikes some commentators as
overwhelmed by the subtlety of supposed Venetian intrigue
(although it is mainly Iago alone who intrigues against
him). His fall, according to various commentators, resembles
that of the main characters in medieval morality plays: his
flawed choices result in the destruction both of himself and
Desdemona. Deceived by Iago, Othello also increasingly

deceives himself. Yet by the end of the play, according to many critics, Othello reclaims his tragic dignity; his suicide has even been interpreted as a heroic reassertion of self-respect and self-control. But the suicide can seem double-edged: it can be read as symbolizing either heroic justice or irrational despair – as a noble act or as the final mistake in a long series of foolish choices Othello has made throughout the play. One might argue that by provoking Othello to kill not only Desdemona but also himself, Iago is the dark victor in an exceptionally dark play.

And it is Iago, of course, who has always fascinated most readers and playgoers. His evil is so thorough, so shocking and so mysterious that he has long been the centre of great critical attention. Although Coleridge famously spoke of Iago's 'motiveless malignity', others have disagreed, emphasizing the ensign's ambition and love of power. Iago at first (some claim) has no grand plan to destroy Desdemona: his plots evolve spontaneously as he responds to unpredictable circumstances. Ironically (such commentators maintain), Iago's reputation as a cynic actually contributes to his reputation for honesty. Some critics see Iago as a psychotic who may be literally insane. For them he is a misanthrope contemptuous of the pleasures (including sexual pleasures) others enjoy. He tries to convince Othello that genuine love is impossible, and some have suggested that he resembles the stage 'Machiavel', a famously vicious and scheming kind of character. Iago may ironically suffer from the same jealousy he promotes, but many critics have seen him as even darker – as an almost satanic figure who takes genuine pleasure in evil for its own sake.

Many commentators have noted that Iago mostly tends to use prose (unlike Othello's characteristic use of verse), and some have suggested that the frequently balanced nature of that prose reflects his calculating personality. His speeches are often cynical and reductive, and one indication of Othello's fall is that he himself eventually begins to talk in similar ways. Iago speaks significantly more lines than Othello – suggesting his importance to the play and his appeal to leading actors. But while, on the one hand, he can seem more psychologically complex than Othello, in other ways he seems a simpler character because he is so purely evil. Part of the fascination of Iago, however, is that he is not only perverse but is also often darkly humorous. He addresses us directly and frequently, forging an odd bond with audiences that Othello himself never really establishes. Iago is perhaps the one Shakespearean character whom we most love to hate.

Both Iago and Othello are, in some senses, outsiders, but Iago selects that role, whereas Othello has little choice in the matter. Yet Iago, despite his profound sense of alienation, speaks intimately, if falsely, to practically everyone else in the play. He is also trusted by almost everyone. Paradoxically, the only character who really begins to see through him is Roderigo, the character he most consistently manipulates. Roderigo, ironically, begins to suspect Iago sooner than does Othello or anyone else. Othello, then, is hardly alone in being deceived by Iago: Cassio, Montano, and practically everyone else in Venice and on Cyprus is deceived, including Desdemona.

Of the play's three major characters, Desdemona has tended to receive the least attention, partly because she seems less complex and mysterious than Othello and Iago. She has often been presented onstage as somewhat naïve and immature, although recent productions have emphasized her self-respect and self-assertiveness, especially in the moments before she dies. Even earlier, however, she had defied her father and had also made such an insistent case to Othello on Cassio's behalf that she had ironically fed Othello's jealousy. Some critics have even wondered how well she and Othello really know each other before they marry, but most readers and audiences agree that the couple quickly dispel whatever doubts we may initially have about their relationship. They prove, especially before the Venetian senate, the strength of their mutual love. Their bond symbolizes all the virtuous values Iago detests: little wonder, then, that he feels compelled to destroy that love. Of the four major tragedies, *Othello* presents the most appealing wife and the most attractive marriage – facts that make the destruction of both so appallingly painful.

Discussion of *Othello* has often centred on the key themes of the play, although commentators have frequently disagreed about which, if any, might constitute a 'central' or controlling theme. Sometimes *Othello* has been thought to illustrate the conflict between reason and passion. Often it has been taken as an extended examination of jealousy. Some have seen, in the movement from Venice to Cyprus, a movement from order to chaos, emphasized by Othello's movement away from Desdemona and towards Iago. Commentators have also emphasized such motifs as deception, self-deception, jealousy, internal psychological conflict, paranoia, psychopathology, mutual misunderstanding, the immaturity of men, the vulnerability of women, and the tendency to treat others as 'outsiders', especially if they are racially or culturally different. Jealousy was the theme most often emphasized by commentators until relatively recently, when race tended to become the central topic of critical concern.

Assessments of the structure of *Othello* have helped illuminate how Shakespeare emphasizes characterization and themes in this play through the work's careful architectural design. The play is full of contrasts and parallels, with one scene often clearly echoing ones that have come before it. The various colloquies between Iago and Roderigo are a case in point, but numerous other echoes might be cited. Thus, Desdemona must answer charges levelled against her by her father at the beginning of the play and then answer similar charges of disloyalty made by Othello shortly before she dies. Othello must explain himself before the senate at the start of the drama and then must do the same before the assembled onlookers just before he commits suicide. The bed that plays such a prominent role in the scene in which Othello kills Desdemona plays a similarly prominent role in the scene in which he kills himself. Here, as in so many of his other works, Shakespeare uses scenic 'echoes' to emphasize both similarities and differences of tone, theme and characterization. This play is very carefully designed. However, one possible structural flaw that is often discussed in published commentary (although hardly noticed in the theatre) is the issue of 'double time'. Critics have often suggested that there simply is not enough time, in the interim between Othello's marriage to Desdemona and their arrival at Cyprus, for her to have been unfaithful to him, especially if she has been unfaithful repeatedly, as Iago claims. More recently, however, this issue has come to seem less important as plausible explanations of the timing of events have increasingly been offered.

Style and phrasing, of course, are two of the most important aspects of any play. The style of *Othello* has been much discussed, especially the style of Othello himself, whose often-lofty language has frequently been noted. This style is especially audible in the scenes in which he eloquently explains himself before assembled groups, particularly in the first and last acts. His speech before the Venetian senate is exotic yet calm, measured yet sublime. It is partly the grandness of his initial (and closing) phrasing that makes him seem such a noble human being and such an appropriate tragic figure. Unfortunately, after Othello becomes infected by Iago's poison, he also begins to speak like Iago: abruptly, cynically and with cold calculation. At one point he even loses the power of speech completely, when he suffers an apparent epileptic fit. At that point, Iago actually speaks to, about, and on behalf of Othello without the latter's knowledge or consent. Iago silences the voice that had once commanded so much respect – a fact that makes Iago's own later, final lapse into silence himself seem all the more ironic. Until that point near the very end of the play, it is Iago who speaks most often and most persuasively to most people. If Othello has a distinctive style of speech, so, too, does Iago – a style that is actually comprised of many different styles, each suited to the specific target he is addressing. Iago is a master manipulator of people because he so masterfully manipulates words.

Discussions of the performance history of *Othello* have become increasingly common and increasingly detailed as interest in Shakespeare's plays *as plays* has expanded enormously, especially in the second half of the twentieth century. Several editions are now devoted chiefly to that topic, and other editions routinely cover this matter in great detail. Right from the start, *Othello* was one of Shakespeare's most popular plays in performance, often evoking impassioned reactions from audiences. Iago, in particular, has provoked heated outbursts from theatregoers over the years; in a few notable cases, audience members have shouted either at or about him from their seats. Iago is an especially challenging and enticing role for actors, and the issue of who will play Iago has often been at least as important to producers, directors and audiences as who will play Othello. Both lead male roles make great demands on performers, although the roles of the lead women have also come to seem increasingly important in recent years.

Othello was one of the first Shakespearean plays to be revived onstage after theatres in England were reopened in 1660 (they had been closed during the period of 'Puritan' domination), and this work is uniformly considered one of Shakespeare's most consistently effective plays in performance. Yet the issue of race has long been a source of controversy, especially onstage, and particularly in racist societies. Many white audiences in the past (often the recent past) frequently disliked the idea of a black man marrying, kissing and bedding a white woman, and often, for that reason, Othello's skin colour has been both figuratively and literally toned down. Yet a 1943 production (directed by Margaret Webster) involving a black actor (Paul Robeson) and white actress (Uta Hagen) was at the time the longest-running staging of any Shakespearean play in the United States, and whereas Othello was for many years routinely played by white actors with artificially darkened skin, today the role is most often assigned to actors who are ethnically black. It is very surprising to think, however, that it was not until the mid-1990s that a black actor (Laurence Fishburne) played the role in a major film production.

Performances and adaptations of the play for modern media – on film, on television, on radio, on recordings – have become increasingly common. The text has long attracted artists working in other media. Verdi's opera *Otello*, for instance, is as important in the Verdi canon as the original play is in Shakespeare's. Producers of films and videos have often adapted the play very freely, turning Othello, for instance, into a teenager in high school or a detective on the streets of modern London. *Othello*, in short, has always been one of Shakespeare's most widely popular plays, and nothing suggests that its popularity will diminish in the years and decades to come.

The essays that appear in the present book inevitably deal with many of the same issues just surveyed. The first chapter, in fact, by Richard Harp and Steven Hrdlicka, provides an extensive overview of critical reactions to *Othello*, from the seventeenth century to the end of the twentieth. In particular, Harp and Hrdlicka discuss such matters as the 'neo-classical' reception of the play, the ways commentators have responded to issues of race, the extensive literature on Iago and Othello, the relatively neglected issue of religion, the matter of marriage, and the ways the play can be (and has been) taught, including through the use of 'close reading'.

Christopher Baker, in the next chapter, offers a rich history of the ways *Othello* has been performed, from the earliest times down to the present day. He discusses the performative choices made by various great actors and actresses and the many different ways the play has been staged and, more recently, filmed. Issues of race (should Othello be portrayed as a sub-Saharan black or as a lighter north African or Arab?) have inevitably been important in most productions, and Baker offers especially detailed discussions of various filmed versions of the play – versions to which most people now have easy access.

Imtiaz Habib, in his overview of twenty-first-century responses to *Othello*, picks up where the two preceding chapters stop. He provides a detailed survey of the most recent discussions of such matters as race, gender and sexuality, love and marriage, politics and power, issues of Venice and Turkey, the play's rhetoric, its sources and contexts, studies of genre, character, adaptations, and editions and textual detail. Habib also offers a very comprehensive overview of recent productions and adaptations, including not only performances on stage and film but also transformations of *Othello* into ballets, operas and other forms of art.

The central section of this book provides four essays offering new perspectives on the play from several distinct points of view. Thus, Matthew Steggle's essay looks at the presence of black people (two in particular) in Shakespeare's England and discusses the relevance of that presence to the conception and reception of *Othello*. My own essay reopens the issue of Iago as a kind of satanic character. In particular, it shows that he in some ways resembles a male witch – a kind of witch not much known about or studied until recently. The essay compares and contrasts Shakespeare's play with King James's famous treatise on witchcraft.

Raphael Falco's essay is also much concerned with King James, discussing the King's poem on a crucial naval battle between Christians and Muslims and the possible relevance of that battle to the play. Falco's work helps situate *Othello* more firmly – if somewhat ambiguously – in its initial historical contexts. Finally, in the last 'new' essay, Lisa Hopkins compares and contrasts Shakespeare's play with several works from the same period that seem to have been influenced by it and/or that share similar characters, plots and themes. Again and again, Hopkins casts new light on *Othello* by viewing it from this comparative perspective.

In the essay that closes the volume, Alison V. Scott surveys many different ways in which *Othello* has been – and can be – approached, especially by students and teachers. Her essay adds to the number of resources already discussed in the opening section of the book and brings right up to date our understanding of the play as a subject for study both inside and outside the classroom.

More than 400 years after it was originally written and staged, *Othello* remains one of Shakespeare's most compelling plays – a play that rarely fails to 'work' onstage and a text that continues to fascinate its many readers. Because its main concerns remain so obviously 'relevant' to life in the twenty-first century, and especially because of the sheer skill with which it is written and structured, *Othello* will almost certainly always remain one of Shakespeare's most powerful and most memorable works.

1

The Critical Backstory

Richard Harp and
Steven Hrdlicka

This chapter will first very briefly survey some of the criticism written about *Othello* before 1800 and then consider particular characters/topics that have interested critics, such as 'Race', 'Iago', 'Heroism', 'Religion', 'Philosophy' and 'Marriage', as well as pedagogical methods that might be used to teach the play such as 'Close Reading'.

Serious criticism of *Othello* began with Thomas Rymer's *A Short View of Tragedy* (1693). Rymer applied to *Othello* the neoclassical principles of his day, but he did this so rigidly that the play inevitably could not measure up. Rymer argued that: drama was meant to be improving; it should not present men and women as they are but rather as they ought to be; and if the demands of the plot made this impossible, there should at least be an edifying moral available. But there was no such moral for *Othello* and Rymer mocked various ones that might be applied – for example: all 'Maidens of Quality' must be careful when 'they run away with Blackamoors' without their parents' consent; or 'all good Wives [should] look well to their Linnen'; or jealous husbands must have their proof 'be

Mathematical',[1] Rymer also found it highly unlikely that a white Venetian woman could love a black man.

Rymer thought the importance given to the handkerchief absurd ('So much ado, so much stress, so much passion and repetition about an Handkerchief? Why was not this call'd the *Tragedy of the Handkerchief*?'). Thus it is no surprise to him that the play has no moral: 'What instruction can we make out of this Catastrophe? ... Is not this to envenome and sour our spirits, to make us repine and grumble at Providence and the government of the World? If this be our end, what boots it to be Vertuous?' Further, Rymer thought the characters in the play are not true-to-life, as Iago bears few aspects of the soldier and in Desdemona there is nothing 'that is not below any Countrey Chamber-maid with us'.[2]

Rymer's objections were unusually strong. They are not absurd, given his adherence to neoclassical principles, but their sarcasm indicates an unusual personal antipathy, perhaps in (large?) part because of the play's interracial love affair and marriage. Such at least some of his language would suggest: 'Should the Poet have provided such a Husband for an only Daughter of any noble Peer in England the Black-amoor must have chang'd his Skin to look our House of Lords in the Face.'[3]

The editor and critic Charles Gildon gave in 1694 the best contemporary rebuttal to Rymer. It is especially striking to see Gildon defending the play's racially diverse lovers: 'Unless he [Rymer] can prove that the Colour of a Man alters his Species and turns him into a Beast or Devil 'tis such a vulgar error to allow nothing of Humanity to any but our own Acquaintance of the fairer hew.' Even more positively, Gildon affirmed that those who know something of the history of Africa must grant that there are 'Negroes' there who are 'not only greater Heroes ... but also much better Christians (where Christianity is profess'd) than we of Europe generally are. They move by a nobler Principle, more open, free and generous, and not such slaves to sordid Interest.' Gildon also effectively countered Rymer's view on Othello's lovemaking sentiments by comparing them favourably with those of Aeneas to Dido in Virgil's *The Aeneid* (thus confronting Rymer the classicist on his own turf) and appealing to human nature as the cause of the tragic action: 'the fatal Jealousie of Othello and the Revenge of Iago are the natural Consequences of our ungovern'd Passions'. Concerning the alleged triviality of the handkerchief's being the cause of Othello's violence – which would exercise many other critics after Rymer – Gildon provides the following moral for the play: 'Jealousie is a fear of loosing a good we very much value and esteem, arising from the *least* causes of Suspicion.'[4] These bracing remarks lead to this comment from Russ McDonald: 'Gildon's views on race and intermarriage, probably not what we would expect from a late-seventeenth-century Englishman, attest to the difficulty of safely generalizing about early modern audiences' responses to Othello.'[5]

Later in the eighteenth century Samuel Johnson removed *Othello* from Rymer's straitjacket of adherence to 'rules' and to the unities of action, time and place. Johnson noted that 'nothing is essential to the fable [plot] but unity of action, and as the unities of time and place arise evidently from false assumptions' and detract from the 'variety' that is one of the drama's attractions. He believed that there is nothing wrong, for example, with *Othello*'s first act taking place in the city of Venice and the second act on the island of Cyprus: those who would object share the same small-mindedness of Voltaire, who could not understand the largeness of Shakespeare's vision. Also (unlike Rymer) Johnson found nothing unsuitable in Desdemona's having fallen in love with the Moor's narration of the marvellous travels and exploits he had undergone: 'It is no wonder that, in any age, or in any nation, a lady – recluse, timorous, and delicate – should desire to hear of events and scenes which she could never see and should admire the man' who had done deeds far beyond her reach.[6]

Johnson's biographer James Boswell, however, also thought that the play lacked a moral and once questioned Johnson on this by-now-standard critical topic. Johnson replied

vigorously – as he often did when Boswell expressed a
decisive point of view of his own – that the play had more
morals 'than almost any play', such as the importance of a
person's marrying someone of his own status and of his not
giving in too quickly to jealousy. In general Johnson found the
play beautiful, admiring particularly the nobility of Othello,
who was 'boundless in his confidence, ardent in his affection,
inflexible in his resolution, and obdurate in his revenge'. In
addition, Johnson thought Iago had a 'cool malignity' and
that Desdemona showed Shakespeare's 'skill in human nature
as … it is vain to seek in any modern writer'. Johnson's
balanced, antithetical style is well suited to his incisive analysis
of the play; he could, for example, easily summarize a minor
(but important) character such as Emilia, whose virtue was
'worn loosely but not cast off, easy to commit small crimes
but quickened and alarmed at atrocious villainies'.[7] John
Dryden had said that Shakespeare needed not the 'spectacles
of Books to read Nature';[8] Samuel Johnson was able to read
Shakespeare's plays with the same facility.

Discussions of race:
The nineteenth century

For most of the eighteenth century, Meredith Anne Skura
has observed, in an important and carefully argued article on
the role of race in the play, 'Othello was a tragic hero whose
colour was irrelevant and whose greatness and savagery
could be considered together without contradiction. Once
his colour became important, that union was no longer
possible.'[9] And his colour did indeed become important in the
nineteenth century. Early in the century, for example, Samuel
Taylor Coleridge asked if we can imagine Shakespeare 'so
utterly ignorant as to make a barbarous negro plead royal
birth – at a time, too, when negroes were not known except
as slaves'. Coleridge, a learned man, showed some historical

ignorance himself here, as white Christians were just as likely to be slaves in the Mediterranean world of Othello as were black Africans. Further, Coleridge could not – or would not – imagine a black Othello on the stage: 'it would be something monstrous to conceive this beautiful Venetian girl falling in love with a veritable negro. It would argue a disproportionateness, a want of balance, in Desdemona, which Shakespeare does not appear to have in the least contemplated.'[10]

Whether Othello had black or only light brown skin colour concerned Coleridge and his age. The essayist Charles Lamb, for instance, said that while one may restrain his revulsion over the love relationship between Othello and Desdemona when reading the text, it is nearly impossible to do so while watching a production. In the latter case, the senses overpower the observer's reason. Reading the play, says Lamb, allows for the 'triumph of virtue over accidents, of the imagination over the senses', while watching the play so focuses upon physical action that one is negatively affected by the 'courtship and wedded caresses of Othello and Desdemona'.[11] As a result a light brown or tawny skin colour was proposed for Othello because some held that the Moors descended from Caucasians who had occupied Spain from the early Middle Ages until 1492. Most actors until Edward Kean (1787–1833) had played Othello in black face – the text is specific about his dark colour – but Kean used a brown skin colour and thereafter this became a fashion. Even where Charles Knight, who edited Shakespeare's play in 1843, acknowledged that it was by no 'means improbable that Othello was represented as a Negro' in early productions, he argued that the 'whole context of the play is against the notion'.[12] Perhaps the vicious eighteenth-century slave trade made critics reluctant to imagine Othello as black.[13] Henry Reed at any rate even suggested that if a black Othello were married to the 'bright, fair-faced Venetian lady', one might be tempted to think that this 'monstrous alliance' received its just deserts in its 'fearful catastrophe'.[14]

This nineteenth-century discussion about Othello's dark skin colour also resulted in some burlesque and farcical productions of the play. After the Civil War a number of outright travesties were even produced; in one such 'a minstrel Othello with an Irish Iago' were paired 'in order to include immigrants in its racial abuse'.[15] Critical comments such as these by Mary Preston were also not uncommon: 'I have always *imagined* its hero a *white* man. It is true the dramatist paints him black, but this shade does not suit the man ... Shakespeare was too correct a delineator of human nature to have coloured Othello black, if he had personally acquainted himself with the idiosyncrasies of the African race.'[16] One other commentator of that era, however, J. E. Taylor, stated that Othello's dark skin 'in no degree affects the character of the Moor'.[17]

Modern discussions of race

The eminent early twentieth-century critic A. C. Bradley regards it as 'nearly certain' that Shakespeare meant Othello to be a black man and not 'a light-brown one'. He finds it amusing that earlier American critics abhorred this idea but is candid enough to observe the same concern in Coleridge. The reason Bradley assigns to critics' prejudice in this regard is the Moor's marriage to Desdemona, but their mistake, he proposes, is to regard the marriage as 'Brabantio regarded it, and not as Shakespeare conceived it'; and he notes the irony of 'our' overlooking her loving a tawny-skinned person but then finding 'it monstrous that she should love a black one'. And yet, even Bradley (like Lamb) thinks that audiences and readers are not as capable as Shakespeare in transcending such matters. Therefore he advises that Othello should not be presented on the stage as a black man, for an audience's repugnance to such 'comes as near to being merely physical as anything human can'.[18] Nonetheless, the issue was not as prominent for most critics of this time as it had been for those of two or three generations earlier; for 'most Victorians,' says Michael Neill, 'and their successors in the first half of the twentieth century, Othello's difference was typically understood not so much as a matter of race, as of the cultural clash implicit in Iago's contrast between 'an erring barbarian and a super-subtle Venetian' (1.3.356–7).[19]

Discussions of race in the play became more prominent in the 1950s and beyond, the era of the American Civil Rights movement and other African-American liberation activities. Lawrence Lerner saw the play as a 'story of a barbarian who (the pity of it) relapses' into violence,[20] a reading reinforced by the 1964 Laurence Olivier stage interpretation of the character. Nonetheless, this performance also 'helped to stimulate serious debate about the significance of race in the play'.[21] Taking another direction was the influential study of Othello's skin colour in G. K. Hunter's 1967 British Academy article, 'Othello and Colour Prejudice'. His argument defending Othello was an idealistic one – Othello represents 'reality' in the play, Iago 'appearances': Iago is the 'white man with the black soul' (and Hunter cited a number of historical references where blackness was associated with the devil) and 'Othello is the black man with the white soul'. Helpful, too, was his citing of the Spanish debate between Juan Ginés de Sepulveda (1489–1573) and Bartolomé de las Casas (1484–1566). The former argued that American Indians were 'slaves by nature', while the latter emphasized their 'natural capacity for devotion'. Previous Christian tradition could also warrant the spiritual potential of blackness, as, for example, when Philip baptized the Ethiopian eunuch in the Acts of the Apostles. Paraphrasing St Augustine, Hunter commented that 'all nations are Ethiopians, black in their natural sinfulness; but ... white in the knowledge of the Lord'.[22]

Hunter called 'powerful' the strain of criticism that goes back to A. W. Schlegel's 1815 essay that paints Othello as 'savage at heart' whose 'veneer of Christianity' collapses under Iago's assault. A stronger critical alternative was needed, though, than his suggestion (and attempted answer to T. S. Eliot's remark that Othello was merely trying to cheer himself up in his final death speech) that the 'perilous and temporary achievements of heroism' have to be achieved 'in *our* minds', that 'catharsis is achieved in ... the Aleppo of the mind'.[23] That such a fine and knowledgeable critic resorted to such vague formulations is a sign of real critical perplexity at this time with the play.

Protests in the 1980s and early 1990s against the South African practice of apartheid also helped bring into focus the play's racial themes. Martin Orkin's essay 'Othello and the "Plain Face" of Racism' found that in its exploration of Iago's racism and in its portrayal of human nobility independent of skin colour 'the play, as it always has done, continues to oppose racism'.[24] Writing about the same time, Anthony Barthelemy believed an audience would be sympathetic 'for [Othello's] struggle to escape his fate' but would not be sympathetic for the explosive temperament that his skin colour seems to demand of him: 'always there to undermine the most positive aspects of Shakespeare's presentation of a noble black is Othello's lapse into ... stereotype'.[25]

Not finding contemporary notions of 'race' and 'racism' necessarily relevant to *Othello*, Kim Hall explored Renaissance ideas of 'Moors' and 'blackness'. After noting discussions by Rymer and Gildon on the subject, her essay concluded by looking at Renaissance associations of 'blackness' with evil and vice, and, interestingly, by also considering Iago's 'whiteness' in relation to such ideas. Hall's Iago was a 'white devil' who is masked until the ending of the play, where his materialistic and malicious language exposes his interior moral blackness: 'he is the evil within who escapes notice by projecting sin onto others'.[26] In a 'recently discovered essay' on *Othello*, C. S. Lewis also considered the difficulties in applying modern notions of race to the play.[27]

Seeking to bridge discussions of race and religion, Patrick C. Hogan argued that 'racial despair' is a secular descendant of spiritual despair. The latter results from a sense that one's

sin is too great even for all-merciful God to forgive, as this
sin blots out one's soul, but the former means that one's skin
is too black for anyone to accept – to forget or to 'forgive'
– that one's skin in fact obscures his soul. Hogan argued
that this 'racial despair' is the real tragedy of *Othello* and
therefore responsible for Othello's suicide and for his murder
of Desdemona. He based his reading significantly on Derek
Walcott's work, which elucidates the process by which one
'see[s] oneself and others through the distorting lenses of
white racism'. Hogan concluded that 'Othello was a greater
Christian than all the Christians in Venice', which is, however,
an overstatement by the critic.[28]

The notion of Othello's 'primitivism', not in the
Enlightenment sense of the 'noble savage' but in a more
violent one, has always received attention in criticism and is
inevitably allied to questions about race. The 'relationship of
the noble and the savage Moor has always caused trouble', said
E. A. J. Honigmann. In the first part of the eighteenth century
Othello's epileptic fit was excised from productions but then
in the nineteenth century it was emphasized. In one rendition
featuring a popular actor, Tommaso Salvini, as Othello, the
Moor grabbed Iago and threw him down but then, as though
coming to himself, reached down and offered his hand to bring
him to his feet again. Honigmann found this a brilliant touch,
serving to remind us of Othello's two sides (perhaps so, if it
could avoid provoking laughter from the audience). Olivier's
1965 National Theatre performance made Othello's fit 'a focal
episode, more prolonged and more unbearably physical than is
usual in the theatre'. Borrowing terms from August Strindberg's
'famous Preface to *Miss Julie*', Honigmann thought that
Shakespeare did not conceive his characters as having a 'fixed
state of soul' and that therefore Othello portrayed as 'conglom-
erate' rather than 'automaton' was entirely natural. He believed
that Othello's 'true inner life' is not accessible to us – an idea
consistent with Hamlet's indignant riposte to Rosencrantz and
Guildenstern's nosiness when they thought they could 'pluck
out the heart of his mystery'.[29]

To what extent, then, is race *the* most important issue in *Othello*? That it is of tremendous current critical interest is evident from the critics discussed in Imtiaz Habib's chapter in this volume. That race is the principal context for Othello's tragedy, however, has been strongly challenged in the twenty-first century by critics such as Meredith Anne Skura. In summing up the role of modern ideas about race and 'racism' (a term that did not exist for Shakespeare) the following comment by Michael Neill is helpful: '*Othello* is a work that trades in ethnic constructions that are at once misleadingly *like* and confusingly *unlike* the twentieth-century ideas of 'race' to which they are, nevertheless, recognizably ancestral.'[30]

Discussions of Iago

Criticism by the English romantics, besides discussing Othello, also had interesting things to say about Iago. According to William Hazlitt, Iago was one of a number of distinctive Shakespearean characters who had 'great intellectual activity, accompanied with a total want of moral principle'. Iago excites a natural love in humans of the sensational and exciting, one of the reasons for humanity's love of tragedy in general. Adopting a term popular in eighteenth-century literature and criticism, Hazlitt said that Iago's 'ruling passion' was 'an incorrigible love of mischief, an insatiable craving after action of the most difficult and dangerous kind'. As part of a series of memorable formulations Hazlitt said that Shakespeare's Ensign is one who 'plots the ruin of his friends as an exercise for his understanding, and stabs men in the dark to prevent *ennui*'.

Hazlitt's description of Iago as one abstracted from the normal emotions of human life, as one who separates reason and moral feelings, who experiments with amoral/immoral actions not in the pages of literature but with his dearest friends and acquaintances, was again a sentiment that persons of any era might recognize. John Milton's character of Satan in *Paradise Lost* attacks the innocent Adam and Eve precisely because they are good and because of his devotion to the principle of 'Evil be thou my good'. Hazlitt noted how the innocent Desdemona arouses Iago's contempt because Roderigo proclaims her goodness, and Hazlitt astutely observed that only the 'genius of Shakespeare' could have convincingly set off the 'elegance' and 'dignity' of Desdemona in the face of such venom. Thus, Iago well analyses his own character when he says 'I am nothing if not critical' (2.1.119). Iago (Hazlitt believed) could hardly be tolerated as a dramatic character except for the reader/audience's interest in the energy and ingenuity he expends to achieve his despicable ends. He is one of the 'supererogations of Shakespeare's genius'.

Hazlitt admired the extreme contrasts between the two leading characters in the play as well as their depth of passion – 'one black and the other white, the one unprincipled, the other unfortunate in the extreme'. Hazlitt believed that in the third act of the drama, for example, Shakespeare gives his best portrayal of knowledge and power, of 'the knowledge of character with the expression of passion, of consummate art in the keeping up of appearances with the profound workings of nature and the convulsive movements of uncontrollable agony, of the power of inflicting torture and of suffering it'.[31]

Coleridge made one of the most famous comments about Iago in *Othello* criticism when he called Iago's musings about why he sought Othello's ruin 'the motive-hunting of a motiveless malignity'.[32] But admiration for Iago's intellectual facility, even divorced from moral ends, caused Hazlitt and Coleridge to be less severe in their judgement of him than Dr Johnson; for Johnson that very ability joined to wickedness causes Iago 'from the first scene to the last' to deserve being 'hated and despised'.[33]

A. C. Bradley regarded Iago as the greatest of all Shakespeare's wicked characters. Given that Iago has no redeeming features and combines evil with superior intelligence, Bradley was

moved to ask the rhetorical question: 'Why is the representation tolerable, and why do we not accuse its author either
of untruth or of a desperate pessimism?' Bradley did not
accept many previous interpreters' view of Iago, finding even
Coleridge's 'motiveless malignity' wide of the mark, as this is a
'psychological impossibility' for a human being. Iago is rather
motivated by the more familiar human failing of egotism –
extreme to be sure – and is moved to action by a jealousy
of Cassio ('He has a daily beauty in his life', Iago says, 'that
makes me ugly' [5.1.19]). Iago is further intoxicated, Bradley
believed, with the diabolical scheme that he has set in motion.
Iago sees himself as an artist in the contriving and executing
of his plot and in this one regard at least 'Shakespeare put a
good deal of himself into Iago'.[34]

Bradley's notion of 'Iago as artist' inspired much subsequent commentary. Not all of it is admiring of the ancient's
subtle wiles. Harley Granville-Barker, for example, said Iago
certainly has the obsessive ambitions of the dedicated artist
but contended that they serve only to mask his lack of any real
abilities. Lawrence Lerner found that the evil Iago takes a kind
of aesthetic enjoyment in his wicked schemes. W. H. Auden
saw Iago's artistic malevolence, which delights in the manipulation and control of circumstance, as connected to the rise
of modern science which (Auden thought) has much the same
end. Sidney Homan was another critic who, like Johnson,
found nothing admirable in an artistic Iago, as he represents
what the Renaissance found negative about art: it substitutes
illusion, often diabolical illusion, for reality and uses invention
to destroy social cohesion. Stanley Edgar Hyman called Iago
an 'artistic-criminal', a role he plays to perfection, being a
master of timing and in knowing exactly how far he can push
his impressionable General to distrust his wife.[35]

The distinguished contemporary Shakespearean scholar
A. D. Nuttall also found much to appreciate in the 'Iago as
artist' theme. It is natural, he thought, for a military hero
such as Othello who is thrust into civilian society to turn to
his brother soldier Iago for support and guidance when the

military props of his old life are completely taken away; this happens, for example, when the Turks suddenly decide not to attack Cyprus. Shakespeare's comedies (Nuttall noted) had shown other struggles between a character's male friend and his female love – for example, *Romeo and Juliet* and *The Merchant of Venice*, but in those plays there was not tragedy because the defeated friends, Mercutio and Antonio, were both good men. But *Othello* is a tragedy rather than a comedy because here 'marriage is defeated by [the] pure hatred of Iago'.[18] For his part, Iago enjoys moulding the suddenly empty character of an Othello removed from military life. Nuttall supported Coleridge's view of Iago's 'motiveless malignity' and said that the Lieutenant's remarks about Othello's having seduced his wife Emilia are merely an attempt to fill his inner emptiness with an excuse for a 'histrionic performance'.[36]

Bernard Spivack gave a helpful genealogy of Iago's character by relating him to the figure of the Vice in medieval morality plays. Thus, the mystery of Iago's hatred of Othello is lessened if we understand him as descended from this earlier type whose very character depended upon his hatred of the equally abstract virtuous characters. According to Spivack, Shakespeare took this tradition and made out of it his fully formed persons of Iago, Othello and Desdemona. In this view, Iago is 'not essentially a man who is provoked to act villainously, but *Villainy* disguised by late convention to act as a man'.[37] Another recent critic, John Gronbeck-Tedesco, performed an extensive reading of *Othello* through recognizing Iago as a 'crucial touchstone' of the play. Iago's motives, he thought, are driven by lust, not reason, and in this way Iago's 'argument falls apart almost comically'. Gronbeck-Tedesco read the end of the play as a tableau, a formal dramatic device, which reinforced the play's parabolic and allegorical elements. 'Love fails in *Othello* because the characters who strive to love do not understand how to sustain a collaborative bond against hostile and impenetrable social contexts'.[38]

Iago's villainy can also be situated within Reformation
controversy. Richard Mallette called him a 'blasphemous
preacher', one who knows what Protestant divines also
knew: that 'belief is best achieved through hearing the
Word preached'. Iago therefore aims to 'abuse Othello's ear'
(1.3.394), as he says in a soliloquy. His strategy is derived from
(but of course distorts) contemporary preaching manuals.
According to Mallette this makes him 'even more diabolical
than hitherto recognized', as he takes a methodology 'that [a]
Shakespearean audience was accustomed to regard as salvific,
and he deforms [it] toward an evil end'. For the ear, thought
Protestant preachers, was 'the avenue of faith'. Mallette noted
that homiletic discourse is absent after Act 4, Scene 2 because
by this point Othello has internalized Iago's words and hence-
forth Iago uses (significantly) more the language of a Roman
Catholic priest, the Moor no longer needing the counsel of his
profane Protestant divine.[39]

Stylistics can also illuminate Iago's character. Catherine
Belsey noted that 'The conflict between Othello's credulity
and Iago's racist resentment, between passionate heroism
and the scepticism that sets out to destroy it, is staged as a
clash of styles.'[40] Othello's speeches are typically poetic and
emotional, very much influenced by Christopher Marlowe's
play *Tamburlaine the Great*, and hence are also similar
to the speeches of other Shakespearean tragic figures who
arouse audience sympathies. Iago's speeches, though, exhibit a
stoical, aphoristic detachment, a characteristic also of Michel
de Montaigne's style. This contrast points to a conflict in the
play of passion and love versus stoical resignation.

Indeed, linguistic matters may be of such relevance to Iago's
role that one can ask, 'Is Iago a deconstructionist? Bonnie
Melchior suggested as much in her discussion of how he
uses words. He exists both inside and outside discourse and
therefore is able to manipulate the meanings of words due to
a sort of phantom presence. By the end of the play it is clear,
Melchior argued, that we cannot even see 'words like *virtue*,
honesty, *love*, and *soul* as originators of meaning', so severely

does Iago distort their ordinary meanings, meanings on which all civilized societies depend.[41]

John Crawford focused on one important word whose meaning is reaffirmed both denotatively and connotatively in the play: 'villainy'. Before it became principally a term of ethical description – obviously important in *Othello* – there was also a social dimension to the word. Crawford noted C. S. Lewis's remark that into the Renaissance the term 'villain' is never without 'some implication of ignoble birth, coarse manners and ignorance'.[42] To establish the point as relevant to the play, Crawford showed the disparities between Cinthio's source text and *Othello* in order to demonstrate that Shakespeare altered the original story consciously in order to foreground social issues.

Finally, Wylie Sypher made illuminating comments about the general historical context of Iago's villainy. Iago, he argued, symbolizes a new sense of time in the Renaissance, quite different from that of the Middle Ages, whose attention moved easily between time and eternity, the here and the hereafter. Sypher compared Iago's (historically) new sense of ambition to that of such an archetypal early modern figure as Leonardo da Vinci. The ancient (Sypher thought) is also a new man in his puritanical intolerance of seeing others – Othello and Desdemona – happily and pleasurably in love. Sypher viewed Othello as having a native trustfulness and patience, typical of an older world, which is undermined by his lieutenant's stirring of the pot.[43]

Discussions of Othello's heroism

After this excursus into commentaries about Iago, let us return to consider more generally A. C. Bradley's criticism. His views are now sometimes regarded as old-fashioned, but the justness of Bradley's many observations on Shakespeare's tragedies makes this opinion difficult to sustain. (In fact, *Shakespearean*

Tragedy has been called recently 'arguably the most influential work of criticism ever printed'.[44] For Bradley, '*Othello* is the most painfully exciting and the most terrible' of the tragedies. He gave due prominence to the theme of sexual jealousy in the play, making perceptive comments on the subject, such as the claim that the green-eyed monster 'splits by poison … the 'golden purity' of passion into fragments'. He thought the suffering of Desdemona is 'the most nearly intolerable spectacle that Shakespeare offers us'. He noted that to have three principal characters in the play, one of whom, Iago, is responsible for the play's intrigue apart from its love interests, is unique in Shakespearean tragedy. Bradley also offered a full and candid account of the title character. He confronted directly Schlegel's view that Othello's nobility and initially civilized demeanour are a thin veneer for underlying barbarian passions waiting to erupt, arguing that while Othello's race is certainly important to the play, 'it makes no difference to the action and catastrophe'.[45] The capacity for such volcanic jealousy, Bradley seemed to feel, is part of human nature.

Bradley affirmed that Othello's exotic background does not merely make him a 'romantic figure; his own nature is romantic'. He also found interesting similarities between Othello and other Shakespearean tragic figures. Both Othello and Hamlet, for example, are 'exceptionally noble and trustful, and each endures the shock of a terrible disillusionment'. In Othello, too, is a quality also commonly found in Shakespeare's later tragic heroes such as Lear and Macbeth, that they are 'huge men' (similar to Michelangelo's figures), survivors of the 'heroic age living in a later and smaller world'.[46]

Some of the very reasons for admiring Bradley's criticism of the play – its concern with *Othello* as mimetic or as an imitation of reality, with the nobility of its hero, with its characters' similarity to persons living in the real world – become for detractors reasons for disowning his criticism. E. E. Stoll, for instance, insisted in his 1915 examination of the play that its characters should not be judged by psychological probability, as one might do with those of a novel, but rather by the conventions of the Elizabethan drama.[47] Othello's precipitous revenge would then not be the manifestation of a barbarian within an apparently civilized and noble warrior, nor the downfall of an unsophisticated foreigner tempted by a demonic subordinate; rather, it is simply a dramatic necessity so that the plot could move forward. However, there is a naïveté to this criticism, as it would make understanding the play unavailable to those not grounded in literary convention. Stoll would require for Shakespeare's modern audience something indeed very like Dryden's 'spectacles of books' to understand the play. This narrowly academic view of literature would not allow for any passionate engagement with the text as proposed by Aristotle's cathartic view of tragedy, where the emotions of pity and fear – emotions present in abundance in *Othello* – are first aroused in the audience by the complications of the play's plot and then purged as a result of its unravelling. Stoll has had relatively few followers among critics, but his views are still often recorded/cited. This kind of 'art for art's sake' approach to literature was notably articulated in the late nineteenth century by influential writers such as Walter Pater, and then by a later, influential twentieth-century philosophy called structuralism.

Such views and those which seek to find in literature a reflection or imitation of a knowable external reality have frequently been in tension in the last a 150 years or so of literary criticism. While we can acknowledge that the structuralists have a point – literary analysis does have its own vocabulary and methods – the very articulation of their philosophy presupposes the use of language held in common with non-structuralists. And any attempt to convince others of its validity will be successful only by using general rhetorical modes of argumentation and persuasion. When Othello cries out to his 'honest' ancient about Desdemona's (supposed) adultery, 'But yet the pity of it, Iago! O Iago, the pity of it ...' (4.1.192–3), most readers and members of the audience – even those who are aware of such things – will be touched not by recognition of dramatic convention and language signifiers but by deep and easily recognized human emotion.

Followers of Bradley's who praise of the nobility of Othello are frequent in twentieth-century criticism – but there are also other challengers. One of the most thorough of the latter was F. R. Leavis (1952). Leavis was intemperately and unjustly harsh to Bradley, but he does give balance to critical appreciation of the play by arguing for serious flaws in Othello's character (and not simply the 'diabolic intellect' of Iago) as a cause for the tragedy. Where Bradley spoke of the 'absolute egotism' of Iago, Leavis sees a 'noble egotism' in Othello, a result of his lack of self-knowledge. While perhaps appropriate on the battlefield, such noble egotism is disastrous in love. However, Leavis pays too little attention to Iago's role, as well as to the genuine nobility of the Othello of the first two acts of the play. To say that Othello has a 'ferocious stupidity, an insane and self-deceiving passion'[48] is to ignore the qualities of character that had made Othello's life a successful one before his fatal honeymoon trip to Cyprus. In discussing this disagreement, E. A. J. Honigmann found that both critics have points in their favour: 'The same speeches [where Othello both attacks and defends Desdemona] suggest that the noble and the savage Moor are both more intimately one than either Bradley or Leavis was willing to allow – and that we misread the play when we put all of our money on either one or the other.'[49] Honigmann's words are wise – but readers' varying temperaments and experiences will make those words a challenge to heed.

Honigmann's own tentative conclusion was that fruitful distinctions may be made between 'character' and 'role playing'. Shakespeare shows his characters playing various roles – none doing so in a more extreme fashion than Othello, with his distinguished bearing and speech in the first two acts, then his terrifying vows of bloody vengeance towards his wife in Acts 3–5.[50]

Another of the mid-twentieth-century's most distinguished critics, Helen Gardner, followed Leavis's attack on the person of Othello with one of the most eloquent defences of the noble Moor. She cited, as evidence of his stature, the eloquence of his poetry, the love he inspires in Desdemona, and the vigour with which he pursues revenge for what he thought was gross disloyalty on the part of his wife. Gardner supported Coleridge's analysis of 'motiveless malignity' as helping explain Iago's destructive drive. She thought Othello's unwillingness to compromise, to live in what (he thought) would be compromised circumstances, with his wife, is at the 'heroic core of tragedy'.[51] His devotion to justice in killing an unfaithful wife is mirrored in his killing himself when he learns the truth.

Discussions of religion

Stephen Greenblatt's 1980 chapter on *Othello* in his landmark book *Renaissance Self-Fashioning* is remarkable but perhaps, at least in this particular case, not for all the right reasons. Greenblatt presents his arguments lucidly and straightforwardly, but it is some of the arguments themselves which might be examined here. He believed that the uncontrollable passion that leads Othello to take Desdemona's life derives from Christianity's insistence that intense romantic passion in itself is wrong; Othello, as a Christian, is unable to reconcile this idea with the great love he feels for Desdemona. Because he believes that his love is itself polluted, it is not a great step for him to accept Iago's call for him to betray that love and ultimately to destroy it at its root. 'Pleasure itself becomes for Othello pollution', Greenblatt writes. Such pleasure becomes a defilement of his property in Desdemona and in himself. It is not Cassio's relations with Desdemona alone that worry Othello; it is the intensity of his own and Desdemona's desire. Othello must 'destroy Desdemona both for her excessive experience of pleasure and for awakening such sensations in himself'.

But perhaps this is exaggerated? Desdemona of course
speaks candidly and with feeling in the play but there is little
in her remarks that should cause even mild insecurity in the
Moor, much less the great anxiety that Greenblatt detected. To
Desdemona's frank and moving expression of love in Act I –

> That I did love the Moor, to live with him,
> My downright violence, and scorn of fortunes,
> May trumpet to the world; my heart's subdued
> Even to the utmost pleasure of my lord ... (1.3.249–52)

– Greenblatt offers an unusual interpretation: 'this moment
of erotic intensity, this frank acceptance of pleasure and
submission to her spouse's pleasure is ... as much as Iago's
slander the cause of Desdemona's death, for it awakens the
deep current of sexual anxiety in Othello'.[52] If that is the
case, there was no hope for the great warrior from the very
beginning – nor for any other man fortunate enough (one
would have thought) who might receive such an honest and
heartfelt declaration of sincere feeling from his beloved.

Greenblatt's essay, too, was an implied indictment of
Christian doctrine about sexuality; he implied that it inevitably
causes the passionate Othello to fashion for himself an extreme
self-loathing. But the essay was not altogether candid in its
citation of certain sources and in its neglect of certain obvious
other ones that might weaken its argument. Greenblatt read St
Augustine's account of the Fall of Adam and Eve in Genesis,
for example, as meaning that mankind's first parents did not
experience any feeling or excitement in their marital relations;
theirs, rather, was an 'ideal of Edenic placidity' (not a phrase
exactly calculated to arouse one's nostalgia for the lost
paradise). Adam and Eve, says Greenblatt, 'would have experienced sexual intercourse without the excitement of the flesh'.[53]

But this is not correct. Augustine in fact made clear that it
is 'lust' – that is, emotion over which we have no control –
that accompanied and was the fatal consequence of the Fall,
not the anterior pleasurable mutual attraction of the sexes in

itself. 'Excitement of the flesh' there still may have been in
Eden – but it was an excitement amenable to the voluntary
movement of the will.[54] Augustinian scholar Peter Brown's
statement on the matter is that 'In Adam and Eve's first state
sexual desire ... coincided perfectly with the conscious will:
it would have introduced no disruptive element into the clear
serenity of their marriage.'[55] In addition, there were available
to Greenblatt any number of other medieval and Renaissance
texts that might have caused his argument to take quite a
different direction. The medieval doctor St Thomas Aquinas,
for example, made explicit that the extreme pleasure of
sexuality was *not* opposed to virtue; his comment on the
matter was this: 'virtue is not concerned with the amount of
pleasure experienced by the external sense, as this depends on
the disposition of the body; what matters is how much the
interior appetite is affected by that pleasure'.[56] Lust is a fact
of life, but in neither the 'Christian tradition' (nor in many
others) is the view held that romantic love inevitably must
dissolve into sensuality. Shakespeare may write in a sonnet
that 'The expense of spirit in a waste of shame / Is lust in
action ...' (Sonnet 129, ll. 1–2), but this is not his exclusive
statement on the subject; he (or his speaker) also hopes that he
will not 'to the marriage of true minds / Admit impediments
...' (Sonnet 116, ll. 1–2), which is the kind of marriage that
Othello looks forward to with Desdemona when he says that
she loved him 'for the dangers I had past, / And I loved her that
she did pity them' (1.3.168–9). Or, as an example from a work
contemporary with Shakespeare, one might take John Donne's
famous poem 'The Ecstasy', which sets forth in memorable
verses the complementarity of mind and body, sex and spirit.
It is a poem drawn from the central Christian tradition on
these subjects and states, among many relevant thoughts, that
'Love's mysteries in souls do grow, / But yet the body is his
book' (ll. 71–2). Thus, to conclude this short digression: while
Greenblatt may have found certain Christian texts in which
even married sexual love was thought to be lustful, there were
also many other obvious and influential ones which would

justify Othello's indulging his 'content so absolute' (2.1.189)
upon meeting Desdemona in Cyprus and his looking forward
to their harmonious and passionate honeymoon . That this
does not happen says more about Othello's own temperament
and constitution and the influence of Iago than about the
supposed shortcomings of contemporary theology.

Stephen Greenblatt's work, however, along with that of
a number of other historically minded critics, has been
constructive in drawing attention to religious issues in the
play. Biblical influences, for instance, have been found in
Othello in a number of different places. Irving Ribner is one
among many critics who sees the Christian view of good
versus evil dramatized in the drama: the Moor is like Adam
in his fall from grace, while Iago serves as the tempter to evil.
Desdemona, on the other hand, embodies sacrificial love –
more of a New Testament rather than an Old Testament idea.
Ribner found Othello at the end genuinely sorry for what he
had done and says that his suicide was expiatory.

Peter Milward also believed that there are structural
similarities between the play and early events in Genesis,
and he further suggested that Desdemona plays the role first
of Mary, then of Jesus, while Othello, in a tragic paradox,
changes from a figure resembling the Christ who is betrayed
by Judas to a Judas himself who betrays and kills his wife.

Harry Morris offered a structural Christian interpretation
of the play, finding it organized around the 'Last Things' –
death, judgement, heaven and hell – whose eschatology must
be enacted upon the stage rather than in the supernatural
hereafter. Desdemona is a Christ figure and Othello's good
angel, Iago a devil, and both fight for the soul of the Moor
– reminding one in these respects of Christopher Marlowe's
Doctor Faustus.[57]

While the play makes clear that Othello is a Christian,
Anthony Hecht did not find him a particularly informed
one, with his conversion suspect. In this connection Hecht
drew upon interesting historical material about the forced
conversions of Moors who remained in Spain after they were

expelled from that country in 1492. Such conversions were not genuine in the eyes of some Christians. Othello's final actions and words towards Desdemona – e.g. 'I would not kill thy soul' – show the superficiality of his Christianity, Hecht believed. Because of his painfully divided nature, however, Othello's final attempt at an accurate summing up of his life does show 'a painful but undoubted nobility'.[58]

In an essay that considers *Othello* one of Shakespeare's most 'theological tragedies',[59] Philip C. Kolin found key theological clues in a biblical parable. Kolin focused specifically on animal signifiers used by various characters in the play that resonate with biblical scripture, especially the goat and sheep language in Matthew 25.31–45. In the biblical text, the language of Matthew is employed towards a parable of judgement, but it also recalls Old Testament parallels, which Kolin considered in order to demonstrate the richness and depth of Shakespeare's use of these biblical allusions in the play. Ultimately, he concludes, at the end of the play Othello has not been able to separate the sheep from the goats, the damned from the saved.

But it is about reformation controversies, Protestant and Catholic and an amalgam of the two, that some of the most interesting criticism has been written in the past few decades. Huston Diehl provides one good introduction to these issues by considering the role of 'sight' – e.g. the ocular proof of the handkerchief – as involving crucial and problematic matters of knowledge and which result from Reformers' scepticism about religious images. The handkerchief itself (she argued) has nearly a sacred aura in the play and Othello's putting overmuch faith in the object leads to the play's tragic conclusion.[60]

Robert Watson placed *Othello* squarely in the midst of contemporary religious debates. Watson argued that although critics have often understood Christian allegory to operate in *Othello*, the play is much more complicated than that because of Reformation politics. Watson saw the allegory in *Othello* to exhibit much anti-Catholic theology and an observable tension

between faith and works. He referred to the play as a kind of
'Protestant Morality Play'. In this allegorical reading, Othello's
obsession (mainly in the first two acts) with works, Iago's
protestations of an injured merit (likened to a contemporary
stigma against Jesuits), and Desdemona's (failed) intercessions
become central to supporting his thesis. Watson also took an
allegorical look at Othello and Desdemona's marriage and
proposed that it 'represents the precious but unstable marriage
between the sinner's soul and its Savior'.[61] Essentially, Othello
has no 'faith' in his wife due to an imperfect conversion.

On the other side of the theological divide, Lisa Hopkins
insightfully looked at the play in relation to the Catholic cult
of the Black Madonna, proposing 'that Othello's interest in
theology and spiritual destinies should be read in light of early
modern Mariology'. Since death is tied to blackness (darkness)
in the play, eschatology becomes a major theme, and Hopkins
relevantly drew attention to Cassio's Calvinist lines in Act 2
('Well, God's above all, and there be souls must be saved, and
there be souls must not be saved' [2.3.98–100]). The early
modern tension between competing views on the afterlife can
be observed in the play by the way the women (Emilia and
Desdemona) 'tend to adhere to the older one: Desdemona
pleads for Cassio 'By'r lady' (3.3.74), and Emilia would
"venture purgatory"' (4.3.76–7) if by her own infidelity she
could make her husband a monarch. The cult of the black
Madonna, of which one of the most famous was Our Lady
of Loreto, becomes a contextual touchstone for this essay as
Hopkins traced many of the myths and facts that she then
related to the play.[62]

Aspects of Catholic theology also inform R. Chris Hassel's
reading of the play. In his article 'Intercession, Detraction, and
Just Judgment in Othello', Hassel argued that the prevalence
of Marian allusions in Othello, of which he cites several, along
with a number of close parallels to the material in medieval
mystery plays, form a 'complex system of analogy [which]
informs Othello with a psychological and a theological depth
that has too often eluded its post-enlightenment audience'.

Hassel places *Othello* in relation to the contemporary anxiety towards the Blessed Virgin and demonstrates how Iago's defamation of Desdemona mirrors the characteristic Reformation view which depreciates Mary. The 'intercession' of Mary between God and man – opposed to such Lutheran assertions as *sola fide, sola gratia* ('salvation by faith or grace alone') – simply cannot occur in *Othello*. Thus, Desdemona's 'prayers' of intercession for Cassio to Othello are not answered.

Hassel also pointed to copious (and lesser noted) material from some medieval Mystery plays such as 'Joseph's Doubt' and 'Troubles of Joseph' in which, as he puts it, 'Joseph's concern that Mary's pregnancy must mean her infidelity' parallels Othello's own anxieties. Ultimately, Hassel contended, the play comes down to a matter of 'just judgment', which, he noted, David Bevington has called 'the ultimate issue for medieval drama'. Hassel concluded by suggesting how 'fifteenth and sixteenth century plays and paintings of "just judgment" may also inform Othello's tortured misjudgment first of Desdemona and then of himself'.[63]

Clifford Ronan stated that 'Like all life conceived by the early modern imagination the action of Othello transpires on both a temporal and an eternal stage.' Ronan is another critic who thinks that *Othello* is Shakespeare's most rigorously theological tragedy. Support for this view can be seen (Ronan believed) in the play's use of symbols (such as water or candles), dialogue, character and allusion. These references do not necessarily suggest a thoroughgoing Calvinism but are extremely diverse; the play, for example, records obvious remarks about 'Turkish ... perfidy, Moroccan innocence and jealousy, African pagan barbarism, occultist spells and fortune telling, cannibalism, and the like'. Ronan concluded by discussing the Samaritan woman at the well (Gospel of John) and the idea that the play actually embraces more of an emphasis on the love of God, rather than emphasizing the views of the 'Calvinist-leaning church in Shakespeare's England'.[64]

A final treatment of religion's role in the play, this time again from a Protestant point of view, is provided by Maurice

Hunt. Hunt foregrounded Protestant debates current at the time of Shakespeare's composing *Othello* (and *Measure for Measure*) as a contextual cultural framework through which to understand the tragedy of the play. A lesser-cited scene in Act 2, where Othello and Desdemona celebrate their nuptials, is looked at closely in order to demonstrate an underlying 'double predestination' rhetoric in Cassio's lines concerning salvation. That Cassio does not believe that good works play a role in salvation is evident enough from these lines (2.3.105–8), but Hunt took this Protestant theological debate as a point of departure for investigating other characters and scenes.[65]

Discussions of philosophy

Philosophical issues of epistemology, or ways of knowing, are closely allied with the play's religious issues. Joshua Avery, for example, argued that since epistemology is a central division between Protestant and Catholic theology, Othello's 'truth-seeking approach, which parallels in key respects a distinctively Protestant epistemology, contributes to his deception and consequent tragedy. Shakespeare's tragic representation may, therefore, by read partly as a cautionary tale for a particular cast of mind.'[66]

Also concerned with the contrast between newer, modern ways of perception and older, traditional ones is John Channing Briggs, who discussed kinds of proof in *Othello*. Briggs argued that Francis Bacon's characteristic understanding of persuasion and proof can be observed in the struggles that comprise the central plot of *Othello*. These struggles are embedded in the titular character's negotiation of 'artificial', that is, 'artful' (oral, based on probable reasoning) and 'inartificial' (visual, based on material signs) types of proof that Shakespeare has put in the play. Briggs closely examined Aristotle's definitions of 'artificial' and 'inartificial' proof, which contextualized Bacon's rejection of rationally reasoned (interpretative) aspects of persuasion, so-called 'artificial proof', in favour of the 'inartificial' variety of proof. Briggs demonstrated the idolatrous tendencies inherent in the privileging of inartificial or ocular proofs that Iago presents as an avenue leading to absolute certainty. Othello destroys that which is important through idolizing the 'ocular proofs' that Iago presents – the handkerchief, the lies about what Cassio said while sleeping beside Iago – thus confirming to himself beyond a doubt the 'worst possibility he can envision'. Briggs summarized his careful and persuasive argument: 'The deterioration of Othello's capacity to express, receive, and interpret the accessible yet relatively immaterial *artificial* proofs of love – gestural and linguistic language of affection, petition, offering, and faith – is matched by his reckless and yet almost anesthetic faith in the revelatory power of artless [i.e., inartificial] proof.'[67]

Discussions of marriage

All these philosophical and theological considerations are raised within very specific material contexts, such as marriage. David Bevington, for example, asked why Othello in Act 3, Scene 3 gives 'perhaps the most insightful definition [of marriage] in all the canon', only to turn completely around just eighty lines later and become a 'stereotype of the anxious male beset by fears of womanly duplicity?'[68] Bevington's answer was that Othello's view of marriage, from the very outset, is somewhat self-centred.

Also considering marriage, Paula McQuade found that the play makes use of the Catholic moral tradition of casuistry (the judging of 'cases of conscience') to show the failure of 'companionate marriage' in *Othello*, that is, the emerging ideal of husband and wife sharing intellectual interests and being each other's help-meets. In looking at the development of the companionate marriage ideal in the Renaissance, McQuade cited seventeenth-century marriage manuals, such as that by Robert Cleaver, to establish 'that the classical understanding of friends as one soul in two bodies is perfected in the theological conception of husband and wife as one flesh'. Protestant manuals in particular emphasized the pleasures of both physical intercourse ('due benevolence') and social intercourse between husband and wife; they also insisted upon the necessity for truth-telling in their mutual relations. Catholic theologians, though, with their greater attention to actual social, concrete circumstances of marital life, found it defensible that the wife, because of her inferior social position, might on occasion lie to her husband in order to protect her life. (The most famous example of the period was called the 'lying adulteress'.) Both Catholic casuistry, then, and the play *Othello*, in which Desdemona justifiably (because of her husband's dangerous emotional state) lies about possessing Othello's handkerchief, indicate the limits of the ideal of the companionate marriage. The play (according to McQuade) demonstrated the 'impossibility of wifely honesty within a marriage relationship that assumes that husband and wife can be "friends" and thus speak truthfully while insisting upon the husband's social superiority'.[69]

Lynda Boose placed the marriage of Othello and Desdemona in the larger context of Shakespeare's representation of marriage ritual and tradition. She argued that it was customary, in plays where a marriage is enacted, to stage some kind of marital rite showing the giving away of the bride by her father. But the demands of tragic convention require that this practice be truncated or deformed; thus, in *Othello* Brabantio's extreme unwillingness to hand over his daughter to the Moor before the Senate (in contrast to Desdemona's playing perfectly her role as willing bride) is a kind of parody of a proper church wedding and is a sign and portent of the ensuing troubled marriage.[70] Carol Thomas Neely considered more generally the relations between men and women and in the process she fruitfully compared

Othello and Shakespeare's comic plays. Neely thinks that Emilia is 'dramatically and symbolically the play's fulcrum', but that the women as a group are both realistic – while still being romantic – and articulate in a way that the play's men are not. The women, Neely argued, are not as lethal nor as fatuously idealistic nor as insecurely suspicious as the men; Neely praised even as marginal and (to some) contemptible a character as Bianca as being as 'active' and as possessing as 'open-eyed enduring affection' as that of the other women. Comparing Bianca to her lover Cassio, Neely said: 'She mocks him to his face but not behind his back, as he does her.' In Neely's reading, apparently incompatible adjectives – e.g. Desdemona and Emilia are 'strong, realistic, and compliant' – were shown rather to be paradoxical and imaginatively fitting for the play.

Neely believed that the men in the play are characterized by their relations to women and also by 'their bonds with other men who guarantee their honor and reputation'. Iago is clever at making himself the intimate of several other men – Roderigo, Cassio and Othello – and at sealing his ties with each man by a 'shared contempt toward another'. Although soldiers by trade, the men are curiously inept at killing (Othello alone is successful and his killing is a suicide) and they are as unable to be friends with each other as to sustain romantic relationships. They do not take responsibility for their own actions, finding (among other explanations) the 'devil' a convenient source of their excesses. Unlike in the comedies, in *Othello* the women are unable to 'transform or to be reconciled with the men' because of the inability of the two sexes to understand one another. According to Neely, Othello does not before his death show any real self-knowledge, and he is the same man at the end as at the beginning – insecure, romantic and 'self-justifying'.[71]

Some of the most useful (and finest) of Shakespearean criticism is in books in which a critic spends a few pages, often without footnotes, talking generally about many or all of the plays. Some major editions of the works have notable introductions

(David Bevington's are especially valuable), and superb single-volume critical introductions have been penned by Mark van Doren, Maurice Charney, A. D. Nuttall, Marjorie Garber and several others. Van Doren located the evil in *Othello* in the hero himself – there is no one else large enough to qualify (his tragedy is both his 'punishment and his privilege') – and the grossness with which Iago awakens Desdemona's father Brabantio in the play's opening scene is paralleled with the vitriolic harshness which Othello himself will use against Desdemona later on. Van Doren's analysis of the majestic poetry which Othello speaks – the 'Othello music' as G. Wilson Knight once called it – is especially illuminating. Van Doren argued that Othello's habitual mode is silence but that he is stung into speech by his love for Desdemona and the cynical manipulations of Iago – thus his capacity for both noble and profane utterances.[72]

Maurice Charney, an admirer of van Doren's criticism, similarly points to Othello's own artistic bent (as opposed to the usually cited 'creativity' of Iago). Othello, Charney argued, can evoke memorably Desdemona's undeniable virtues even as he is tortured by her presumed infidelity ('O, the world hath not a sweeter creature: She might lie by an emperor's side and command him tasks' [4.1.180–2]). Charney found a particularly telling example of Othello's impressionableness in the way he often echoes Iago's speech. Iago first gains his general's attention about possible infidelity by uttering the interjection 'Ha' when he sees Cassio leave Desdemona in Act 3, Scene 3, following it with 'I like not that', which of course leads Othello to demand what was wrong. Othello then repeatedly uses this same expression throughout the rest of the play, and Charney proposes that 'Ha' 'becomes the spoken sign of betrayal' in the play.[73]

Marjorie Garber pointed out that, as often happens in Shakespeare's plays, the middle of *Othello* transports us from a 'civilized place to a wild one'. The play's change of locale from Venice to Cyprus reminds us of the island's association with the goddess Venus – and of her adulterous relationship with the god of war, Mars. They were caught in bed with each other by Venus's jealous husband Vulcan, the lame god of the forge, who entrapped them with a golden net of his own making. Garber argued that *Othello*, among many other things, re-enacts this myth, with Iago serving as the jealous voyeur seeking to throw his own net over the bedded lovers – whose 'affair' is of course not adulterous but perfectly legitimate; this, says Garber, is a significant change to the myth. Another insight offered by Garber: Othello is so used to seeing himself as superhuman through his incredible martial exploits that he is unable to be a merely normal human husband, so that 'it is Othello's very refusal to trust the personal, to trust his own feelings, that gives Iago the opportunity he seeks'.[74]

A. D. Nuttall's essay on *Othello* had other notable comments besides those cited earlier about Iago. Just as *Hamlet*'s central problem is the reason for the hero's delay, said Nuttall, *Othello*'s is the reason for the hero's gullibility. Noting that Rymer found it contemptible that the great military hero is 'overwhelmed by small domestic details', Nuttall said that this is in fact exactly what the play is about: 'this man who should have died on the field of battle is destroyed by small-scale household stuff'. Bertram's comment in *All's Well That Ends Well* is apposite here – 'War is no strife / To the dark house and the detested wife' (2.3.291–2).[75]

Discussions of pedagogy and close reading

In an imaginative and practical discussion of pedagogical issues in teaching Shakespeare's tragedies, Andrew Hiscock proposed that 'embed[ding] the study of *Othello* in a collection of (excerpted) early modern documents (the source tale from Cinthio's *Gli Hecatommithi*, *Titus Andronicus*, Peele's *Battle of Alcazar*, relevant extracts from Hakluyt's *Principal Navigations*) and others might revitalize students' understanding of familiar plays. Another means to the same

end, Hiscock suggested, is to draw together contrasting
critical discussions on a well-known play – again, he chooses
Othello as an especially suitable example, which can have
an 'emancipating effect on discussion and can produce lively
results encouraging a plurality of response to critical scenes or
to the plays as a whole'.[76]

The Modern Language Association has a series of
pedagogical books discussing how to teach great literature.
Othello is discussed in the series, and Maurice Hunt had a
number of suggestions on how teachers and students might
approach the play. He suggested first that teachers begin
with a thorough consideration of Iago's motivation, perhaps
through re-examining Aristotle's discussion in the *Poetics*,
which considers motivation in drama. Hunt then broadly
surveyed historical perspectives that might be applied to the
play, as wide-ranging as how Shakespeare's contemporaries
might have seen Iago (as a 'conflated ... stage villain or
vice and the satanic figure of stage devil') to the notion of
Coleridge and E. H. Seymore that 'Iago seems to have too
many motives for his evil and thus, paradoxically, no motives
for it at all'.[77]

Ultimately, close reading – looking at the play line by
line, scene by scene – is as useful as any critical method,
for scholars as well as for teachers and students. Robert C.
Evans has profitably examined a number of different texts
in this manner, including *Othello*. His particular thematic
focus on the play is friendship. He used common language
and a relaxed style to look comprehensively at the subject
throughout the entire play. At the play's opening, for example,
he noticed the shallowness of Iago and Roderigo's friendship
as well as Iago's hypocrisy in complaining that 'Preferment
goes by letter and affection / And not by old gradation'
(1.1.35–6) after having himself 'used mediators to try to
win promotion'. Here, said Evans, 'the grasping, ambitious
individualist poses as a defender of dying traditions'. One
of the play's principal themes, he thought, is whether or not
non-sexual friendship can exist between a man and a woman;

and while Evans did not discuss this subject – he said the topic would take an article unto itself – similar commentary could also usefully be written on the play's portrayal of friendship between a black man and a white man.[78]

In a complementary article on flattery and friendship Evans considered how Plutarch's *Moralia*, which discusses 'How to Tell a Flatterer from a Friend', and Sir Thomas Elyot's *The Book Named The Governor* might both have influenced *Othello*. One conclusion from this study is that 'Othello is less a foolish dupe who falls victim to the connivings of a satanic Machiavel (as some critics have alleged) than a basically (if flawed) good man betrayed by an apparently good friend.' Evans noted that concern about the dangers of false friends nearly superseded the pleasure enjoyed with true friends in the extensive Renaissance literature on friendship in the second half of the sixteenth century. Evans closely read Act 4, Scene 1, a scene often 'chopped to bits' by modern productions. This is particularly unfortunate, he argued, because here Iago 'convincingly manages to play the false friend before three separate targets – Othello, Cassio, and Lodovico, none of whom seems for a minute to doubt the ensign's solid integrity'.[79]

Much might also be said of the setting of the play, as Venice, at the crossroads of Europe and Asia, was an important trading centre in the Renaissance. Shakespeare used the setting for *The Merchant of Venice* as well as *Othello* and James Andreas has noticed some pointed similarities between the two plays. These include the fact that, in both works, 'ethnic minorities or aliens are tolerated and even encouraged for the 'service' they provide to the state – lending money and military expertise' – but their 'social and especially sexual interaction with native Venetians is tightly circumscribed'. There is also a 'theft' of the daughter from the father (by marriage) in both plays. In addition, Shakespeare leads audiences (through his rhetorical and dramatic mastery) to sympathize to some degree with both Othello and Shylock. Andreas then spent a portion of the essay examining how Jews and Blacks were linked by Elizabethans, not only in terms of 'complexion', but also of moral behaviour, as 'thieves and murderers'.[80] The essay concluded with an extended comparison between Othello and Shylock. Also on the topic of setting, David McPherson's *Shakespeare, Jonson and the Myth of Venice* offered an excellent full account of Venice's role in the two plays.[81]

And, finally, for readers who may have trouble following the play's story, Jay Halio proposed 'Reading *Othello* backwards'. The textual question of composition is a relevant one, he showed, because Shakespeare's source for *Othello*, the Venetian 'novella' written by Giraldi Cinthio in 1566, does not include any of the material that we find in Acts 1 and 2 of the play. Halio then suggested 'reading the play backwards', due to his definition of 'tragedy' as 'often including an alternative to disaster, one that we are invited to recognize'. These alternatives in *Othello*, he argues, are presented in Acts 1 and 2, where audiences and readers perceive an Othello who is rational, calm and in full possession of his wits. Iago tries to move Othello to rash action in the disturbances that he incites after Othello's wedding but is unable to do so because of the Moor's calm demeanour and poised speech: 'Keep up your bright swords, for the dew will rust them' (1.2.59), as he says to the armed guard that came to take him to the Duke to explain his marriage. The investigation which then ensues is a model of probity and fairness, allowing each of the affected parties – Brabantio, Othello and Desdemona – to have their say, with a judgement that is objective and consistent with the facts. 'Shakespeare invented [these] scenes', says Halio, 'to include a standard of behaviour and justice against which the actions of acts 3 through 5, the events in Cinthio's novella, might be judged.'[82]

Why then, one might ask in concluding this survey of over three hundred years of *Othello* criticism, does Othello so wildly depart from this procedure when investigating Iago's case against Desdemona's fidelity? Is it because the barbarian within will ultimately have its way, as Schlegel and a number of other critics have said or strongly hinted, an interpretation more than slightly tinged with prejudice? But surely this is unlikely in a work of what many believe is the world's greatest writer? And Halio helps us see, for example, that Shakespeare's own contribution to the Othello story is to establish vividly and dramatically the nobility of the Moor, an embodiment of what Aristotle considered one of the finest types of character, the magnanimous or great-souled man.[83] There is much truth in the notion that he was so quickly taken from his life-long occupation of soldier and placed into the circumstances of domestic life in a foreign culture that he must have felt insecure and easily upset. Although, again, Act 1 showed little evidence of this.

Halio's own explanation is perhaps as good as any. Because Othello 'is an absolutist', that is, one who insists upon knowing the truth in matters that are close to him, he is prey to an 'anxiety that ultimately undoes him'.[84] Othello understood this himself at the end of his life, that he was one 'who loved not wisely but too well' (5.2.342), as his excessive insistence upon 'ocular proof' of his wife's faithfulness led him to give credence to material evidence that was either falsified (Iago's report of what Cassio had said in his sleep) or irrelevant (the handkerchief). There is perhaps no more lamentable fall of a great man from prosperity to ruin in all of Shakespeare's plays than that of Othello. But if the play is read backwards, many readers may best remember the Othello of Acts 1 and 2, the hero as Shakespeare distinctively imagined him.

2

'Let Me the Curtains Draw': *Othello* in Performance

Christopher Baker

In Act 5, Scene 2 of *Othello*, just after the Moor has murdered Desdemona, he draws the curtains around her bed before Emilia enters the room, momentarily hiding his crime from her but also bringing down the curtain on his most tragic performance, ending what he knows to be the play's most intense scene: 'O, come in, Emilia. / Soft, by and by, let me the curtains draw' (5.2.102–4).[1] A mid-nineteenth-century promptbook directs that Othello 'Goes up to bed, – touches the side of the drap'y curtains, they descend, and enclose them from the audience.'[2] Othello's awareness of his own theatricality at this moment – his sense of how his behaviour might 'play' for an onlooker – is a notable metadramatic feature of the play: 'I know this act shows horrible and grim' (5.2.201). Thomas Rymer's notoriously critical *Short View of Tragedy* (1693) singles out this moment as yet another reason to condemn the play: Othello hesitates before killing Desdemona 'that he might have a convenient while so to *roul his Eyes*, and so to gnaw his *nether lip* to the spectators'.[3] Despite Rymer, the scene nevertheless reinforces that it is not only the audience that is both involved in the play and yet outside it as observers of the performance, but likewise the hero himself, who often seems conscious of both his own identity within his story and of himself as the object of others' gaze.[4]

But Othello's self-awareness fails him when he needs it most; only with agonizing slowness does he realize what the audience knows full well, that he is not merely a passionate husband but the tragically unwitting victim of a drama directed by his most trusted officer and lethal foe. Perhaps no other Shakespearean tragedy makes such successful use of dramatic irony, forcing us to witness Othello transformed into a creature of jealousy. We feel compelled to warn him of his enemy, like the spectator in a Victorian performance who shouted his advice to actor Charles Macready: 'Choke the devil! choke him!'[5] The play's irrepressible ability to arouse its audiences' most ardent affections and animosities marked its earliest performances. Recollecting a performance by the King's Men in 1610 at Oxford, Henry Jackson recalled, 'truly the celebrated Desdemona, slain in our presence by her husband, although she pleaded her case very effectively throughout, yet moved (us) more after she was dead, when, lying on her bed, she entreated the pity of the spectators by her very countenance'.[6] As Marvin Rosenberg has observed, 'Not by accident was it a leading tragedy – perhaps the leading tragedy – of the early 1600's.'[7]

A play's performance history can be approached from the dramatic and critical theories of the eras in which it is staged, to the cultural and social assumptions which influence its production, to its audiences' artistic preferences and tastes. This chapter explores the play's history through the inter-pretations offered by significant actors over time, performers who, especially in the nineteenth century, could arouse fierce loyalties. Tracing the play's stage interpreters reveals critical problems posed by the tragedy, especially concerning Othello himself. As the Ghanaian-born actor Hugh Quarshie has said, 'the main difficulty about playing Othello is getting plausibly from the magnanimous and dignified warrior of the first half to the obsessive, homicidal, gibbering wreck of the second half'.[8] The relationships between such extremes are neither simple nor obvious. Are Othello's grandeur and violence both of a piece, or is one more central to his personality than the other? At what point do we witness the transition from the general to the degenerate? If he was considered 'great of heart' (5.2.359), then actors traditionally were praised for conveying a thoughtful, heroic Moor, a stranger to Venice now acculturated and valued for his military prowess and widely deserving of admiration 'for the dangers [he] had passed' (1.3.168) – in eighteenth-century productions, the very model of a modern Augustan general. However, if he were considered more truly the 'circumcised dog' (5.2.353), actors were lauded for depicting a man – as often African as Moor – who was 'savage' in his excitable credulity, in his naïve trust leading to a self-justifying vindictiveness.

Neither of these options alone fully defines Othello's character; they shade into each other in a fine *discordia concors*. Many colliding binaries – love and hate, African and European, jealousy and trust, superior and subaltern, and more – have been used to probe the play and its hero. Which 'Othello' an actor preferred, or which unique combination of or transition between these poles he sought to portray, influenced the role of Iago as well, which grew to rival the general's. If the passionate African predominated, then Iago's character may have tended towards the *agent provocateur* whose task was to awaken the uncivilized urges already present beneath the general's civilized veneer to disclose the fragile yet vindictively jealous husband.[9] If Othello's native civility were foremost, then Iago seemed almost a perverse *auteur*, devising ways to corrupt an apparently sterling character, engendering an inexorable hatred within the civilized, Christianized foreigner. Iago's presentation of himself offered another opportunity for dramatic invention, perhaps as cold, premeditating sociopath; jovial but conniving barracks buddy; jealous husband wounded, like Othello, by fears of being cuckolded; or, eventually, as rejected subordinate fraught with homosexual longing. Myriad oppositions are held in tension within Othello and drive actors' varied interpretations.

The production of *Othello* seen by Henry Jackson in 1610 must have starred Richard Burbage (1567–1619), Shakespeare's famous tragedian. Burbage's competitor for tragic roles, Edward Alleyn of the Admiral's Men, had starred as a variety of Marlovian overreaching heroes at the Rose and Fortune theatres. His comparatively bombastic style suited those personalities as well as the dramatic rhythm of Marlowe's mighty line. However, *Othello* was mounted not only in the public Globe but also in the private Blackfriars theatre, an enclosed space for audiences eager for more nuanced styles. If, as Martin Holmes suggests, Shakespeare was composing his tragic heroes with the skills of his actors and the conditions of his stages in mind, we can presume that Burbage's Blackfriars Othello enacted a subtlety of character that Alleyn lacked. The play's atmosphere of intense, private emotion was well suited for a theatre 'where a small, intimate audience can hear every word without having to be assailed with loud declamation', and Burbage seems to have excelled in generating the Moor's character in this enclosed space.[10] An anonymous elegy singles out his success in this part:

> But let me not forget one chiefest part
> Wherein, beyond the rest, he mov'd the heart,
> The grieved Moor, made jealous by a slave,
> Who sent his wife to fill a timeless grave.[11]

On 2 September 1642 the theatres were closed by the London authorities, now dominated by Puritans convinced that the stages menaced public morality. They reopened in 1660 to audiences attuned to the freer views of the Restoration court. Female actors now performed women's roles instead of men, and male actors attempting female parts (pre-Civil War stage veterans) were mocked:

men act that are between
Forty and fifty, wenches of fifteen,
With bone so large and nerve so incompliant,
When you call *Desdemona*, enter *Giant*.[12]

These lines from the prologue to a 1660 production of *Othello* document the play's staying power; it was one of the first dramas to be revived when the stages reopened. Though it received judicious cuts later in the century, *Othello* did not undergo a full-scale recasting like the happy ending Nahum Tate imposed upon his revision of *King Lear* (1681), but the popular conception of the heroic protagonist who arouses admiration even when gripped by tragic flaws – perhaps most admired when most flawed – fed the Restoration portrayal of a tainted yet regal Othello.

The Augustan 'improvements' made to Shakespeare sought to conform his plays to neoclassical expectations of tragedy and prune away 'primitive' features. The Dublin Smock Alley Theatre promptbook reveals that suggestive or bawdy language, outmoded words, or references to Othello as anything but refined and commanding were cut, as also Emilia's frank discussion of the sexes and Desdemona's willow song and recollections of her mother's maid Barbara.[13] Despite Rymer's frustration at Shakespeare's having cast a Negro as his protagonist, Othello's blackness did not diminish audiences' enthusiasm; in a favourite theatrical tactic, James Quin played up the contrast between the Moor's white gloves and his black skin. Casting Othello's tragic nobility in deeper relief, Iago was a low comic villain as played by Samuel Sandford. '[H]is figure', wrote Anthony Aston, 'was diminutive and mean, (being Round-shoulder'd, Meagre-fac'd, Spindle-shank'd, Splay-footed, with a sour Countenance, and long lean Arms) [that] render'd him a proper Person to discharge *Iago* … and (as King *Charles* said) was the best Villain in the World'.[14]

Thomas Rymer's attack on *Othello* was based on the strictest application of rigid expectations: characters should behave exactly as would their social counterparts in real life (English life, that is – Othello typically wore the uniform of a British officer until 1744 when he was given 'native' attire).[15] Decorum of speech must be consistent; motivation should be appropriate for heroic personages; and a clear moral should inform the work, with good rewarded and evil punished according to 'poetic justice' (a term Rymer coined). Measured against such standards, Shakespeare's original *Othello* fails miserably. The protagonist and his wife are simply unbelievable: 'never in Tragedy, nor in Comedy, nor in Nature was a Souldier with his Character'; Othello is 'like a tedious, drawling, tame Goose'; and 'there is nothing in the noble *Desdemona* that is not below any Countrey Chamber-maid with us ... A Negro General is a Man of strange Mettle', sneered Rymer, not realizing that Othello's strangeness is central to his dramatic power.[16] But audiences who flocked to the play were clearly responding to a different set of standards. The uplifting examples and admonitions that Rymer expected to be *taught* by a tragedy were instead expected by other critics to be *caught* by an audience swept up in the play's lively 'Passions'.

The actor Thomas Betterton (1635–1710) was equal to this task. He dominated the part of Othello on the Restoration stage until his death, when Richard Steele's memorial in *The Tatler* (#167; 4 May 1710) praised his skill: 'The wonderful agony which he appeared in when he examined the circumstance of the handkerchief in *Othello*; the mixture of love that intruded upon his mind upon the innocent answers Desdemona makes, betrayed in his gesture such a variety and vicissitude of passions as would admonish a man to be afraid of his own heart and perfectly convince him that it is to stab it, to admit that worst of daggers, jealousy.'[17] Experiencing such a 'vicissitude of passions' led Steele to reflect 'upon the emptiness of all human perfection and greatness in general'.[18] Betterton extended Burbage's reading of the 'grieved Moor', and other actors attempted their parts with similar emotional effect. On 11 October 1660 Samuel Pepys attended a performance starring the first Restoration actor to play Othello, Nicholas Burt (?1621–after 1689), and his diary recorded that 'a pretty lady, that sat by me, called out, to see Desdemona smothered'.[19]

James Quin (1693–1766), David Garrick (1717–79), Colley Cibber (1671–1757), Spranger Barry (1719–77) and Barton Booth (1681–1733) all acted prominently in *Othello* after Betterton. In the three decades between Betterton's death and Garrick's rise at the Drury Lane Theatre, *Othello* appeared in all but two London seasons. Summarizing the role's demands, Francis Gentleman wrote in 1777 that Othello should be 'amiably elegant and above middle stature; his expression full and sententious, for the declamatory part; flowing and harmonious for the love-scenes; rapid and powerful for each violent climax of jealous rage'.[20] Acting styles were changing. Quin (also known as 'Bellower' Quin) belonged to an older, declamatory tradition which came to seem monotonous, whereas Barry and Garrick were noted for their intensity. By mid-century London was a hotbed of theatrical enthusiasts, as Virginia Mason Vaughan notes: 'Drury Lane partisans versus Covent Garden devotees, Garrick fans versus Barry fans – none hesitated to join the fray'.[21] Barry excelled at the Moor's nobly heroic grief; one observer remarked on his 'muscles stiffening, the veins distending, and the red blood boiling through his dark skin – a mighty flood of passion accumulating for several minutes – and at length, bearing down its barriers and sweeping onward in thunder, love, reason, mercy all before it. The females, at this point, used invariably to shriek, whilst those with stouter nerves grew uproarious in admiration ...'[22] Another observed that in Barry audiences saw 'that mere color could not be a barrier to affection'.[23] In contrast to Barry, Garrick strove for a more fiery, unshackled Othello, believing that in 'Othello [Shakespeare] had wished to paint that passion [jealousy] in all its violence, and that is why he chose an African in whose being circulated fire instead of blood, and whose true or imaginary character could excuse all boldnesses of expression and all exaggerations of passion'.[24] Garrick moved interpretation of the character in a more spontaneous direction, prompting Quin to say, 'If this young fellow is right, I and the rest of the players must have been all wrong.'[25]

Fewer details remain of eighteenth-century Desdemonas, but Sarah Kemble Siddons (1755–1831) was noted for her 'elegant deportment, cordial manners, and smothered anxiety, on the landings at Cyprus' as well as her 'intense sympathy'.[26] The phrase 'smothered anxiety' neatly captures the tension between intense feeling and proper deportment that shaped both leading roles. Charles Macklin was often paired as Iago to play up their contrasts, emphasized through Iago's makeup as a 'broad-breasted, bald-headed, shaggy browed, hooked-nosed individual, as rough and husky as a cocoa-nut, with a barking or grunting delivery more peculiar than pleasing'.[27] Cibber's portrayal of Iago to Booth's Othello seemed notable for its hyperbole to one observer: he 'shrugs up his shoulders, shakes his Noddle, and, with a fawning Motion in his Hands, drawls out' his lines, so that 'Othello must be supposed a fool, a stock, if he does not see thro' him'.[28] Such contemporary accounts reveal not merely the divided popular opinion about both the actors and the character of Othello but the likelihood that a key to the play's popularity was the *frisson* offered by witnessing the Moor's emotions clashing with prevailing tastes and canons, of which Rymer's essay was an extreme example. One suspects that theatregoers, accustomed to the demand for propriety, loved the play for the opportunity it gave to break with convention: females attended for the chance to shriek, and men like Pepys attended for the chance to watch them do it.[29] Garrick believed that the need for black makeup hindered the character's expressiveness, while actors like Quin purposely called attention to the Moor's blackness, but actors and audiences alike responded sympathetically to Othello's race more as a reflection of his exotically admirable character than as a cause of Venetian ostracism.

Gradually the stage conception of Othello was shifting, the pendulum swinging more towards a freer expression of his uninhibited side, an alteration also emerging in literary criticism. Unlike earlier attempts to define him against pre-established social or literary norms, Romantic critics of the early nineteenth century read Othello more inductively, finding his nobility and violence to be intimately mingled rather than discrete emotional states. William Hazlitt, for example, was less concerned with Othello's social persona than with his tragic psyche:

> It is in working his noble nature up to this extremity through rapid but gradual transitions, in raising passion to its height from the smallest beginnings and in spite of all obstacles, in painting the expiring conflict between love and hatred, tenderness and resentment, jealousy and remorse, in unfolding the strength and the weaknesses of our nature, in uniting sublimity of thought with the anguish of keenest woe, in putting in motion the various impulses that agitate this our mortal being, and at last blending them in that noble tide of deep and sustained passion, impetuous but majestic, that "flows on to the Propontic, and knows no ebb", that Shakespear has shewn the mastery of his genius and of his power over the human heart.[30]

Hazlitt stresses how Othello's 'noble nature' is dynamically transmuted 'through rapid but gradual transitions' into 'deep and sustained passion' as coterminous elements within a more organically complex self, each element contributing to the other's intensity.

Barry and Garrick would likely have agreed with Hazlitt's insight, but it took Edmund Kean (?1787–1833) to realize such a conception on stage. Byron wept at Kean's performances; 'To see him act', said Coleridge famously, 'is like reading Shakespeare by flashes of lightning.'[31] Despite his short stature, Kean conveyed for Hazlitt 'all the fitful fever of the blood, the jealous madness of the brain: his heart seemed to bleed with anguish, while his tongue dropped broken, imperfect accents of woe ...'[32] Just as Quin had emphasized Othello's blackness by carefully peeling off his white gloves, Kean too had his moment of racially charged stage business. As one observer wrote: 'One of his finest instantaneous actions was his clutching his black hand slowly round his head as though his brains were turning, and then writhing round and standing in dull agony with his back to the audience.'[33] After witnessing a performance, John Keats was moved by Kean's demand that Iago 'prove [his] love a whore', especially the line 'blood, blood, blood' (3.3.454); it was 'direful and slaughterous to the deepest degree', recalled Keats, 'the very words appeared stained and gory ... His voice loosed on them like the wild dog on the savage relics of an eastern conflict.'[34] Keats's use of animal imagery here and the adjective 'savage' may have a racial overtone, but it is noteworthy that Kean conceived of Othello as not African but Moorish, and used bronze, rather than black, makeup.

Unlike Kean's uninhibited portrayal, the one by William Charles Macready (1793–1873) was more restrained, creating the sense of passions held in check until the very end. More devoted to historical realism than Kean, Macready, with his detailed costumes and scenery, drew on his memories of personal trips to Venice. Prompted more by Victorian propriety than Augustan decorum, Macready erased the play's more violent and erotically charged words (e.g. 'whore' and 'strumpet') and relied on the plot of supposed infidelity without risking any of the potentially offensive original language. He succeeded on both sides of the Atlantic, but, while disturbed by first-hand encounters with American slavery in the 1840s, he put no special emphasis on Othello's race, though he played in blacker makeup than had Kean. While less violently distraught than Kean in earlier scenes, at Desdemona's murder, according to George Vandenhoff, he was 'less the noble Moor ... than an enraged and desperate African, lashed into madness and roused to thirst for blood by vindictive wrath and implacable revenge'.[35] Any sense that

Othello may have been an early incarnation of the Victorian gentleman was shown to be a mere façade for the alien within, an interpretation that may account for Macready's favourable reception in the slave-holding American South.

Macready's physical energy in murdering Desdemona was vigorous enough to cause anxiety in Fanny Kemble (1809–93) who played his ill-fated wife numerous times. He once broke her finger during a performance. 'My only feeling about acting it with Mr. Macready', she stated, 'is dread at his personal violence. I quail at the idea of his laying hold of me in those terrible passionate scenes.'[36] For his part, Macready confided to his diary about Kemble that 'I have never seen [a Desdemona] so bad, so unnatural, so affected, so conceited.'[37] Kemble, English by birth, had in 1834 married Pearce Mease Butler, a prosperous Georgia slave owner; her criticism of the harsh treatment of his slaves contributed to their divorce in 1849. In an 1839 letter to a friend, Kemble noted that if Othello were in fact an African rather than a Moor, it 'would at once settle the difficulties of those commentators who, abiding by Iago's very disagreeable suggestions as to his purely African appearance, are painfully compelled to forego the mitigation of supposing him a Moor and not a Negro'.

Kemble disliked portrayals of Othello's wife as weak, objecting to Desdemonas who would 'acquiesce with wonderful equanimity to their assassination'.[38] More outspoken in this view was late Victorian actress Ellen Terry (1847–1928), renowned for her productions of Shaw, Ibsen and Barrie. 'The general idea', she complained, 'seems to be that Desdemona is a ninny, a pathetic figure.'[39] In fact, she concludes, Desdemona is 'by nature unconventional', 'the kind of woman who being devoid of coquetry behaves as she feels', and 'is not a simpleton, but a saint'. Desdemona is made of sterner stuff than at first appears; her 'love for Othello is not of the sort which "alters when it alteration finds"', and she is proof that 'Shakespeare is one of the very few dramatists who seem to have observed that women have more moral courage than men'. No wonder that Desdemona should find such a close friendship with Emilia, whom Terry praises as a woman with 'plenty of courage', one who, condemning Othello, performs 'an ecstasy of rage', becoming 'a human volcano in eruption, pouring out a lava of abuse'.[40]

Any actress playing Desdemona to the Othello of Tommaso Salvini (1829–1915) had cause to fear the sort of physical maelstrom that Fanny Kemble dreaded. Salvini electrified his audiences with a brutality that exceeded even Kean's. Though using lighter makeup, Salvini, who spoke all his lines in Italian amplified by histrionic gestures, was often described as animalistic when murdering Desdemona: 'he drags her to his feet ... grasps her neck and head with his left hand, knotting his fingers in her loose hair, as if to break her neck ... You heard a crash as he flung her on the bed, and growls as of a wild beast over his prey.'[41] Salvini's controversial portrayal distanced Othello still further from his opening self-possession. An obviously foreign actor, a non-English speaker, was enacting a darker-skinned foreigner who could seem beyond the pale of civilization. Henry James struggled to rescue his own judgement from consigning Othello to an almost subhuman level: 'My remarks may suggest that Salvini's rage is too gross, too much that of a wounded animal; but in reality it does not fall into that excess. It is the rage of an African, but of a nature that remains generous to the end; and in spite of the tiger-paces and tiger-springs, there is through it all, to my sense at least, the tremor of a moral element.'[42] James wishes to retain a vestige of Othello's exotic grandeur, but there is no escaping the racial essentialism of his late Victorian verdict. All one can hope for from this enraged 'African', who so resembles a 'tiger', is but the 'tremor' of any real ethical sensibility. Female approval of Salvini could also be tinged with a racially erotic overtone. As Clara Morris exclaimed, 'his gloating eyes burned with the mere lust of the "sooty Moor" for that white creature of Venice. It was revolting, and with a shiver I exclaimed aloud "Ugh, you splendid brute!"'[43] As seen by Joseph Knight in 1875, Salvini's rendering of Othello's death was inimitable: 'he rises, and at the supreme moment cuts his throat with a short scimitar, hacking and hewing with savage energy, and imitating the noise that escaping blood and air may together make when the windpipe is severed'.[44] Such responses document Virginia Mason Vaughan's conclusion that Othello at the turn of the century tended to be perceived as neither a gentlemanly officer nor an uxorious husband but as an 'exotic Oriental or African whose nobility cloaked the passionate fury of an uncivilized savage'.[45] The latent theme that had been upstaged for so long, the issue modern audiences now see as the play's *raison d'être* – not love, gullibility, jealousy, or honour, but race itself – had taken centre stage.

Unsurprisingly, the earliest black actor to call attention to this theme had to leave America to gain recognition. Ira Aldridge was born in New York in 1807, acted in an all-black company in the 1820s, and at 17 appeared as Othello at the Royalty Theatre in London. Denied access to Covent Garden and Drury Lane, he nevertheless gained notice for an interpretation marked by what Alex Ross terms a 'carefully controlled dramatic arc' in place of Salvini's overwrought gyrations.[46] Though he too displayed an impressive physical anger, Marvin Rosenberg perceptively comments that 'he usually seemed not the barbarian African he was rather expected to be'.[47] In 1852 he played to great approval in Germany and later in Zurich to audiences that included Richard Wagner but had his greatest successes in Russia, where, taking a leaf out of Salvini's book, he acted in German productions of the play, but spoke his lines in English. Later praised by Langston Hughes, W. E. B. DuBois and James Weldon Johnson, Aldridge was, notes Bernth Lindfors, 'the most visible black man in a white world in the middle of the nineteenth century'.[48] However, though stereotypically termed a 'tiger' by some critics, at least one Russian reviewer caught the point of Aldridge's interpretation: 'From Othello is torn the deep cry, "Oh misery, misery, misery!" and in that misery of the African artist is heard the far-off groans of his own people, oppressed by unbelievable slavery, and more than that – the groans of the whole of suffering mankind.'[49] For his Russian and Polish audiences especially, 'Aldridge, as a mere "Negro," was not only one of the best and most effective emissaries of Shakespeare, but also a compelling representative of the antislavery movement and an effective ambassador for the politically, socially, and culturally abused.'[50]

It was left to Paul Robeson (1898–1976) to establish the influence of a black actor in the role in a way that Aldridge could never have achieved in his own country. When English critic James Agate commented that Othello could be any white Englishman, Robeson wryly suggested that he 'try to produce it in Memphis'.[51] Robeson was the first black performer successfully to play Othello on the American stage with an intentional awareness of the play's reflection of the racial predicament of his own society. After opening the play in London in 1930, he took the production to Broadway under Margaret Webster's direction in 1943. For Robeson, Othello was an honourable African of noble lineage; there was no thought of deflecting negative audience opinions by depicting him as a lighter-skinned 'Moor'. As Robeson put it, 'Othello came from a culture as great as that of ancient Venice, came from an Africa of equal stature, and felt he was *betrayed*, and his *human* dignity was *betrayed*.'[52] His voice, stature and stage presence impressed audiences profoundly with an Othello as a living figure of black oppression. John Dover Wilson wrote of seeing the 1930 London production (generally regarded as inferior to the later Broadway version): 'I felt I was seeing the tragedy for the first time, not merely because of Robeson's acting, which despite a few petty faults of technique was magnificent, but because the fact that he was a true Negro seemed to floodlight the whole drama.'[53] Robeson's famed baritone voice lent the part a hortatory grandeur; his was an Othello not merely to be seen but to be heard. Certainly he also intended that audiences feel a certain shock, as 'every night there was an "audible gasp" from the audience when Robeson first kissed Desdemona on Cyprus'.[54] Some harsher judgements of the production sounded academic: 'Shakespeare wrote this part for a white man', declared Herbert Farjeon.[55] Despite the debate it aroused – or perhaps because of it – the 1943 production ran for 296 performances and was 'the longest running and most successful Shakespearean production yet staged in the United States'.[56]

It is difficult to overestimate the impact that Robeson's performance and the questions it raised had on subsequent productions, not least the issue of whether a white actor could or should attempt the role. Was the play to be experienced no longer as a work of dramatic tragedy in its own right but more properly as social commentary? Was it, in Ibsen's sense, a 'problem play'? Was it exclusively about the black experience in a white society or was it a metaphor for the harsh realities faced by any oppressed minority, conveying what Robeson called Shakespeare's 'superb sympathy for the underdog'?[57] Did Desdemona's murder affirm racial prejudices or did it instead verify the insidious victimization of all marginalized persons? Can we call this a racist play, or does Othello's death result from the schemes of a misanthropic sociopath who does not hesitate to kill anyone in his path regardless of race and 'never … speak word' (5.2.301) about what Coleridge called his 'motiveless malignity'?

By the time Robeson's first production of *Othello* had been staged, no fewer than six silent films of the play had appeared in Europe and the United States. Of these, the most notable was the 1922 version starring Emile Jannings and directed by Dimitri Buchowetzki.[58] Less than ninety minutes long, it cuts the role of Bianca entirely – Othello discovers Iago has the handkerchief only when Iago (Werner Krauss) wipes Jannings' forehead with it after the Moor's fit. Also missing are the willow song of Desdemona (Ica von Lenkeffy), her conversation about sexual mores with Emilia (Lya De Putti), and the racially and sexually tinged language that Iago and Roderigo (Ferdinand von Alten) hurl at Brabantio (Friedrich Kumlautuhne). Werner Krauss, with plastered hair and stringy moustache, eerily evokes a portly Hitler and injects slapstick into his role. Dressed in a sexually ambiguous filmy black blouse and black tights, at one point he pulls leaves from a bush and munches them while chatting with the buffoonish Roderigo and skitters across the stage like a gleeful fiend. Douglas Brode is right to say that Krauss is 'guilty of embarrassing overacting', but this portrayal reminds us of Iago's descent from the medieval Vice and classical clever slave, more akin to *Volpone*'s Mosca than to *King Lear*'s Edmund.[59] In height and girth Jannings dominates the cast, impressing with a stolid, Eastern grandeur in a striped burnoose and wearing a scimitar. But at Iago's comment 'I like not that' (3.3.34) his suspicions grow, and Janning's face registers uncomprehending fury and profound shame, his large eyes standing out against his black facepaint as he glares into the camera. Upon seeing Desdemona's handkerchief in Iago's hand, he tears it apart with his teeth in grotesque rage. When he tosses her across the bed we witness the unleashing of inarticulate anger before he kills her, offscreen, and then cowers in a corner. Because of the silent medium and heavily cut text, we miss his subtle descent into revenge; Jannings conveys the onrush of irresistible anger too suddenly, oversimplifying Othello's complex motivation.

Much more accomplished and widely discussed was Orson Welles's 1952 film version. The opening title announces that this is an adaptation, a disclaimer authorizing Welles's liberties, such as inserting a voiceover and giving Roderigo a pet dog. Othello's transition from confident married commander to jealousy-crazed murderer is the tragedy's central dynamic, but Welles brackets his film with scenes of Othello's funeral ('cliché Eisenstein', remarks Kenneth Rothwell), making the play essentially a flashback framed by the hero's death.[60] This strategy undercuts the Moor's hopeful expectations at the start, diminishing the effect of his fall into murderous hate. Pamela Mason finds 'an impressive stillness' in his opening speech to the Senate, but in the context of the opening funeral scene this seems a sepulchral stillness, not the self-assured public assertion we expect at this early point.[61] The musical score, marked by a simple, threatening piano refrain, enhances the stark effect of light and shadow. Samuel Crowl calls the film Welles's 'most cinematically complex and baroque adaptation of Shakespeare'.[62]

Welles's blackface varies in intensity throughout the film; though he is often shot in shadow to deepen the tint, the effect is uneven; at times he appears merely smudged and sweaty. Micheál MacLiammóir's Iago is too predictably sinister. With heavy eyebrows and large, dark eyes he is a brooding and one-dimensional presence, lacking Iago's chameleonic ability to exploit every situation. As Patricia Tatspaugh has pointed out, although Welles himself felt that Iago should display 'no conscious villainy', 'MacLiammóir's Iago is passionless, even somewhat mechanical'.[63] Suzanne Cloutier is a waiflike Desdemona, blonde, petite, always bathed in a light as intense as her husband's shadow. Her defence of Cassio is more fearful pleading than energetic request; only at the moment of her death, begging for life, does she express genuine emotion. The shimmering veil Othello strangles her with emphasizes her oddly diaphanous, unearthly demeanour. Fay Compton's Emilia is perfect as the earthy, plain-spoken foil to Desdemona.

Viewers of his earlier 1948 film of *Macbeth* will recognize Welles's characteristic desire to have setting and camera work convey the inner world of characters. The interior shots make rather heavy-handed use of arches, doorways, staircases, pillars or ceilings, at times suggesting that Othello is caught in an Escher drawing of endless, labyrinthine perspectives from which there is no escape. This *Othello* is staged in the architecture of a troubled mind, though at times rapid cuts, close-ups, and low- and high-angle shots, especially between Othello and Iago, come too rapidly and without a clear relationship to the narrative moment. The camera itself thus becomes a disconcerting character. Welles also emphasizes bars, windows, lattices, screens or slatted openings – Iago's cage is the most obvious example – literal and figurative demarcations or barriers, repeated in his use of light and shadow, to underscore confinement and separation. The effect is striking, but once again the Wellesian medium appears to overwhelm the Shakespearean message. As Anthony Davies notes, 'Welles's *Othello* invites us to respond primarily to the image. Shakespeare's *Othello*, more perhaps than any other of his plays, insists that we relate – at times obsessively – with actor and with character.'[64]

Moving from Welles's vision of the play to Laurence Olivier's 1964 film is to shift from a daring expressionism to an equally daring yet clearly more traditional interpretation. This film, however, poses problems because, though it seeks to capture a copy of a stage experience, it necessarily cannot *recreate* that experience. Olivier's affecting rendition on the stage under John Dexter's direction becomes gratuitously hyped in Stuart Burge's film whenever tighter camera shots or close-ups are used; the stylized, exaggerated result strikes many as more distortion than convincing characterization. Olivier admits in his book *On Acting* that this is 'one hell of a difficult part', yet he clearly felt motivated to rise to the challenge of playing a *black* tragic hero, a task requiring careful makeup.[65] But more than makeup was required, and here, in a play and film produced during the height of the American Civil Rights era, was a remarkable – some might say presumptuous – decision by a white actor who believed that it might be possible for him to 'throw away' his own race:

> Black ... I had to *be* black. I had to feel black down to my soul. I had to look out from a black man's world. Not one of repression, for Othello would have felt superior to the white man. If I peeled my skin, underneath would be another layer of black skin. I was to be beautiful. Quite beautiful.
>
> Throwing away the white man was difficult, but fascinating. Of course, you can never truly do this, but there were times when I convinced myself that I had.[66]

Any actor seeks the 'soul' of a part, yet Olivier's declaration that there were 'Moments when I think I am Othello, when I am convinced I am black' seems rather gratuitous (however well-intentioned) for assuming 'blackness' to be a fixed identity inhabitable by anyone willing to expend enough effort.[67] Yet the total theatricality with which he immerses himself in the part (however we judge its success) is so all-consuming that we admire his effort to capture the dilemma of an alien caught in a Venetian web. Apart from his makeup, Olivier put great effort into creating a figure who physically resembled no other Othello on stage or screen, especially in his fluid stride and his low voice for which he had received coaching. As Ronald Bryden reported of a 1964 performance in London,

> He sauntered downstage, with a loose, bare-heeled roll of the buttocks; came to rest feet splayed apart, hip lounging outward ... The hands hung big and graceful. The whole voice was characterized, the o's and a's deepened, the consonants thickened with faint, guttural deliberation ... It could have been caricature, and embarrassment. Instead, after the second performance, a well-known Negro actor rose in the stalls bravoing. For obviously, it was done with love ...[68]

But as the play progresses, what had been the casual, confident saunter of an 'extravagant and wheeling stranger' (1.1.136) degenerates into an off-kilter shuffle; his eyes cross; Othello's formerly commanding voice now booms and screams; his sentences sometimes fade into incoherent squeals.

Frank Finlay plays Iago with fine attention to facial expression that more suits the screen than Olivier's broad gestures. Olivier (who had played Iago himself in 1938) told Kenneth Tynan that he didn't want 'a witty Machiavellian Iago. I want an honest-to-God N. C. O'.[69] For Bryden, Finlay's Iago was 'bony, crop-haired, staring with the fanatic mule-grin of a Mississippi redneck'.[70] Rolling his eyes with impatient disgust, he easily manipulates Robert Lang's Roderigo, a pouty, diffident dandy with bright red hair. Finlay is more expressive than Micheál MacLiammóir and suggests Kenneth Branagh's later combination of easy confidence and diabolical intent in the same role. After Othello's epileptic fit, Finlay crouches behind Olivier's

back to give him a massage, rather like the sinister Vice of a
morality play suggesting evil designs on his victim or perhaps
hinting at Iago's possible homosexual attraction to the general.
Maggie Smith's Desdemona is a poised, refined Venetian,
earnest and loving. With red hair coiled above her head she
is almost of Othello's height, projecting a sense of equality
rather than resembling Suzanne Cloutier's diminutive wife to
Orson Welles's hulking general. She is not fearful or petulant
when arguing Cassio's cause, but bold and insistent, so that
Othello's slap comes as the dramatic shock it should be. Derek
Jacobi's Cassio is energetic and lively, showing a streak of the
short-tempered Hotspur when he gets drunk. At the loss of
his reputation he is appropriately filled with angry self-disgust
rather than sunk in weepy despair like Nathaniel Parker's
Cassio in Oliver Parker's 1995 film. This strong supporting
cast makes Olivier's film very memorable. His decision to black
up for the role, coupled with the hyperbolic tone of its filmed
version, has fed the debate over the relevance of an actor's own
race to the identity of the lead character.

   In 1981 Jonathan Miller directed Antony Hopkins in the
title role for the BBC series of televised Shakespeare plays.
This was the last (and may perhaps be the final) time a major
actor played Othello in blackface on film. Hopkins is more
bronze than black; he affects no changes in his speech or gait
as did Olivier, but his wig is an unruly shock of black hair
often accentuated by a white ruff. The result is a production
that seems less about race *per se* and more about the betrayal
of a naïve husband. Shot almost entirely in candlelit, indoor
settings suggesting the intimacy of the enclosed Blackfriars
playhouse, the play acquires the air of an intense domestic
drama rather than a tragedy played out within the larger fates
of warring city-states. Hopkins enunciates his lines beautifully
but with a curiously halting, almost diffident tone that seems
especially out of place when he arrives to stop the fracas
outside Brabantio's house in Act 1. His emotional reaction
is controlled and subdued, his attitude one of condescending
irritation rather than public anger at this threat upon his

father-in-law and civic peace. His speech to the Venetian senators similarly is reduced to a quiet conversation over a desk rather than the more familiar, rhetorically impressive defence of his marriage designed to move all listeners. Miller seems to take a consciously anti-Olivier approach to the play by downplaying the discourse of the early scenes; certainly this method offers a contrast to Othello's later emotional outbursts in the final acts delivered at full volume, interspersed with his tears of angry frustration and curious, cat-like, open-mouthed hisses. Hopkins is the most introspective of filmed Othellos, especially in the opening acts a reserved and patient man. It is hard to imagine this Othello on the 'tented field' until he later releases his shattering rage; even his first kiss of Desdemona is a modest peck that underplays their love.

Desdemona (Penelope Wilton) is more the mature and loving spouse than the fresh newlywed. Unlike Suzanne Cloutier's ingénue or Irene Jacob's sensual paramour, Wilton conveys a forthright vigour that, while sometimes matronly, allows her to defend herself vigorously against Othello's suspicions and to press Cassio's case with intelligent force. She develops a fine onscreen relationship with Emilia (Rosemary Leach); Miller presents the 'willow' scene sensitively, ending it with Desdemona gazing thoughtfully if apprehensively into the distance, lit only by a single candle. Such a Desdemona is not going to go gently into the night; her murder is violent enough to leave Othello panting and wide-eyed, its erotic subtext rather pointedly evoked by Hopkins' striped codpiece.

Against this somewhat introverted Othello, Bob Hoskins plays a constantly frenetic, even manic Iago, whose theatrical quirk is a frequent laugh of some type; Hoskins runs the gamut of amused giggles and smirks expressing smug self-satisfaction while envisioning his success. Observing Othello's epileptic fit, he literally leaps for joy at seeing his 'medicine' at work (4.1.45). A short actor, he plays Iago as a bumptious 'little man', the officious wheeler-dealer, the sinister Machiavel who is clearly a sadist but also a malevolent trickster; Hoskins himself said that he 'sought to do him like Rumpelstiltskin'.[71]

Below large, black eyebrows his face is almost half covered by a simian black beard which he often strokes thoughtfully, his lower-class speech contrasting thuggishly with Hopkins' clipped diction. In keeping with his devious and prevaricating nature – and notably unlike either Frank Finlay or Kenneth Branagh – he almost never makes eye contact with the camera during his soliloquies, his eyes darting about evasively as he devises his schemes but never resting for long on any single object. Although Iago can change his manner to suit any person or situation he happens to confront, on the deepest level his personality has a flat, pathological, sameness. Hoskins' sporadic laughter directs our attention to this subterranean level of his psyche, even to the final scene when, though stabbed and bleeding, his grisly chuckles echo down the hall as he is taken away to be tortured.

Since Miller's *Othello*, numerous black actors (such as Morgan Freeman, Avery Brooks and David Harewood) have played the role. Yet this is not to say that the part now 'belongs' to black performers, for *Othello*'s representation of race continues to rankle for some as the portrayal not of an individual but of the stereotyped white perception of a group. Thus, in an often-quoted remark, Hugh Quarshie has written:

> If a black actor plays Othello does he not risk making racial stereotypes seem legitimate and even true? When a black actor plays a role written for a white actor in black make-up and for a predominantly white audience, does he not encourage the white way, or rather the wrong way of looking at black men, namely that black men or "Moors," are over-emotional, excitable, and unstable …? Of all the parts in the canon, perhaps Othello is the one which should most definitely not be played by a black actor.[72]

As if in answer to Quarshie, James Earl Jones (whom British Equity barred from Jonathan Miller's production) has insisted that Othello is at heart a man of even greater nobility than the Venetians he serves. Othello, says Jones, 'is a superior human being, but not a superman who would exploit others. He possesses grace.'[73] The debate as to who should be able to play Othello – an actor justified by his race or one justified by the weight of dramatic tradition (and authorial intent?) – will probably continue, but it seems unlikely that blacked-up portrayals will return among the most prominent white actors. Jude Kelly's 1997 'photo-negative' version, in which Patrick Stewart appeared as a white Othello amid an otherwise all-black cast, is one ingenious response to the whole question.

Among black actors in the title role, John Kani in Janet Suzman's 1988 South African production ranks high. This version, produced in 1988 to protest against apartheid, was a resounding if controversial success. In her commentary on the film version, Suzman states that white actors are 'no longer appropriate' to play Othello; of Shakespeare's great tragedies, this is in her view 'the least philosophical, the least intellectual, and the least overtly political – except in South Africa'.[74] Kani, a native South African and member of the Xhosa tribe, recalls Edmund Kean as an Othello of rather short stature who nevertheless conveys coiled energy. With a scarred, weathered warrior's face and speaking in a marked but not distracting accent, Kani's Othello is intriguing and sympathetic. He enters smilingly confident, holding a single rose that recalls Olivier's similar prop. His authority over those around him is accentuated by his frequently standing slightly above them, and his early scenes with Desdemona are affectionately tender. As Iago's web begins to close, Kani becomes increasingly puzzled and teary-eyed. When he reaches the emotional nadir of 'The pity of it, Iago' (4.1.193) he is a crushed soul, but then immediately explodes with 'I will chop her into messes' (4.1.197). The effects of his epileptic fit linger: 'Goats and monkeys!' (4.1.263) becomes a practically inarticulate shriek. In the death scene, Othello's shadow looms enormously on the curtain behind Desdemona's bed before he fairly quickly kills her. Kani's dominant emotion is profound grief; he wails with anguish while holding her body, as Lear howls over the dead Cordelia. At 'Blow me about

in winds' (5.2.277) he waves his arms pitifully but without
Olivier's theatrical grandiosity.

Kani's emotional impressiveness is matched by Richard
Haines's utterly repulsive Iago, whom Suzman terms in her
film commentary a 'local bigot' with a 'cramped world view'.
The salacious Haines gesticulates constantly, rubbing his
hands with anticipatory glee, sticking his fingers in his nose
to mimic a baboon, braying like an ass, and exploiting every
familiar obscene gesture. Iago's idea of sexuality is intimately
linked with violent abasement, and there is nothing remotely
titillating about Haines's spitting, grinding, jerking behaviour.
He becomes a psychotic sadist when he screams, 'Work on, /
My medicine' (4.1.44–5) and slaps the fallen, epileptic Othello.
His wicked laughter is less persistent than Bob Hoskins' but
more pointed; at 'Divinity of hell' (2.3.345) he drops to the
floor, cackling maniacally. His soliloquies are delivered while
he glares defiantly into the camera, and at 'I am your own
forever' (3.3.482) he speaks directly to the audience, not to the
departing Othello, as if to link his perverted outlook with that
of the prejudiced South African society and its 'tight-lipped
doctrinaire Calvinism' that Suzman is condemning.[75] When
Othello finally stabs him – in the genitals – 'the justice of it
pleases' (4.1.206).

Joanna Weinberg's Desdemona is beautiful and composed.
In a low-cut gown and red cape, she exudes a refined
sexuality, with a resilient personality that defies her father's
angry opposition. Suzman saw 'a very rare and mature sort
of fatalism emerging from her, born of her goodness of heart
and her deep love of the man that she married against all
odds'.[76] Desdemona and Othello share several moving kisses
onstage but most surprisingly when Othello says, 'Your
napkin is too little' (3.3.291). Beginning to sense that she
might be unfaithful, he clasps her intensely, kisses her, then
says with a guttural, lusting eagerness, 'Come, I'll go in with
you' (3.3.292). Her death struggle is comparatively brief, her
body almost a prop for her husband's outpouring of grief.
Dorothy Ann Gould plays Emilia as a thoroughly embittered

wife; her final lines at the end of Act 4 ('their ills instruct us so' [4.3.102]) are spat out in disgust, a mood that only intensifies in the death scene. When she reveals Iago's guilt he cruelly slaps her in the groin, a brutal signifier of their certainly abusive marriage.

The year after Janet Suzman's production was staged, Trevor Nunn directed *Othello* with the Royal Shakespeare Company at The Other Place in Stratford-upon-Avon, an intimate theatre of less than two hundred seats. If Laurence Olivier wanted 'an N.C.O.' for his Iago, he would have prized Ian McKellen's reading of that role, as McKellen portrays probably the most repressed and buttoned-up Iago of the play's recent stage history, neatly folding the blanket on his cot before lying down or tidily closing his cigarette case as he chain-smokes. Sporting a clipped moustache and choppy hair, and speaking most of his lines through barely moving lips, this Iago is adept at a false front of ingratiating military efficiency and brittle joviality that hides a brutally amoral heart. McKellen excels at acting a character who is playing a part. In his soliloquies he looks directly into the camera with unblinking, heavily bagged eyes, his face that of a jaded, dissolute reprobate who has a bottomless need for power. Unlike Hoskins or Haines he rarely gives evidence of being pleased with himself. He physically embraces everyone he victimizes – Cassio, Roderigo, Othello, Desdemona, Emilia – but does so in such an emotionally detached way that the effect is of someone who is exploiting even his own feelings for ulterior ends. In the play's final scene a single spotlight illuminates his face has he gazes impassively at the 'tragic loading' (5.2.363) of Desdemona's bed. He has little difficulty manipulating Roderigo (Michael Grandage) and especially Cassio (Sean Baker), who is disconcertingly obsequious and unmilitary.

Zoë Wanamaker brings Emilia to life more subtly than does Dorothy Gould, though she too is a woman who has had to settle for an unfulfilled marriage. For instance, after she presents Iago with the handkerchief, he ardently kisses her but then suddenly pulls away. Her ensuing expression of

wounded yearning suggests years of emotional neglect which
her finding of that token might ideally have ended. Her silent
glances, often in tight close-ups, reveal a complex depth of
character long before her anguished defence of her murdered
mistress, while her anger in her final scene captures not only
her outrage at Desdemona's death but her pent-up hatred of
her husband and her self-disgust at having been duped by
him. Imogen Stubbs is a sprightly, girlish Desdemona, clearly
younger than Othello; she impulsively clings to Emilia in the
'willow' scene, conveying an intelligent yet childlike fragility,
but does not hesitate to share passionate, public kisses with
her husband. Both she and Emilia wear small crosses, and her
religion comes briefly to the fore while answering Othello's
accusations: she clings to the prie-dieu in her room, clutching
her Bible and acting out the 'angel' to Othello's 'blacker devil'
(5.2.128–9). The depth of the Emilia–Desdemona relationship
in this production receives careful attention, and Robert
Smallwood notes 'the compassionate affection of the disillusioned Emilia supporting the bewildered anxiety of the
grief-stricken girl'.[77]

Othello is played by Willard White, the Jamaican-born
operatic star, who, apart from a slight lilt in his speech,
displays none of the 'West Indian' mannerisms Olivier prized.
His physical size and imposing voice, at times lending an
almost parental air to his exchanges with Desdemona, are
balanced by an expressive face that registers his increasingly
confused rage. In Act 3, Scene 3, it takes him longer than
many modern Othellos to succumb to Iago's innuendoes;
he even smiles slightly at 'Look to your wife' (3.3.200) as
if hoping to remain above this insinuation of infidelity.
But when he notes how nature can be 'erring from itself'
(3.3.227), his mood turns sharply dark. At 'Thou hast set me
on the rack' (3.3.338) he threatens Iago so physically that
McKellen must defend himself with a chair, but at Iago's 'I
am your own forever' (3.3.482), he kisses the ancient's hand.
By the start of Act Four, when White weeps out 'the pity of
it', Iago embraces him and strokes his hair expressionlessly.

White's large physical size offers a dramatic contrast to his own emotional weakness; he is a general who is totally lost on his own emotional battlefield. He enters his bedroom to kill his wife dressed in a white burnoose, the first time in the play we see him out of his European-style uniform. After smothering Desdemona, who puts up an intense defence, he rolls off her body with all passion spent in a scene that intentionally mingles the murderous and the erotic.

Perhaps the mostly widely seen black actor in the role has been Laurence Fishburne in Oliver Parker's 1995 film, a lush production with the location settings, impressive musical scoring, and colourful cinematography typical of Hollywood Shakespeare. Kenneth Branagh competes with McKellen and Haines as the best contemporary example of an Iago who threatens to steal the play from its eponymous hero. By turns conniving and ingratiating, cold-heartedly vicious and quick-wittedly sarcastic, he dominates Fishburne's brooding, confused and frustrated general, who is more prone to express his anguish not with White's operatic voice or Olivier's oratory but with frequent tears that simultaneously convey pain, anger, love and shame. Throughout the film (but especially in the play's final frames, when Iago – now sprawled wounded on the bed with Othello, Desdemona and Emilia – slowly looks up at us with just the hint of a superior smile) Branagh's penetrating stares, glares and asides confront and even seek to control the camera itself, unlike Bob Hoskins' intentionally less frontal soliloquies. Othello, on the other hand, is always the subject of the viewer's gaze, as if in a subservient position throughout the film that reflects his victimization by Venetian authority. Irene Jacob, in her first film spoken entirely in English, plays Desdemona with an energetic naïveté; though her native French-Swiss accent seems at odds with her role as a Venetian daughter, it lends an appropriate distance to her character that makes her love for her equally foreign husband believable. Her bedroom conversation with the frankly earthy Emilia (Anna Patrick) is a convincing scene of feminine insight into male behaviour.

Unfortunately, Parker is not content to let Shakespeare's language convey the barely concealed sexuality that pervades the play (something Olivier does well), but insists that we must see Cassio and Desdemona as Othello imagines them *in flagrante delicto*, see Othello and his wife disrobe before a night of lovemaking, see Iago slide his hand up Roderigo's thigh with more than a suggestion of homoeroticism while both are lying beneath a wagon in which another couple vigorously enjoys each other, and see Iago mount Emilia to ensure that we understand that the 'thing' she has for him is more than just a handkerchief. Parker condescends to his audience, reaching for a gratuitous sensationalism that confuses sensuality with prurience. Similarly, in a visual cliché, we see Iago rearrange pieces on a chessboard lest we forget that the lovers are merely pawns in his game. A danger with Iago is to define his motivation too readily (as essentially a case of sexual revenge, for example) and dispel the deeper obscurity that cloaks the roots of his misanthropic hatred. The dramatic power of his final 'What you know you know' (5.2.300) is that we actually know so little. The temptation to pluck out the heart of his mystery should be resisted.

The erotic charge in the scenes of Fishburne's unclothed athletic body have struck some commentators as a concession to stereotypes of black physicality which demeans Othello's 'great[ness] of heart' (5.2.359). Recent productions of the play starring black actors have foregrounded their bodies so as to place 'the black male's sexuality, but also his energy, beauty, and virility into bolder relief. Cast in the subject position of sexually magnetic lover and husband, the Othello in question also becomes the not-so-obscure object of audience desire, and often the desires of a film's Iago or Iago-surrogate.'[78] It remains arguable whether modern productions employing black actors have the unintended effect of objectifying Othello's race more or less than did older productions, in which audiences knew they were witnessing Othello at 'two removes' so to speak: a mimetic, interpreted racial identity over and above the imitated character himself.

Another impressive black Othello is Eamonn Walker, who starred in the 2007 Globe production directed by Wilson Milam. Milam sees the play's armed, male characters as 'near pirates' in the 'wild wild west' world of 1570 Cyprus, the last year in which that island enjoyed independence from the Turks.[79] Like Orson Welles, he also turned to the paintings of Caravaggio for models of his costume design. This production uses a practically bare stage and almost no props, but, unlike most directors, Milam retains the Clown (Paul Lloyd) who angrily reads his lines while constantly interrupted by several oafish musicians; in a further nod to the Elizabethan stage, the cast concludes the play with their version of a jig. Walker brings to his role a strong voice and muscular physique, less rotund than White but still able to command respect. His sense of dignity is enhanced by his expressive eyes that powerfully register a variety of emotions, frequently sweeping the full gallery of the Globe as he speaks. Whereas White depicts a defeated and trapped Othello at the end of the play, Walker becomes a betrayed and enraged general. His affectionate moments with Desdemona are truly tender, but his final revenge hints at what we know of Salvini's physical style in this scene. As she pounds on the door of her bedroom, screaming for help, he lifts her up bodily and throws her violently on the bed, then manhandles her into submission, screaming insanely 'I would not have thee linger in thy pain' (5.2.87). Walker's final rages are so intense that our pity for Othello is nearly swept away by our fear of him.

Unlike Trevor Nunn's production, this is an *Othello* in which the Moor truly dominates the play, owing not only to Walker's dynamic performance but also to Tim McInnerny's oddly one-dimensional Iago. McInnerny speaks most of his lines in a loud, raspy voice that modulates only slightly during his soliloquies. He is an Iago who seems devoid of the inner, lurking malevolence that is central to the role; while anger is certainly part of Iago's personality, a constant, abusive ire should not be his only *modus operandi*. McInnerny's Iago jovially joins Cassio in the musical drinking scene, but we lack the sense that Ian McKellen expresses of a clever strategy unfolding before us. Neil Forsyth has suggested that McInnerny's Iago 'is an isolated, rather lame tempter, not simply alone for the soliloquies, but lonely'.[80] We believe that he can manipulate Sam Crane's impudent but vacant Roderigo (whose part Milam regards as a 'mini-tragedy'), but it is harder to accept that the feisty and dynamic Cassio (Nick Barber) would so readily be conned by such a phleg-matic intriguer. Zoë Tapper creates an energetic and defiant Desdemona despite her rather small stature, far different from the older, more composed Desdemonas of Maggie Smith or Penelope Wilton. Totally devoted to her husband, she is never-theless engagingly assertive, with none of Imogen Stubbs's girlish dependency. The black actress Lorraine Burroughs plays an equally demonstrative Emilia.

Like other Shakespeare plays, *Othello* too has had its popular film spinoff – Tim Blake Nelson's *O* (2001). As the star of his prep-school basketball team (the Hawks), Odin James, or 'O' (Mekhi Phifer), is coached by 'Duke' Gouldin (Martin Sheen). The Duke's son Hugo (Josh Hartnett), jealous of O's skill and fame, is also stung by the fact that the coach, who is also his father, has publicly claimed that he loves and respects O like a son. O loves Desi Brable (Julia Stiles) a white girl and daughter of the school's Dean Bob Brable (John Heard), a name that tries a bit too hard to mimic 'Brabantio'. Hugo follows the actions of Iago fairly closely, though Desi and her roommate Emily (Rain Phoenix) lack as close a bond as Desdemona and Emilia have. Roger (Elden Henson), the Roderigo character, is a chubby admirer of Desi who is driven to violence after being taunted and bullied. The film was set and shot in Charleston, South Carolina, a location that establishes a racially tense background for Dean Brable's suspicions about O's intentions towards his daughter. Exterior scenes are often shot through trees draped with Spanish moss, a heavy hint that Odin's inter-racial love will fare no better here against ingrained prejudices than did Othello's in Venice. Despite being respected for his athleticism, he cannot hope to prevail over Hugo's selfish bigotry, whose jealousy on the court is as great as O's jealousy over Desi. In a final voiceover as he is driven away in a police car, Hugo says that 'Odin is a hawk, he soars above us, he can fly … One of these days everyone is going to pay attention to me because I'm going to fly too.' This is more insight into his character than Shakespeare gives us into Iago's, but it would probably be unrealistic to burden a teenaged Hugo with Iago's motiveless malignity for popular audiences. Nelson makes sure to include details of dialogue that echo Shakespeare; when Odin shows Desi his scar from a skateboard fall, she tells him, 'You have the best stories', and Iago's 'Look to your wife' (3.3.200) becomes Hugo's 'Watch your girl, bro.' In a quick inside joke, when Hugo's English teacher asks him to name a poem by Shakespeare, he deadpans, 'I thought Shakespeare wrote movies.' And in a spinoff within a spinoff, the film opens and closes to the 'Ave Maria' from Verdi's opera *Otello*. The film succeeds even for those who do not know *Othello*, and for those who do it offers another example of Shakespeare's persistent influence upon popular culture.

Predicting the vagaries of Shakespearean production is risky, but despite likely attempts at non-racial readings of the play – based on the conviction that Shakespeare's intent is to comment on the fate of all discriminated minorities, Othello just happening to be a black instance of this – *Othello* will continue to be seen primarily as a study of racial bigotry. It seems equally probable that, despite Hugh Quarshie's reservations about black actors in the role, and even if white actors still continue to perform it, the part will increasingly be seen as the province of black performers. As modern renditions of the story such as *O* or Suzman's South African production suggest, it will also be as impossible to disengage productions of *Othello* from an awareness of contemporary racial friction as it has been for audiences to separate *The Merchant of Venice* from a post-Holocaust context. And finally, as Laurence Olivier said of playing Othello, 'It's a hell of a part.' Its artistic challenge alone will be enough to ensure its enduring vitality on the stage.

3

Othello: The State of the Art

Imtiaz Habib

In the late 1960s a respected scholar famously declared *King Lear* 'the play of our times'.[1] Yet four decades later *Othello* was called the 'greatest' of the tragedies and the pre-eminent Shakespeare text of the moment.[2] Similarly, Michael Neill in 2006 declared that *Othello* had begun to displace both *Lear* and *Hamlet* as the Shakespeare tragedy of greatest contemporary interest, 'as critics and directors alike began to trace in the cultural, religious and ethnic animosities of its Mediterranean setting, the genealogy of the racial conflicts that fractured their own societies'.[3] Likewise, Edward Pechter called *Othello* the present generation's 'tragedy of choice', and Julie Hankey wrote that 'Over the last twenty years or so *Othello* has leapt into focus as the play of our times.'[4] As of September 2013, 722 items on *Othello* were listed in the *MLA International Bibliography* as having appeared since 2000, and of course that figure is surely incomplete. Yet if there are 'new trends' in *Othello* studies of any sort now, they are related to earlier critical developments, either as outgrowths of those developments or as reactions against them.

Race studies

Although discussions of race, colonialism and imperialism in *Othello* have a long history, positive interest in Othello's race (and in race in *Othello*) began with Eldred Jones in 1965, Ruth Cowhig in 1977 and G. K. Hunter in 1978, and exploded in the late 1980s and the 1990s (see Barthelemy, Newman, Neil, Loomba, Bartels, Donald, Hendricks and Parker, Hall, Singh). This concern also implied growing interest in the play's imperial and early colonialist aspects.[5] Lena Owen Corlin, for instance, succinctly described the play as 'a case study' for 'tracing the course of critical thinking about Shakespeare in the late twentieth century', because it 'registers all the concerns of the newly politicized readings of the last decade: gender, power, sexuality, race', and the 'continuing legacies of empire and enslavement'. Orlin also calls *Othello* a key text for introducing 'poststructuralist theory in the interpretation of English literature in the Renaissance'.[6]

These new trends, however, are precisely what Edward Pechter had protested against three years earlier, and Philip Kolin, while tracing in 2002 the history of responses to race in *Othello*, mainly surveys scholarship along familiar formalist lines of character analyses and reviews of performances.[7] Kolin's survey implies his preference for a balance of older and newer approaches, yet the volume he edited *begins* with five discussions of race – the highest number of examinations of any topic in the collection. Similarly, an essay collection edited by Peter Erickson and Maurice Hunt in 2005 opens its survey of modern criticism by simply declaring that they 'begin with two topics – gender and race',[8] and in fact most of the essays deal with these topics. The simple firmness of their critical preference is evident in the lucid, precise sketch they provide of scholarship on race in *Othello*, including in adaptations and derivations of the play.[9]

The vigour of studies of race in *Othello* is further signalled by a 2002 essay by Erickson himself. It studies the play's discourse of blackness by focusing on the subtly rather than starkly prejudiced language community in which Othello is enmeshed.[10] Meanwhile, Sujata Iyengar discussed the efficacy of selecting either white or black actors to play Othello,[11] while Denise Albanese described a blackface 'photonegative' casting of the play in 1997, with Patrick Stewart as a white Othello but the rest of the characters as blacks. Albanese believes this production reflects the wishful assumption of an age that imagines itself as post-racial, a modelling of 'a utopian space in which race doesn't matter anymore – especially when it comes to [a] Shakespeare that is the universal property of all humanity'. For Albanese, it is precisely through this problematic instinct of 'cross-racial desire' that the 'the racial repressed' 'returns' and 'force[s] itself on a viewing public'.[12]

The issue of blackface representation in *Othello*, and in modern Shakespearean performance generally, has exploded into what has been called 'a contentious debate over racial surrogacy and representation'.[13] The debate involves on the one hand Virginia Vaughan's 2005 argument that Othello 'should not be played by a black actor at all [because] Shakespeare's tragedy is not about Africanness but the white man's *idea* of Africanness',[14] and on the other hand several formulations by Ayanna Thompson. Like Albanese, Thompson first asserts that colour-blind casting in Shakespeare assumes 'that we are in a post-racist era: that is the conservative line. Racism doesn't exist anymore.'[15] Yet Thompson subsequently suggests that 'the conflicting desires for a return to Shakespeare's original intent [of having a white actor play Othello in blackface] may signal the problems with Shakespeare and Shakespeare's cultural capital rather than any inherent problems with the performance of blackface itself', and she also suggests that the force of Shakespeare's cultural capital is 'too strong to forego the fantasy of the Bard's intentions as race neutral or even race progressive'.[16] The debate in effect highlights the complex intertwining of the essentiality and non-essentiality of race, that is, of race as an ontological identarian self-marking which is good, and race as an epistemological construction learned and imposed on subjects by others, which is bad, resulting in rac*ism*. Because the one phenomenon often can and does pass as the other, the issue of the blackface representation of race is difficult to resolve. Critical attention to the politics of playing *Othello* in blackface, exemplified by this debate, was started in recent decades by Joyce MacDonald in 1994.[17]

Reaffirming the black/African strain of the race topic and complicating it is James Andreas's novel move of overlapping Othello's African genealogy with a Judaic one through the curse of Ham, thus connecting *The Merchant of Venice* and *Othello* as Shakespeare's comic and tragic versions of the same idea.[18] Taking a different tack, John Ford points to the play's 'mixed dramaturgy' of race and gender that, quoting Kent Cartwright, he says produces in the audience 'a disorientating double response' of sympathetic or 'heroic' engagement and detached or 'unheroic' understanding, exemplified surprisingly by Roderigo.[19] Meanwhile, Michael Neill, while masterfully tracing discussions of race in the play, highlights the conceptual challenges of the race question (including what it meant for Elizabethans and what it does, can, and should mean for us now) – an approach resembling Vaughan's observation that the undecidability of the play's racial and racist charge is neither resolvable nor avoidable.[20]

The density of contention about Othello's exact ethnicity is nicely caught in Emily Bartels' *Speaking of the Moor*, a systematic examination of the construction of the 'moor' figure in early modern Europe. Bartels usefully highlights the complex and contradictory overlays in the idea of the Moor, which she sees as 'continuous' and 'discontinuous', a 'collage', and 'a progression', simultaneously 'augment[ative]', 'supplant[ive]' and 'supplementary' in the Derridean sense, and that merely 'points to the instability of "race" as a term or concept in our ... recent history'.[21] Similarly, Kim Hall concludes that 'rather than trying to pin Othello down to a specific geographic location, Shakespeare took advantage of the rich and sometimes disturbing network of allusions associated with "Moor",' so that 'Othello's "race" becomes a matter for, or barometer of, aesthetic judgment – the critics' as well as Shakespeare's'.[22] Likewise, Lara Bovilsky suggests that 'early modern racial logics have much in common with modern or contemporary ones',[23] while Lisa Hopkins, associating the race and skin-colour issue with Desdemona, connects the violence Desdemona suffers not just to post-Reformation English violence against Marian images but also specifically to images of the Black Madonna.[24] Comparably, Celia Daileader examines Desdemona in light of both the powerful early modern taboo against miscegeny and modern feminist deconstructions of historical attacks on women. She traces 'a Shakespearean racialized rhetoric that pairs a black man and a white woman' so 'as to render the former a vehicle for misogynistic figurations of a woman's sexual sullying'.[25]

Ian Smith offers an interesting new discussion following from an influential essay by Lynda Boose. After pointing to a 'critical orthodoxy … of seeing or positing whiteness in the handker-chief', Smith argues that the handkerchief was in fact black and suggests how it and 'its relation to Othello' help construct 'an idea of blackness and race that places severe constraints on black subjectivity'.[26] Smith's essay should be juxtaposed with two others, by Sheila Cavanagh and Janelle Jenstad.[27]

In an approach now fast becoming conventional, Millicent Bell, while acknowledging traditional perspectives on Othello, firmly frames him as a racialized colonized coloured subject who tries to achieve 'a new personhood' but cannot.[28] (For a contextual frame for this approach, see, for instance, works by Thomas Cartelli, Imtiaz Habib, Arthur Little Jr, and Ania Loomba and Martin Orkin. A later work, by Lisa Hopkins, includes a valuable primer of this school of thought.[29])

Gender and sexuality narratives

Arguably, studies of gender and sexuality have been even more influential than those of race in approaching both *Othello* and

Shakespeare. As marginalized populations, ethnic minorities, women, and sexual minorities simultaneously complement one another and compete for representation in cultural and literary critiques.[30] Thus Lynda Boose argues that the play employs a lethal male spectatorial voyeurism focused singularly (for Elizabethan drama) on the 'bed' as a site not for dying but for male sexual violence. Boose sees *Othello* as singular among Shakespearean tragedies in ending without leaving an alternative male hero when the protagonist dies. The voyeuristic aesthetic, Boose believes, is implicitly misogynist and racist and causes the uneasiness the play arouses in modern (and, by implication, predominantly male and white) commentators.[31]

Equally symptomatic of the growing fertility of gender studies of *Othello* is an important essay by Emily Bartels, who argues that to ignore the play's gender narrative is in fact to weaken perception of its race discourse and vice versa. She focuses on Desdemona's suit to help Cassio in Act 3, Scene 3, a scene she identifies as 'structurally and ideologically central … [because] it adds the missing link of gender to the spectacle of race'.[32] Similarly, Cynthia Marshall, arguing that 'gender ideologies' shape 'identities in the play', contends that when Desdemona says in Act 1, Scene 3 that after hearing Othello's story she wished 'Heaven had made her such a man', her phrasing suggests that she wished not only that she could find such a man but also that she could *be* such a man. This moment (Marshall believes) symbolizes a counter-fantasy, by the play's disempowered women, to the dominant males' 'code of expectations' that organizes 'characters' actions along gendered lines'.[33]

The fantasy of gender-crossing implied by Marshall extends naturally to queer studies, as when Nicholas Radel shows the play's investment in 'same-sex desire', specifically 'sodomy', and 'the place of such desire in the early modern period'.[34] Similarly, Daniel Boyarin, arguing that 'the open secret at the heart of the play is the secret of Islam in Europe', believes that 'Othello's ambiguously circumcised penis is as important

– and even more important – as a signifier of his "race" than
the colour of his skin': it is a hidden marker of his 'bestial[ity]'
despite his Christian baptism. For Boyarin, this aspect of the
play 'provides an exemplary early instance of the queering
of the very identity markers that form our contemporary
markers of race, gender, religion' [35]

Love and marriage

A notable strain in recent critical interest in love and marriage
in *Othello* focuses on the failures of these experiences. Thus,
John Gronbeck-Tedesco finds in the play's action 'the breach
between morality and ethics'. The demands of each are
initially 'adjusted' successfully by love, but they eventually
diverge with catastrophic results because 'the characters
who strive to love do not understand how to sustain a
collaborative bond against hostile and impenetrable social
contexts'.[36] Eric Mallin and David Bevington also concentrate
on marriage, with Mallin calling *Othello* 'Shakespeare's only
marital tragedy … underscor[ing] the wretched difficulty of
the wedded condition', including its 'revelatory constrictions'
and 'demands on men for self-exposure', and with Bevington
describing Othello as 'a stereotype of the anxious male beset by
fears of womanly duplicity'. Unfortunately, Othello's anxiety
undermines what is, for Bevington, 'arguably … the most
rich and compatible [marriage] in the Shakespeare canon'.[37]
While Sandra Logan examines the breakdown in the play of
the well-known early modern 'family/state homology' because
of the 'violent' collisions of 'the personal and the political',
Theodore Leinwand masterfully extends this line of thinking
by seeing marriage as '*Coniugium Interruptum*', in which
by 'staging domestic heteroeroticism, and the orgasms to
which it aspires, Shakespearean tragedy intimates temporary
stays against the 'repudiation of assured significance', so that
marriage 'teeters unsteadily on a fault line between the public

and the private ... thus crowding the "body social" into a fraught relation with the "individual body"'. This relation expectedly ruptures, Leinwand believes, because 'The early modern literary moment lacks either the publicly sanctioned space or the requisite private imaginary in which intimacy can stand on its own.'[38]

State, power

Thomas Moisan traces the relationship of the state to 'the subject of *Othello*' by tracking the many occurrences of the word 'state' and its multiple, prolifically connected allusions to 'Venice the city state', 'the Venetian body polity', 'Venice's governing authority and power' and 'estate' as 'condition'. For Moisan, 'the state' and Othello are linked in a 'mutually exploitative and mutually revealing relationship'. Bryan Reynolds and Joseph Fitzpatrick, in contrast, study Venice's 'transversal' state power,[39] while Elizabeth Hansen examines state power exerted on women, specifically through torture, by studying Desdemona as 'an epistemologically resistant female subject' who is the object of a misogynous anxiety.[40]

Venice, Turkey

Another topic of renewed interest is Venice and, concomitantly, the Ottoman regime. Many discussions of these topics break from existing critical assumptions that Shakespeare's Venice resembles London to argue that the play's city is a 'representation' of Venice itself. According to Virginia Vaughan, *Othello* simultaneously explores both Mediterranean geopolitics and Venice's state politics, while according to Eugenie Freed *Othello* invites Shakespeare's audience to question their assumptions about Venice's fame and renown. John Drakakis sees the play as offering a disillusioned, anti-idealistic view of

Venice, while Graham Holderness sees Shakespeare's Venice as 'a place where myth and reality meet and merge'. Discussions of the Ottoman world of the play include seeing it, variously, as the literary representation of a historically flexible and expedient – rather than a rigidly hostile – English relationship with a superior power (Jonathan Burton); as a political and religious entity that was many-coloured rather than monolithically hostile (Linda McJannet); as a construction that wasn't simply Orientalized (Daniel Vitkus); and as a culturally superior power from whose view *England* was marginal and backward (Peter Stallybrass).[41]

Rhetoric

Rhetorical studies of Shakespeare have a distinguished lineage exemplified by Joel Altman's *The Improbability of Othello*. Altman meticulously invokes Aristotelian ideas of rhetoric, ethics and politics to show how the 'dramatis personae – with varying intermittent awareness and varying degrees of consciousness – all inhabit a phantom sphere in which a finely woven mesh of supposition creates the illusion of connection between knowledge that cannot be had, judgments that must be made, and actions that need to be taken'. Alan Sinfield offers a comparably expert essay on the 'politics of plausibility' in the play, albeit from a cultural materialist standpoint.[42] Stefan Keller 'combines rhetoric and pragmatics' to analyse Iago's 'extreme' 'manipulation of language' to destroy Othello, while Stephanie Chamberlain examines 'narrative strategy' and its conflict with 'juridical authority' in the play.[43]

Source/context studies

Among recent source or historical context studies, Bernadette Andrea examines the relevance of Leo Africanus, one of the first historical figures scholars connected to Shakespeare's fictional African; Christopher Baker also re-examines Othello's literary derivation, but from Ovid's 'Pontic Scythians';[44] and Katrina Attar reasserts the play's derivation from its principal source, Giovanni Giraldi or Cinthio, by demonstrating fresh historical Venetian details taken from Cinthio for the play's characters and locales.[45]

Genre studies

Recent re-examinations of the play's genre include Jean Howard's profitable consideration of *Othello* as an 'adventure' play, Douglas Bruster's reflections on it as a 'Tragedy and Comedy', Cynthia Lewis's pedagogic framing of it as an '(Anti) Revenge Play',[46] and Catherine Bates's formulation of the play as 'a tragedy of love'.[47] Additionally, Sean Benson has recently examined the play as a 'domestic tragedy'.[48]

Character studies

The continuing hold of A. C. Bradley's character criticism is evident in an essay by Enrique Camara Arenas that explores not just Iago's but also Othello's motivation by reinterpreting Bradley's analyses of these characters. Arenas uses H. H. Kelley's 'Covariance Theory of Causal Attribution' to extend Bradley's 'humanizing approach onto a higher level of method-ological sensitivity'.[49] Nicholas Borrelli and Tea Cammarota examine Iago as 'A Case Study in Mental Illness and Sexual Deviation', invoking Freudian psychoanalysis to do so and perceiving 'Iago as a neuropathic personality, drifting into borderline disorder'.[50] Maurice Hunt, surveying the critical history and analytical challenge of Iago's motivation, cites both Stanley Hyman's important dismissal of the idea of a fictional character having a psychology and motivation and

James Calderwood's rebuttal of Hyman's literalism. Hunt adopts an inclusive strategy, using Aristotelian ideas to vet both positions. Hunt also discusses views that see Iago both as 'satanic' and as allegedly homosexual, but he cautions against conflating such readings.[51]

Marxist critics, of course, eschew interest in individual psychology, preferring to study social discourses. Thus Catherine Belsey, in studying Iago as an essayist, demonstrates how his 'purposive, blunt' style clearly contrasts with Othello's passionate Marlovian language. She links Iago's phrasing not to the medieval Vice character but to the trenchant humanist discourse of Montaigne.[52] Using a different kind of close reading, Harry Berger shows that contrary to a modern tendency to see Iago as more clever or sophisticated than Othello, Iago is actually 'a needy actor' who constantly 'solicits the audience's admiration', and who 'is manipulated, by his victims, more than he knows or would like'.[53] Alternatively, Ken Jacobson sees Iago as a military strategist whose 'rhetorical performance' is 'deeply informed' by Niccolò Machiavelli's *The Art of War* rather than by *The Prince*.[54]

Adaptation studies

Among adaptation studies, Karley Adney's new historicist approach suggests that even adapters of *Othello* for children incorporate narrative elements which are neither present in nor even suggested by Shakespeare's text.[55] Jill Levenson offers a useful history of changes in the roles of women in the many *Othello*s staged between Shakespeare's era and the nineteenth century, while Alexander Leggatt traces differences in the nature of the Othello–Desdemona relationship in Shakespeare's play and in Boito's libretto for Verdi's *Otello*.[56] Joyce Green MacDonald shows how Gayl Jones's novel *Mosquito* reorients our understanding of the play from the perspectives of African-American women, rather than men, although a male-centred perspective has been typical of national reconstructions of Shakespeare's text.[57]

Editions and text studies

As could be expected, since 2000, new editions and reprints of Othello have proliferated. These include volumes edited by Russ McDonald in 2001; Thomas Woodman in 2002; Norman Sanders in 2003 (reissued in 2012); Edward Pechter in 2003; Michael Neil in 2006 (reissued in 2008); Barbara Mowat and Paul Werstine in 2004 (a reprint); Burton Raffel in 2005; Jibesh Bhattachrya in 2006; Kim Hall in 2007; Jonathan Bate and Eric Rasmussen in 2009; and Adrian Coleman and Shane Barnes in 2010. A multiple text edition prepared by David Bevington and David Scott Kastan includes not only *Othello* but also *Hamlet*, *King Lear* and *Macbeth*.[58] As could also be expected, most of these editions contain extensive introductory discussions of the play's racial, sexual and national-colonial critical contexts. Two major critical guides are those by Nicholas Potter and Nicolas Tredell in 2000 and by Andrew Hadfield in 2003.[59] Additionally, two foreign-language editions of the play appeared in 2007 and 2010.[60]

Among the many scholarly imponderables of the histories of the printed texts of Shakespeare, the text of *Othello* has seemed 'notoriously problematic',[61] especially the differences between the texts of Q1 (First Quarto) in 1622 and that of the F (First Folio) of 1623, both published many years after the play's original performance. Which version is more accurate? Briefly but precisely surveying modern critical theories on this problem and their solutions to it by A. W. Pollard, W. W. Greg, Nevill Coghill and others, Scott McMillin in 2002 proposes a new explanation: instead of being authorial and performance copies respectively, both Q1 and F were performance copies, in which 'F [was from] one of the disposable backstage scripts prepared for performances over two decades of its stage life before publication', and 'Q1 [came from] a performance which was abridged from something like a performance envisaged by F', so that the 'differences between Q1 and F are not primarily between [authorial] foul papers and prompt copy, but the differences of two kinds of theatrical script'. The distinction of McMillin's view is that it shifts the focus of textual studies from 'resurrecting' authorial copy and revision (an approach typical of modern textual scholars such as E. A. J. Honigmann) to the 'stage practices' of the popular theatre itself.[62]

Leah Marcus, subscribing to the traditional position that the revisions are by Shakespeare, argues that they represent his 'intensif[ication]' of racist elements and '"additions" of pornographic specificity and negativity to the images of inter-racial love'. Marcus thinks this conclusion was avoided by earlier scholars because of their own 'uneas[iness]' about the 'more benign construction of racial difference offered in Q'.[63] A new summary work of Shakespearean textual scholarship in general is that of Gabriel Egan, *The Struggle for Shakespeare's Text: Twentieth-Century Editorial Theory and Practice*.[64]

The play in performance and adaptations

In the twenty-first century, Shakespearean film studies constitute a vigorous field, as is evident in the appearance of such volumes as *Shakespeare, Film, Fin de Siècle* (2000); *Shakespeare in the Cinema* (2002); *Shakespeare, the Movie: Popularizing the Plays on Film, TV, Video, and Dvd* (2003); *Shakespeare from Stage to Screen* (2004); *A Concise Companion to Shakespeare On Screen* (2006); *Screening Shakespeare in the Twenty-First Century* (2006); *The Cambridge Companion to Shakespeare on Film* (2007); *New Wave Shakespeare on Screen* (2007); *Studying Shakespeare on Film* (2007); and *Who Hears In Shakespeare: Auditory Worlds on Stage and Screen*

(2012). Such titles complement the list of standard earlier sources on the topic provided by Philip Kolin.[65] Expectedly, studies of *Othello* on stage and film make a busy category of commentary about the play, something pointedly visible in Kolin's allocation of 34 pages, in an 86-page essay, to this topic alone. A conservative listing of productions of the play in *any* media, including spin-offs, amounts to no less than 14 items in the US and abroad in the first 13 years of the twenty-first century. This figure seems especially significant in light of the claim by Mark Thornton Burnett and Ramona Wray that a 'smaller number of major Shakespeare films [were] produced in the immediate post 2000 period' than before that date. Thus *Othello* seems to have had an unusual impact in popular media of the twenty-first century.[66]

Recent major productions or adaptations have often been non-traditional. Thus the National Asian Theater Company's version in New York in 2000 used all Asian performers except for the role of Othello, who was played by a white. This production, though, did not win wide approval: one reviewer commented that Joshua Spafford's 'never passionate' Othello was 'more like … a grad student experiencing exaggerated stress over a term paper than a man tormented by fierce love or primitive desire', and another that 'this Othello's fall [was] pitiable but it [did] not make the earth tremble', although both commentators found Joel de Fuente's Iago impressive.[67] Even more indicative of the distinctiveness of twenty-first-century renditions of *Othello* were two powerful productions in 2001 – one on film and one on stage. Tim Blake Nelson's film *O* set Shakespeare's story in a southern US prep school and involved the tangled relationship of an African-American basketball player, Odin James, the 'O' of the title, played by Mekhi Phifer, and a white girl, Desi, played by Julia Stiles. The film, according to one reviewer, used 'Shakespeare's play as a base for a story of teenage love, jealousy and violence … [while still capturing] 'the awkwardness in a cross-racial dating angle' and was, in the words of another, 'one of the most important films of our generation', not only 'because of its honest depiction of sex, drugs, and violence among teens, [but also] because of its true and raw depiction of race'.[68] Other commentators also in general praised the film. One argued that it 'present[ed] the issue of a race in a way that is pedagogically useful';[69] another liked the film's insight into race (but not into Shakespeare);[70] and yet another described it as 'realistic and jarring'.[71]

The other major production of 2001, televised in Britain, starred the black actor Eamonn Walker as Othello and the white performers Christopher Eccleston as Iago and Keeley Hawes as Desdemona. This adaptation was set in the contemporary London police department. (It was released in Canada by CBC in 2002 and was also staged in London six years later.) Maitland McDonagh praised the 'excellent performances and … sharp screenplay that seamlessly updated Shakespeare's text', an updating that Tom Cartelli later praised as being done 'for reasons other than for mass legibility'.[72] However, Michael Billington, reviewing the stage version in 2007, said that it was 'a decent, middle-rank production' but complained that Walker's Othello lacked the magniloquence found in Shakespeare's character.[73]

In 2002 a ballet in three acts, based on the original Cinthio novella and Shakespeare's play, was choreographed by Lars Lubovitch and performed by the San Francisco Ballet. It was later performed again on PBS television and nominated for an Emmy Award. The first version starred Cyril Pierre in blackface as Othello and Lucia Lacarra as Desdemona. Mary Ellen Hunt (citing the director's opinion that in this production, as in the sources, '"race is not an issue"'), asked, 'Why make it an issue now? This ballet could have played exactly the same without any indication as to ethnic background. It is the story of a man driven to jealousy and murder by the envy and scheming of an unscrupulous friend. Why does Othello have to be black? Why should Desdemona be white?'[74] Of the PBS television version, featuring the black dancer Desmond Richardson as Othello and the Asian dancer Yuan Tan as Desdemona, one commentator asserted, 'It's impossible not to point out that political correctness seems to have played a part in the casting of … Richardson.'[75] The same year also saw an intriguing digital feature film adaptation done by Australian director Brenden Dannaher. Titled *Eloise*, it won several Australian film awards and starred Mark Jensen (as the Othello character named Michael) and Melanie Holt.[76]

Most remarkable and ambitiously complex among recent adaptations was Richard Eyre's metatheatrical and sexually loaded film, *Stage Beauty* (2004), which depicted a performance of *Othello* in Restoration London while simultaneously foregrounding and marginalizing the race dimensions of Shakespeare's play. The film projected a seventeenth-century England in which, according to A. O. Scott, 'politics were as theatrical as theater was political', and featured both a blackface Othello (played by Tom Wilkinson) *and* a cross-dressing Desdemona (played by Billy Crudup), as well as a character named Maria Hughes (played by Claire Danes) who is his fictional understudy and who in the end successfully challenges him for that role. As the plot unfolds, some characters eventually take off their costuming and come out of their sexual roles. This film, according to Scott, was 'at once common-sensical and brazenly revisionist' and offered some insights into theatre history and (through Maria's successful bagging of the Desdemona role) into the 'triumph of feminism and realism'. Yet overall, according to this same reviewer, 'such playacting compromised the tragic force of Shakespeare's work' and produced a 'timorous and ungainly' effect.[77] The film's racial, sexual and theatrical deconstructions were even more bluntly interrogated by Richard Burt: 'If *Othello* [was] so central to the film, why marginalize it? … why, if *Othello* [was] so important, are there no actors of colour in the film?'[78]

Internationalization of the play continued in 2005 with Eubulus Timothy's South African cinematic adaptation, *Othello: A South African Tale*, in which both Othello and Iago are black and Emilia is white,[79] and in which Othello is 'the first Admiral of colour of the South African Navy'.[80]

This production not only followed Janet Suzman's lead in her famous stage production of 1987 but also extended it by complicating and partly reversing the play's race politics along the lines of a resurgent black African postcolonial nationalism. Next, in 2006, came a major, award-winning and internationally acclaimed Indian film version of *Othello*, *Omkara*. Set in western India and evoking 'India's political underworld … [and] issues of caste instead of race' (Jiminez), it was described as 'Shakespearean to its core' and 'a work of cinematic brilliance', although some called it 'dark and disturbing'.[81] In 2007 Kirk Peterson's two-act *Othello* in Calgary, Canada, offered another balletic adaptation. Race or colour politics was clearly not the focus. The emphasis was much more on Iago and even on a hint of homoeroticism between him and Othello, projected by the 'suggestiveness of their varied grappling',[82] recalling a similar undertone in Kenneth Branagh's 1995 film of the play. In contrast, race politics clearly *was* the focus in the Canadian Broadcasting Corporation's stage production, directed by Zaib Shaikh in Montreal in 2008. Although Denise Duguay thought it not 'a full adaptation', she found its depiction of the lead character 'as a Muslim rather than as a black man … stunning'.[83]

The trend of international adaptations appeared elsewhere as well, as for instance in the 2008 Malaysian film *Jarum Halus* ('web of conspiracy'), produced and directed by the young Malaysian-born but British-trained Mark Tan. One critic said it depicted 'the fragility of relationships, and how "little sins" can easily snowball into great tragedy'; another called it an 'incredibly violent and macabre' recreation of Shakespeare's play as 'a corporate drama in Malaysia, substituting the Moor/Venetian conflict with the multiracial (Chinese/Malay) context'. A third critic commented that it mixed 'the Western story with Eastern values … where Muslim calls for prayer are played out against the backdrop of the dramatic capitalist world of corporate Kuala Lumpur'.[84] In 2006, a Japanese Kabuki adaptation of *Othello* was performed at Illinois State University. It was a rendition by Shozo Shato of Karen

Shunde's *Othello's Passion: A Kabuki Play* which used Kabuki theatre's 'direct expositional address by characters' and heavy visual elements to focus on 'passion' but was, in the words of one reviewer, only partially successful.[85]

An interesting theorization of Eastern/Asian adaptations of Shakespeare's play, and a direct refutation as well as an extension of pointed postcolonial denunciations of the Western cultural exploitation of non-Western materials inherent in the play itself, is provided by Chungfung Fei and William Sun in their analysis of the Beijing opera's performances of *Othello*. They assert that such performances mark deliberate Asian importations of Western materials to enrich Chinese life.[86] A good collection of discussions of varied Asian media adaptations of Shakespeare is the volume *Shakespeare in Asia: Contemporary Performance*.[87]

Capping the cultural politics of these productions and clearly highlighting the play's racial and sexual provocativeness in 2009 was 'a four-hour, futuristic, high-tech "Othello"' staged by Peter Sellers. The performance derived from an argument between Sellers (who felt the play had outlived its usefulness) and the celebrated African-American novelist Toni Morrison (who felt otherwise). Each agreed to script a version of the play, both of which Sellers would stage, beginning with Sellers' version. This production used a Latino actor for the lead role (and combined the roles of Bianca and Montano, which were played by a Middle Eastern actress) to diffuse, according to one reviewer, 'any lingering uneasiness about Othello's race' and indicate that 'racial tensions were not the focus of the production'.[88] Sellers' work 'was greeted with mixed reviews in Europe and criticized in New York'.[89] In contrast, Morrison's version, titled *Desdemona* and staged in 2011, was 'Part play, part concert ... an interactive narrative of words, music and song about Shakespeare's doomed heroine, who speaks ... from the grave about the traumas of race, class, gender, war – and the transformative power of love.'[90]

The year 2011 saw another musical adaptation: an Indian choreographic interpretation titled *White Orchids*, by Reetu

Patel. It showcased 'a total of 20 unmatched, exclusive and nonrepeating choreographies',[91] including 'dance styles and traditions ranging from modern to Bollywood and even a Spanish flamenco'. It was inspired by 'the love story in Shakespeare's tragedy',[92] and according to Patel sought to appeal 'to the general American community, as well as Indian-American audiences'.[93] Later, in 2013, a major new production, set in a Cypriot military garrison and starring a black actor (Adrian Lester) as Othello and a white one (Rory Kinnear) as Iago went on the boards at the National Theatre in London. This production drew upon British audiences' knowledge that military bases in Cyprus are interim stops for soldiers en route to and from Afghanistan. Critic Susannah Clapp called it 'a terrifically exciting, exceptionally coherent *Othello* … [and] a major reinterpretation batting away the notion that Shakespeare's drama is dominated by racism'.[94] Also in 2013, a 90-minute hiphop stage rendition called 'Othello: The Remix' debuted in Chicago. In this version, Othello is 'a ghetto-born musician, pumped up on the American Dream as he skyrockets to success. Like Shakespeare's Othello, who seduced Desdemona with his stories, this Othello seduces with his songs.'[95]

This formally multifarious and politically heterogeneous proliferation of *Othello* on stage, in film, in musical renditions and in public media worldwide is perhaps best described as the contemporary revival of the emergent early modern worldliness of Shakespeare's play, framing Europe from without and within, and backcrossed inevitably with conflicted racial, sexual and colonial-national hues. The many denials by recent directors and commentators of the importance of race in *Othello* do not necessarily announce the end of a racial-sexual-national-postcolonial perspective on Shakespeare that Katherine Eggert proclaimed, but rather, as Richard Burt has argued, the vacuity of attempts to declare that death. For Burt, there is no longer any authentic Shakespeare left because now *both* authentic and adapted Shakespeares are fakes.[96] But this in itself is a post-postmodern meta-mimetic position, suggesting that representations of race, sex, class, nation, are representations of representations of being. The absent centre to which Burt points, that vacuity, is itself made visible, enabled, by the artificial performances of artificial ontologies – of imagined states of being. This conclusion would seem both to point back to the self-conscious 'play'-fulness of the Elizabethan stage itself, its delight in foregrounding its performance of illusion, and also to mark a closer affinity between our performative moment now and the playwright's then. The racial-sexual-national-colonial components of *Othello* that preoccupy us in the twenty-first century thus can only be the nuclear elements of the play's first incarnation and not the 'poisons' of modern thinking as Pechter claimed.

Prospects

The epochal events of September 2001 changed cultural politics, leaving a world not just of endless wars of the West on Muslim terrorists worldwide and vice versa but also a perpetual suspiciousness of foreign-ness itself within and across national communities, including the United States. Yet the MLA International Bibliography lists only one recent item pertaining even in passing to the impact of those epochal events on our understanding of *Othello*.[97] If critical commentary has invoked the grim parallels of a world after 9/11 in Shakespeare at all it has been not in connection with *Othello* but in connection with *Romeo and Juliet*.[98] Worth noting is that the third and latest incarnation of the ground-breaking *Alternative Shakespeares* critical anthology series contains not a single essay on *Othello*.[99] Remaking the new should not mean abandoning the gains of the racial, sexual, national-imperial cultural politics of the moment, but reinforcing them, especially in response to the growing and determined attacks in contemporary public discourse against the very relevance of the Humanities. In that project, Shakespeare's charged drama about the Moor of Venice cannot but have a vital role to play.

4

New Directions: Othello, the Moor of London: Shakespeare's Black Britons

Matthew Steggle

Had Shakespeare ever met a Moor? Did he count any black people among his acquaintances, or even, in the language of a previous generation's prejudice, among his best friends?

This is a potentially troubling line of questioning for readers of *Othello*, not so much because it is seemingly impossible to answer definitively – although it is – but because it opens up the whole problem of how to think about early modern racial discourse, a field which goes far beyond individuals to encompass, in Margo Hendricks' influential formulation, 'a multiplicity of loci, of axes of determinism, as well as metaphorical systems to aid and abet its deployment across a variety of boundaries in the making'.[1] Much recent work on the play has explored the global and extended dimensions of the early modern racial experience, while paying, perhaps, less attention to local networks and personal relationships of the sort problematized by the question posed here.[2] In this chapter, I read *Othello* in the light of the growing evidence that there was a small but significant black presence in Shakespeare's England. The argument is anchored around the life records of two black individuals, Edward Resonable and John Accomy, who might, in theory at least, have been present at an early performance of Shakespeare's tragedy.

For early critics of *Othello*, it was an axiom that the central character's colour put him far, far outside the direct experience of the audience. At the beginning of the twentieth century, A. C. Bradley wrote that Othello 'does not belong to our world, and he seems to enter it we know not whence – almost as if from wonderland'.[3] G. K. Hunter, writing in 1964, demonstrates the assumption in action, in the course of an essay about the word 'Moor':

> The word 'Moor' was very vague ethnographically ... [In English minds] [t]here seem, in fact, to be Moors everywhere, but only everywhere in that outer circuit of non-Christian lands where, in the *mappa mundi*, they appear with the other aberrations – 'salvage' men, satyrs, apes, skiapods, and the creatures that Othello knew of old:
>
> > The Anthropophagi, and men whose heads
> > Do grow beneath their shoulders.
>
> Throughout the Elizabethan period, indeed, there seems to be considerable confusion about whether the Moor is a human being or a monster.[4]

By 1997, the axiom of Bradley and Hunter – that Shakespeare's England was radically unfamiliar with Moors – was starting to weaken. For instance, E. A. J. Honigmann's introduction to the Arden 3 edition of *Othello* discusses the events of 1600, when the ambassador of the King of Barbary visited London. For his knowledge of Moors, therefore, 'We now know that [Shakespeare] did not have to rely on literary sources: not long before he began *Othello* he had the opportunity of observing a Moorish embassy at first hand … The first audiences of *Othello* could compare Shakespeare's Moor with these much-discussed foreigners.'[5] Honigmann also cites the notorious 1601 proclamation ordering the expulsion of all black people from the kingdom: 'Whereas the Queen's Majesty is discontented at the great number of "negars and blackamoores" which are crept into the realm … her Majesty hath appointed Caspar Van Zenden [sic], merchant of Lubeck, for their transportation.'[6] He adds that correspondence from the following year indicates that 'the "annoyance" lingered for some time'. Thus, Honigmann's introduction starts to doubt the orthodoxy that Shakespeare would never have met a Moor. However, it does not proceed very far along that road. Another indicator of scholarly opinion at around the same date is Dympna Callaghan's deservedly influential essay on the play in *Alternative Shakespeares*, Vol. 2. Callaghan documents numerous instances in early modern England of 'the display of people from Africa and the New World motivated by curiosity and profit'. This leads her to ask:

> [W]hy is it that an African never trod the boards of a Renaissance stage? Given that Africans and representations of them were so popular in exhibitions, and such a potential box-office attraction, one might expect some venturesome theatre owner or playwright to have included an actual African in his group of players, problems of training and apprenticing a foreign actor notwithstanding.[7]

This is the starting point for Callaghan's subtle meditation on early modern theatre's representation of difference, of all sorts. What I want to pick on here, though, is the implicit belief that theatre itself, both in its personnel and in its audiences, was an all-white institution. While Callaghan's essay differs from Honigmann's perspective in many respects, it shares something of Honigmann's assumption, prevalent elsewhere throughout critical writing about *Othello*, that it was a play produced by an all-white theatre for an all-white audience.

A number of new archival studies have mounted a sustained challenge to the idea that early modern England had no place for black people. A centrepiece of this new work is Imtiaz Habib's book, *Black Lives in the English Archives*. Habib collects 448 documentary records, of many varieties, which attest to the presence in Britain of numbers of black people between 1500 and 1677: men, women, and children, in cities and in the countryside, working often as servants, but also in a range of occupations as various as trumpeter, diver, prostitute, needle-maker, and soldier.

Early modern records are, of course, both cryptic and very incomplete. What records there are focused mostly upon male landowners rather than women or the poor, and servants are notoriously ill documented. But '[T]he un-seeability of early modern English black people', writes Habib, 'is also due to the sedimented racial etymology of their naming'.[8] Black servants' names are quickly Anglicized or else replaced altogether, and skin colour is rarely mentioned at all in most types of record. Thus, the collection of detectable references represents only a trace of what, Habib argues, can be thought of as a largely invisible presence.

Habib's work is part of an upsurge of interest in this topic. Duncan Salkeld has provided other primary citations, in a survey of sex workers in early modern London.[9] Gustav Ungerer has described numerous hitherto unknown documents showing the presence of black Africans in Britain in this period. Miranda Kaufmann and Justin Champion have also added new documents. An excellent recent article by Kaufmann suggests that the notorious 1601 'proclamation' is only a proposal, drafted by Caspar Van Senden himself. His scheme was to make money by kidnapping black residents of England and selling them abroad as servants, and the idea that black people discontented the Queen was made up by Van Senden, argues Kaufmann, in the hope of providing justification for the abductions. The proclamation was almost certainly never issued.[10]

English attitudes to slavery were interestingly conflicted, tolerating English slaving activity abroad, although at home slavery itself was firmly illegal under English law.[11] As William Harrison wrote:

> As for slaves and bondmen, we have none; nay, such is the privilege of our country by the especial grace of God and bounty of our princes, that if any come hither from other realms, so soon as they set foot on land they become so free of condition as their masters, whereby all note of servile bondage is removed from them.[12]

When, in 1587, Hector Nunez complained to an English court that a black man he had bought as a slave refused to do his bidding, he discovered to his dismay that he had no legal recourse.[13] Tudor and Stuart England was proud of possessing 'too pure an Air for Slaves to breathe in', and one of the alienating aspects to *Othello*'s Venice, one of the things that makes it apparent that it is *not* contemporary London, is its attitude towards slavery.[14] The Venetian institutionalization of slavery was long established and well known.[15] In Shakespeare's earlier foray into Venice, for instance, it forms the basis for one of Shylock's most startling complaints:

> You have among you many a purchased slave,
> Which, like your asses and your dogs and mules,
> You use in abject and in slavish parts,
> Because you bought them. Shall I say to you,
> 'Let them be free, marry them to your heirs?
> Why sweat they under burthens? let their beds
> Be made as soft as yours and let their palates
> Be season'd with such viands?' You will answer
> 'The slaves are ours:' so do I answer you:
> The pound of flesh, which I demand of him,
> Is dearly bought, is mine, and I will have it.
> If you deny me, fie upon your law!
> There is no force in the decrees of Venice. (4.1.88–102)[16]

Placed near the start of the courtroom scene, this is a telling moment, because the slave-owning Venice is suddenly defamiliarized: the speech's English audience will be momentarily on Shylock's side. Although *Othello* is less explicit, there are allusions in it which remind an audience that Venice is *different* to contemporary London in respect of its attitude to slavery. For instance, Brabantio complains that if Othello is allowed to get away with the marriage, 'Bond-slaves and pagans shall our statesmen be'. Brabantio, then, does not live in William Harrison's England. There is perhaps something of a similar implication in Othello's story of being sold into slavery and 'of my redemption thence' (1.2.99, 1.3.139).[17] The religious overtones here are so loud that a modern reader may not notice the factual implication, that, again, Venice is a society in which one has to be bought out of slavery, unlike Harrison's England in which (in theory) slavery is almost magically dissolved when one arrives there.[18] Twice in the pivotal scene Act 3, Scene 3 (lines 137 and 161), Iago rattles Othello by referring to slavery as a fact of everyday life, which in Britain it was not.

British attitudes to slavery would change profoundly in the second half of the seventeenth century, when slave plantations in the colonies became lucrative. The merchants involved pressured law-courts to give slavery a legal basis, pressure which led in 1677 to the shameful judgement that 'Negroes, being usually bought and sold by merchants, and so merchandise', could therefore be considered as unentitled to human rights.[19] But before 1677, those black people who found themselves in Britain, whether through travel or through forcible abduction by traders, were in a strange position. They were, to be sure, at massive social and cultural disadvantages, in a deeply racist (or proto-racist) culture.[20] However, they did not yet have, as later they did, the legal status of an unperson. Instead, individuals and groups attempted to accommodate themselves within Tudor and Stuart Britain, with some success. For Imtiaz Habib, the first half of the seventeenth century can in fact be thought of as a 'renaissance of English black people in the early modern age'.[21]

The idea of an English or British black person at this date may seem an anachronism. But it is one that is explored directly – albeit as a paradoxical possibility – in one comedy of the period, Richard Brome's *The English Moor* (1638), a play which revolves around the (supposed) black maidservant of a moneylender living in central London, and which features a (supposed) larger community of black servants working for merchants in the city.[22] *Othello*, too, I want to suggest, is responding not just to the abstract idea of blackness; not just to the growing importance of economic relationships with Africa and overseas, as much recent work has explored; but also directly to the 'renaissance of English black people' described by Habib. In what follows, I pursue this question by discussing two black men who might – might! – have attended an early performance of *Othello*: Edward Resonable and John Accomy. Both are identified in early records using the word 'moor' or 'blackamoor', although both are long-term residents of England.

It should be said at once that we do not have any direct documentation of a black person attending an early performance of *Othello*. Indeed, we have very little documentation of anyone identifiable attending an early performance of *Othello*, a fact that speaks to how generally incomplete our evidence is about early modern theatre.[23] All the same, the idea of black audience members at the Globe may bring to the fore some of the ways in which Shakespeare's great tragedy seems different in the light of the emerging new information about early black Britons.

Edward Resonable (*b*.1587)

Between 1578 and 1594 a silk-worker named (arguably) John Resonable, and his family, can be traced living in Southwark, in close proximity to – and potentially, at least, doing work for – Philip Henslowe's Rose Theatre. John Resonable was black.

The Resonables offer a challenge to the conventional idea, not just of the all-white audience, but also of the all-white theatre.

John Resonable has been known to critical race studies since the 1990s, under the name 'Resonable Blackman', a name derived from the baptismal record of his son Edward in 1587. However, recent intensive investigation by Imtiaz Habib suggests that in that record 'Resonable' functions not as a forename but as a surname. Habib concludes that church records from St Saviour's Church in Boroughside, Southwark, and from the adjoining church of St Olave's, Tooley Street, contain '14 direct and indirect notations of a black man variously named as Resonable, Reson, John Reason, [and] John Resonne'. John Resonable (as this chapter will now standardize his name) is first recorded to have lived in the area in 1578; to have fathered children there including Edward; and to have died around 1594, as attested by further archival references to 'Johan Blackmore widow'.[24]

In addition, Habib makes some unverifiable but very plausible guesses about John Resonable's working life. The combination of his name and his trade suggests that he may well have arrived in London as a family servant to the Huguenot silk-worker Nicholas Reason, who is recorded living in St Bride's in 1571. The Reasons were originally from Picardy, in north-east France, and came to England in the 1560s, probably as refugees from the siege of Antwerp. As Habib notes, 'Dutch-influenced Antwerp had a long-standing coloured population, made up largely of enslaved Africans arriving as market commodities from Portugal, and as servants of Portuguese factors'.[25] Once in London, Huguenot silk-workers – their English rivals complained – routinely taught their family servants the mysteries of the trade, bypassing and weakening the English guild system.[26] They also frequently freed their servants, and John Resonable could well have been such an unofficial apprentice, left behind on their probable return to Antwerp later in the 1570s.[27]

Both St Bride's, the parish where Nicholas Reason is recorded in 1571, and St Olave's, Tooley Street, where

John Resonable is recorded, are parishes associated with theatrical activity. In particular, St Olave's is the home of Henslowe's Rose Theatre, and of a large number of actors and associated theatrical personnel. Henslowe's was an enterprise that generated a large demand for silk-work, and, given what we know of Henslowe's practice with other commodities, he is likely to have dealt with suppliers very local to his theatre. Habib suggests: 'there are 274 "sylke" and "lace" items listed in Henslowe's *Diary*. Of these, 139, or 50 per cent, are from the (probable last) years of Resonable's life, 1591–4. Could these items have been provided by Resonable?'[28] No documentation has yet been found to confirm such a connection, nor is any likely to be: but in principle it seems plausible enough.

We can say nothing about John Resonable's wife, nor even hazard a guess at her ethnicity. But we know that the Resonables had at least five children. A boy named Edward was baptized at St Olave's, Tooley Street, in Southwark, on 19 February 1587: 'Edward, the sonne of Resonable blacman silkweaver'. It should be said at once that this is the only documentary evidence of Edward's life. Two of his siblings died in infancy, and the same may well be true of Edward. The uncertainties around his surname, a recurring theme in studies of black individuals in early modern England, make it impossible to trace his subsequent career, if any. We shall consider in a moment how *Othello* might have appeared to the young Edward Resonable, but first one should note how fascinatingly close his father John Resonable is, in biographical terms, to Shakespeare himself.

Most obviously, Shakespeare was making his early career in the area where John Resonable lived. His professional life at this date is bound up with the Southwark theatres, and numerous friends and associates are documented living there. St Saviour's parish, where Resonable is recorded, is where William Kemp lives at this date; and where Shakespeare's brother Edmund lives, or at least where he dies and is buried in 1607.[29] Like John Resonable, Shakespeare was a figure on the edges of Philip Henslowe's business empire in the early 1590s.

Writing, like silk-working, figures in Henslowe's *Diary* as an ancillary trade of the theatre industry, and like silk-working the work required could comprise both the creation of new items and the refurbishment and repurposing of existing stock. Both Shakespeare and Resonable were, possibly, among Henslowe's suppliers (although he names neither of them). In time, in place, and to an extent in trade, John Resonable and William Shakespeare inhabit the same milieu in the early 1590s.

Furthermore – and not, I think, hitherto noted in this connection – Shakespeare later in his career had close biographical links with another textile worker connected to Huguenot Picardy. In the period c. 1603–5 Shakespeare was a lodger in Silver Street with the family of the immigrant Christopher Mountjoy, whose trade of tire-making was closely allied to silk-working. Shakespeare has a recurrent fascination with the trade of silk-working, documented by Charles Nicholl in connection with the Silver Street plays, but present in plays from much earlier in his career.[30] One need not posit any causal link between Shakespeare's putative familiarity with John Resonable and his later actual familiarity with Christopher Mountjoy, but the Mountjoy connection shows that Shakespeare (himself an outsider to London) does not appear unwilling in principle to engage with immigrant alien silk-workers.

It has even been proposed that *The Merchant of Venice* may make a direct reference to the Resonables, in the banter in Act 3, Scene 5, around Lancelot having made a Moor pregnant so that now 'It is much that the Moor should be more than reason.' This may link, Duncan Salkeld has argued, to a record from 1595 suggesting that Resonable's widow was pregnant, a connection particularly piquant if, as seems likely, Lancelot was played by the widow's neighbour Will Kemp.[31] The connection is unproven, but it is certainly possible.

John Resonable's son Edward cannot, as yet, be traced in subsequent archival records (although there are various tantalizing 'Edward Blackmans' and 'Edward Blackmores' recorded in Jacobean London).[32] If he was still alive, he would have been around sixteen at the time that *Othello* was staged. He stands in, in our argument here, for the class of unattached black people recorded, just barely, in the parishes of London around this date. Other documents that bear upon the lives of this group of people include the burial notices of Christopher Cappovert, seemingly a metal worker, who died in St Botolph's, Aldgate, in 1586; and of 'Francisco, a nigro', who died in St Olave's, Hart Street, in 1590; and the numerous records described by Duncan Salkeld of black individuals in the Bridewell records.[33]

If Edward *did* see an early performance of *Othello*, what would he see? He would see a play produced in his native city by an institution to which – if his father had indeed done silk-work for Henslowe in the early 1590s – he would have a personal connection of sorts. Silk-working is prominent in *Othello*, that play which hinges on a silk handkerchief woven in Africa:

> ... there's magic in the web of it.
> A sibyl that had number'd in the world
> The sun to course two hundred compasses
> In her prophetic fury sewed the work;
> The worms were hallowed that did breed the silk,
> And it was dyed in mummy ... (3.4.57, 71–6)

This is not, of course, anything so crass as an allusion to the Resonables, but it addresses a connection between silkworking and black Africa, and emphasizes – as does Iago's later allusion to the international scenes of drinking in London's taverns – the international and intercontinental traffic of objects, ideas and people through the major cities of the Renaissance.

Equally indirect, and yet still significant, is the play's recurrent fascination with ideas of reason and reasonableness. From the start, Iago assumes that a black man cannot be fully rational: 'The Moor is of a free and open nature ... / And will as tenderly be led by th' nose / As asses are' (1.3.398–401). Othello, in contrast, makes a speech which seems the epitome of reasonableness, and is employed by the state on the Cyprus mission 'With such loud reason' (1.1.148). The word 'reason' itself occurs 12 times in the play, from the opening scene onwards, in the mouths of Desdemona (who appeals to 'our common reason' [3.3.64]), Othello, who at one point asks Iago for 'a living reason she's disloyal' (3.4.412), and most of all Iago himself. Iago is a great admirer of rationality: 'If the balance of our lives had not one scale of reason to poise another of sensuality, the blood and baseness of our natures would conduct us to most preposterous conclusions: but we have reason to cool our raging motions ...' (1.3.327–30). 'Reason' is a word often on Iago's lips, and yet the word itself is part of what Coleridge called the 'motive-hunting of motiveless malignity'.[34]

This observation links to the play's long-noted obsession with problems of cause and causality. Madhavi Menon offers a further meditation on the play's interest in cause:

> From Bianca, who understands that cause is always retrospective, and exclaims after Cassio has given her Desdemona's handkerchief to copy the work – 'O, Cassio, whence came this? / This is some token from a newer friend. / To the felt absence now I feel a cause' (3.4.205–7) – to Cassio at the end of the play when he learns that Othello has colluded in the plan to murder him – 'Dear General, I never gave you cause' (5.2.351), the text repeatedly tries to understand the cause of actions, the motive for passions, and the reason for disasters. And each time it insists on coming up with nothing.[35]

Appropriately, given the play's interest in things without reasons, I am not suggesting that the existence of the Resonables has anything directly to do with the play's interest in the question of how race intersects with reason. However, the name recorded for the Southwark silk-worker John Resonable, and this play's fascination with 'reason', are both specimens of early modern English culture's wider struggle to conceptualize the relationship between racial difference and human intellect.

And this, I would argue, is where Edward Resonable's (possible) presence in an early audience most changes our sense of the dynamics of *Othello*: not just in terms of what the play contains, but in terms of how it plays in front of its initial audience. Iago assumes that black people are unutterably alien and inferior – 'an old black ram' ... 'you'll have your nephews neigh to you, you'll have coursers for cousins and jennets for germans' ... an image of monstrosity which many have taken as indicative, perhaps not of Shakespeare's attitudes, but certainly of the attitudes of his London (1.1.87; 1.1.111–12). This may not be a safe assumption. It is not that the existence of one Edward Resonable would stop the whole community of London being racist, as bitter experience shows. But it changes the relationship between play and audience.

Early modern thinking about European identities and alliances – about Catholic and Protestant Christians, about Turks and Moors – was often fluid, as when the Spanish, mounting a seaborne raid on the far west of England in 1595, described the Protestant church at Penzance as a *mesquita* or mosque.[36] By a similar logic, in this play the Moor Othello is a plain-speaking outsider defined by his straightforward, masculine contrast to a Venice stuffed with an almost overdetermined collection of Catholic stereotypes: jealous Italians, ineffectual rulers, effeminate men like the 'curled darlings of our nation' who have courted Desdemona in the past (1.2.68). In some lights, he looks almost like an Englishman abroad. Conversely, Iago, his chief tormentor, is associated with England's most obvious and dangerous international rival. If Catholic Iago voices such a strongly racist attitude in front of Protestant Londoners, and if those Protestant Londoners are themselves at all of mixed race, it is an implied criticism of London, and he commits a crime against politeness in the theatre, which puts further distance between himself and the theatre audience whom elsewhere he woos.

If Edward Resonable's (hypothetical) presence in the audience of *Othello* challenges assumptions about the all-white audience: what about the challenge that John Resonable's (hypothetical) connection to Henslowe poses to the idea of theatre as an all-white institution? Callaghan is confident that no black actor *did* appear on the Renaissance stage. But given the fragmentariness of the theatre history, not to mention the fragmentariness of the racial history, can we be at all sure of this? Might the Aaron of the Henry Peacham drawing be, indeed, a picture of a black actor at work? Work such as Habib's challenges us to think differently, looking for records that *might* indicate black presence as well as ones that certainly do indicate such presence. Here, then, are some possible records of black involvement in early modern theatre.

A player named Gilbert Reason appears in a number of theatrical records between 1610 and 1625. Nothing is known about his background. Habib notes that, in theory at least, he could be related to John Reason/Resonable. Intriguingly, Reason's one identifiable role is as a 'Priest of the Sun' in a performance of *A Looking Glass for London and England*.[37] The player 'Black Dick', mentioned in an Admiral's Men record of 1597, and the otherwise unidentified player 'Blackson', named in a manuscript of Middleton's *Hengist, King of Kent*, have names that could be allusions to skin colour.[38] Surprisingly, at least two players christened their daughters 'Africa': Henry Hamerton in 1626, and former player William Hall in 1644.[39] None of these names by themselves prove anything, and doubtless most if not all are red herrings, but they are representative of the type of evidence one has to work with in rethinking whether the early modern English theatre community was necessarily, as Callaghan assumes, an entirely white one.

John Accomy (*fl.*1596–1638)

Black people from another social category altogether, however, could also have attended the theatre at this date. Our representative example here is John Accomy, a black manservant in the employ of the very rich, and slightly literary-minded, Capell family of Hertfordshire and London. Accomy is particularly interesting because he has not previously been known to scholarship on the black presence in Britain. His very existence, and the fact that he has not been discussed hitherto, is further evidence of the scale of the black presence in early modern England.

John Accomy is first heard of in 1596, when 'Accame the negro' is listed in the Muster Roll of East Hertfordshire, among the servants of Henry Capell of Hadham Hall in Little Hadham.[40] Nothing can be said for certain about whether he came to England willingly or unwillingly, nor about whether he came to England straight from Africa or indirectly through the African diaspora of continental Europe. But that he arrives in Hertfordshire unbaptized, and that he bears a name which seems to preserve traces of an African heritage, are, perhaps, two indications that he was born in Africa and not in Europe. Beyond this suggestion of international abduction, his past remains as unknowable as Othello's. The only constraints on his age are provided by the Muster record, implying that he is in theory old enough for military service by 1596, and his death in 1638. It is therefore most likely that he was born between about 1570 and 1580.

The Capells were extremely wealthy gentry based in Hertfordshire. Sir William Capell had been a successful cloth merchant, serving as Lord Mayor of London in 1503, and subsequent generations had consolidated this success, building a fine Elizabethan house at Hadham, which still stands, and entering into marriage alliances with local and national gentry, notably the Manners family.[41] Henry's grandfather and namesake Henry Capell (I) entertained Queen Elizabeth herself at Hadham Hall during her progress of 1577. Arthur Capell (1557–1632), the son, succeeded in 1588, and our Henry Capell (1579–1622) was in turn son and prospective heir to Arthur, although Arthur's unusual longevity meant that Henry never, in fact, inherited.[42] A flavour of the family's wealth is given by Cornelius Johnson's

portrait of our Henry's son, with the gardens at Hadham
visible in the background.[43]

The Capells are perhaps best known to Elizabethan
literary studies because of their later progeny, the great
eighteenth-century Shakespearean editor Edward Capell,
but they have connections to early modern literature
besides. Arthur Capell had a personal relationship with
Gabriel Harvey, being the recipient of one of the letters
preserved in Gabriel Harvey's *Letter-Book*.[44] The family are
mentioned in Spenser's *Shepheardes Calendar*, since it was
at Hadham, E. K. tells us, that Harvey presented Queen
Elizabeth with her personal printed copy of his panegyric
to her, *Gratulationes Valdinenses*.[45] Arthur and our Henry
Capell were among the dedicatees of the English translation
of Camden's *Annales* (1625), and Henry's wife was among
the dedicatees of a printed sermon by the moderate Puritan
William Perkins.[46] Most impressively of all, the eighteenth-
century antiquarian John Brand stated that he possessed a
1596 *Faerie Queene* containing Henry Capell's ownership
inscription, and the date 1598, together with a manuscript
note about Spenser's funeral: an event which (James Shapiro
argues) Shakespeare may well have attended.[47] Regrettably,
this volume's whereabouts are currently unknown, and the
veracity of Brand's report has been questioned.[48] But even
without it, the Capells certainly have connections to English
poetry.

At the time of John Accomy's first appearance in the
records, his master, Henry Capell, was around seventeen
years old. Henry Capell himself can be traced in a series of
references through his youth and young manhood. On 11
May 1592 he was admitted at Queen's College Cambridge as
a fellow-commoner.[49] He became a student at Lincoln's Inn
on 5 May 1596; married, on 11 August 1600, Theodosia,
the daughter of Sir Edward Montague, MP, from Boughton,
Northamptonshire; and in 1601 he entered parliament himself,
as MP for Boston in Lincolnshire. He gained a knighthood on
7 May 1603.[50] This is a London-centric *cursus honorum* of

the sort one might expect for the son and heir of a powerful gentry family.

Accomy himself appears in further records over the next few years. '[John?] Accomy' was baptized at Little Hadham on 17 June 1599, becoming a Christian like Othello.[51] On 9 January 1603, in the same parish, 'John Accomy' married Peronell May, *vid*' (i.e., widow).[52] We can say a little about his wife. She was born Peronell Wright, and the Wrights were a long-established and fairly numerous Little Hadham family. A Peter Wright, probably a relative, appears alongside Accomy on the 1596 list of Henry Capell's retinue. Peronell's birth is not recorded, but her first marriage was to one of the 'Chief inhabitantes and householders' of Little Hadham, William May, on 28 January 1580.[53] By 1603, then, she was a middle-aged and independent widow marrying a younger man, and she would not have Desdemona's problem of an overbearing father objecting to an interracial marriage: 'a maid so tender … Run from her guardage to the sooty bosom / Of such a thing as thou'. Peronell died in 1613 in Little Hadham and was buried there under the name 'Peronelle Accomy'.[54]

In 1614, Henry Capell gained possession of his family's second home, Raine Hall in Essex, and moved there.[55] John Accomy did not follow him, since a new series of archival records places him in the town of Hertford, some 12 miles from Little Hadham. On 9 May 1614 'John Ockamie' married Temperance Swain in St Andrew's, Hertford.[56] Children to John Accomy, Giles (1618), Elizabeth (1621) and John (1625), appear in the baptismal records of the neighbouring parish, Hertford All Saints, a parish that extends south of the town to include the liberty of Brickendon.[57] By 1631, in Brickendon, 'John Accomy, a Moor' had an adult daughter named Penelope living at home with him in contravention of the Statute of Artificers, and she may, I suggest, be the otherwise unidentified Penelope, daughter of an unidentified John, baptized at All Saints, Hertford, on 20 March 1614.[58] In this case, she would have been born out of wedlock and (presumably) legitimized by the marriage six weeks later.

There is seemingly yet a fifth child, since an otherwise untraced 'Dambrose [i.e., Damaris] Ochymy' marries a man named Richard Clarke, in the neighbouring town of Ware, on 4 February 1632.[59] Over the next ten years, Richard and Damaris Clarke went on to have at least three daughters and a son.

One more thing is worth noting about John Accomy's choice of names for his own children. Neither 'Giles' nor 'Penelope' is a common name. However, both are associated with the Capell family, and in particular both names belonged to siblings of Henry Capell. Accomy is, in Habib's term, 'compliant', proclaiming allegiance to his Capell employers even after he has, seemingly, left their employment.[60]

To summarize the above paper trail: at the time of the first performance of *Othello*, John Accomy was servant to a wealthy, powerful and literary-minded young man who spent time in London. His service to Capell is recorded directly in the 1596 record; indirectly in the 1599 and 1602 records, showing his continued presence at Little Hadham; and, most intriguingly, in the names of two of his later children. The eleven primary citations referring to him directly or indirectly, taken together, suggest a good degree of integration within the communities of Hertfordshire, and only two of them mention his colour.

Accomy is a representative, in our argument here, of a class of black servants working for conspicuously rich families, and serving, arguably, as 'trophies of the rich ... sold into domestic servitude'. There are a number of documented examples of black servants, from Queen Elizabeth herself downwards.[61] Robert Cecil had a black personal servant named Fortunatus, of whom the only archival trace so far found is his burial in London in 1601.[62] (It is a sign of how invisible such servants are in the records that even the massive archive of the Cecils seems to preserve no reference to Fortunatus.) So did the merchant William Winter, whose Guinean servant Domingo, who may have been in his service for up to seventeen years, is also only known of from his burial record in London in 1587.[63]

In 1600, a black maidservant with the doubly evocative name of Augustina Patra was whipped for truancy at Bridewell. She belonged to the household of Lady Berkeley, daughter of Henry Carey, who had been patron of Shakespeare's own theatre company between 1594 and 1596.[64] Another, equally otherwise untraceable, black servant appears in a Jacobean-era picture of Anne of Denmark by Paul van Somer, dressed in the enviably opulent clothing appropriate to a royal servant, and holding her horse.[65] Such servants give their aristocrat status by acting, in effect, as a 'cultural trophy': in exchange for a certain prestige, they gain precarious and temporary access to the lord's resources, power and protection. Shakespeare might well see a deeper sympathy between the lot of the black servant and the lot of a poet courting the household of, say, the Earl of Southampton.

Further examples show that John Accomy is not the only one of this group of servants to achieve, ultimately, a good deal of integration into the community. Dame Anne Bromley's unnamed 'negro' maid, in Dame Anne's service from before 1603 until around 1625, left a legacy of £10 to the church of St Mary, Putney, and was commemorated for doing so.[66] A little further down the social ladder, surviving documents record figures like Polonia, the 12-year-old blackamoor maid of Mrs Piers, who took her to a consultation with Dr Simon Forman in 1597; and Mary Phyllis, blackamoor, servant to a seamstress in St Botolph's, Aldgate, baptized in 1597.[67] Evidently, many more black Britons are unrecorded, or – extrapolating from the paper trails of Accomy and the Resonables – are in plain sight, in records that do not allude to their skin colour. Such black Britons would have been part of Shakespeare's daily experience.

There is, perhaps unsurprisingly, no documentation of Accomy ever attending the theatre. In principle, though, we can say that Accomy might have done so as a servant in the retinue of his master, a practice for which there are various primary references. Equally, he could have attended the theatre in his own time.[68] In either case, he would have been wearing the livery of one of the wealthiest families in London.

For Accomy, if he saw it, *Othello* would have been of obvious interest as a play about an interracial marriage, of the sort into which he would enter in 1603 (and again in 1614). Karen Newman observes of the interracial marriage in *Othello* that the play's Venetians are appalled by it: it is one that 'all the other characters view as unthinkable'.[69] This is a fair observation, but it is worth noting that such revulsion is not shared within the play either by Othello or Desdemona. What is more, in early modern England interracial marriages, such as Accomy's, did in practice take place, several other examples being documented by Habib. The play's Venice is at odds with Shakespeare's England in this respect too.

As a member of the retinue of the very prosperous Henry Capell, Accomy would also see a play about a black man whose position of service grants him a potentially enviable degree of prestige and power. Indeed, ideas of service, servanthood and slavery have a central importance in the language of *Othello*.[70] Iago early on registers his discontent with 'the curse of service' (1.1.34), even while himself betraying the whole idea of service in his dealings with his master Othello. Conversely, when Othello is first attacked, he defends himself in terms of his service relationship with the state of Venice: 'My services, which I have done the signiory' (1.2.18). Michael Cassio frequently mentions the idea of service, in senses which are – for a suspicious ear – all too open to interpretation in terms of the Petrarchan convention by which a lover is servant to his lady.

As the play develops, language of service and slavery continues to be to the fore. Iago seems to confuse service and slavery, as when he argues that Othello should not abuse his service obligations by questioning him further about Desdemona – 'Though I am bound to every act of duty, / I am not bound to that all slaves are free to', he argues disingenuously before letting himself be compelled to speak his thoughts (3.3.137–8; cf. 3.3.161). The phrasing here is designed, of course, to jangle the nerves of the former slave in a slave-owning society. And while Othello still dies insisting on his service relationship with Venice – 'I have done the state some service' – the word 'slave' has come free of its moorings in the last acts of the play, being applied in more or less metaphorical registers to Cassio, to Roderigo, to Othello, and, four times over, to Iago himself.[71] *Othello* is interested in the whole intel-lectual question of service: what it gains you, what its limits are, how it is internalized, to what extent service identity trumps other markers of difference such as racial identity, and how service relates to slavery. These concerns chime, I would argue, with the presence in Shakespeare's England of John Accomy and his ilk: black servants who are visibly different and whose presence in Britain derives ultimately from former possible enslavement. While not necessarily wealthy themselves, they are now embedded in structures of wealth and prestige which Iagos might find enviable.

Conclusion

The black presence in early modern England is more substantial than was recognized by Hunter in 1964, or even Honigmann in 1997. Indeed, it is now better documented even than it was in 2007 when *Black Lives* was published, thanks to the ongoing work of numerous scholars. Shakespeare shared his city with numerous unattached black people including the Resonable family, and also with numerous black servants such as John Accomy. The case of Accomy, little investi-gated before this chapter, shows that much still remains to be discovered in the archive.

Othello's early audiences were, for sure, overwhelmingly white, and doubtless, by modern standards, racist, partici-pating in the strongly racially prejudiced discourse of the period. But they were not necessarily entirely white; their assumptions were not yet conditioned by legally sanctioned slavery; and they were not members of an all-white city. We have seen, in specific terms, some of the implications of this for *Othello*, in terms of ideas of topics such as slavery, marriage and service. But I would argue too that the potential presence of black Londoners in *Othello*'s early audiences – as unattached people, or as servants representing powerful households – should make us attend to the differences between the Venice it portrays and the London in which it occurs.

Finally, the presence in Britain of Resonable, Accomy and others, gives a new angle on a long-noted feature of *Othello*: the play's doubleness, its ability to be both a story of exuberantly exotic, highly political geography, and one of detailed domestic tragedy set off by rows over mundane objects such as bed sheets and handkerchiefs. This doubleness is particularly visible in the play's attitude to sex. In *Othello*, sex is both an overdetermined cultural mystery and a practice of daily life conducted with bodies in a bed such as that which features so prominently in Act 5. The same is true, I would argue, of the play's treatment of race. For an audience whose extended community includes people like Edward Resonable and John Accomy, the play's achievement is to offer us racial difference both as a cultural construct with all its freight and complexity, and *at the same time* as a fact of life, a simple and potentially uncontentious matter of skin pigmentation. Iago delivers his sermon on the evils and monstrosities of miscegenation, and this is certainly part of early modern Britain's experience of race: but in practice, in the audience's Britain, John Accomy will have at least five mixed-race children and at least four grandchildren, who melt unobtrusively into the gene pool of Hertfordshire.

5

New Directions: King James's *Daemonologie* and Iago as Male Witch in Shakespeare's *Othello*

Robert C. Evans

[A witch, Agnes Tompson, intending to kill King James of Scotland] kept the same venom close covered until she should obtain any part or piece of foul linen cloth that had appertained to the King's Majesty, as shirt, handkercher, napkin, or any other thing; which she practiced to obtain by means of one John Kerr … being attendant in his Majesty's chamber … [She said] that if she had obtained any one piece of linen cloth which the king had worn and fouled, she had bewitched him to death, and put him to such extraordinary pains as if he had been lying upon sharp thorns and ends of needles.

NEWES FROM SCOTLAND, DECLARING THE DAMNABLE
LIFE AND DEATH OF DR. JOHN FIAN, A NOTABLE SORCERER
[LONDON, 1591]

*And God wrought no small miracles by the hands
of Paul, So that from his body were brought unto
the sick, kerchiefs or handkerchiefs, and the diseases
departed from them, and the evil spirits went out
of them.*

ACTS 19.11–12, GENEVA BIBLE

Although witchcraft is a prominent theme in Shakespeare's
Othello, the topic has been relatively little discussed, and
some of the best relevant scholarship is decades old.[1] Iago,
admittedly, has often been seen as satanic, but the possibility
that he may be a kind of male witch remains comparatively
unexplored. Partly, of course, this is because we rarely
think of witches as males. Usually we imagine them as old,
poor, relatively isolated women. Yet as the case of Dr John
Fian in Scotland (mentioned above) suggests, male witches
were far from unusual in Shakespeare's era. In fact, in some
places males were the persons *most* likely to be accused
of witchcraft. The presence of the malevolent Iago in
Shakespeare's *Othello* might have reminded many original
viewers and readers (perhaps including even King James
himself) that witches were often imagined as males, especially
since the play itself mentions witchcraft so frequently. If any
character in *Othello* resembles a witch, that character is
Iago.

As the case of Fian (alias John Cunningham) suggests,
male witches were not only known in Shakespeare's day but
were sometimes especially notorious for attacking prominent
people. Fian, for instance, was called a 'clerk to all those that
were in subjection to the Devil's service bearing the name
of witches'; he took their oaths and 'wrote for them such

matters as the Devil still pleased to command him'.[2] Readers of *Newes from Scotland* might be forgiven for assuming, then, that Agnes Tompson merely followed John Fian's satanic instructions to try to acquire a piece of linen cloth, such as a handkerchief, in order to torment and kill King James.

Fortunately for James, however, the plot involving *his* linen (unlike the one involving Othello's handkerchief) failed, partly because John Kerr (unlike Emilia in *Othello*) told Tompson that 'he could not help her'. Yet readers of the *Newes* who also know *Othello* cannot help being struck by various similarities. Thus, the *Newes* reports that Fian, after being apprehended and accused of witchcraft, would at first (like Iago) 'confess nothing' and then stubbornly continued to refuse to confess. Even when he was tortured, initially 'his tongue would not serve him to speak', although eventually he did admit his guilt. Among other acts of evil, he confessed to:

1 causing a gentleman to fall 'into a lunacy and madness' because Fian was jealous of the man's involvement with a 'gentlewoman' Fian himself desired;

2 causing the same gentleman to embarrass himself through rash, irrational behaviour before the King and members of the royal court; and

3 conspiring to use witchcraft 'to obtain his purpose and wicked intent of the same gentlewoman'.[3]

In all three respects, intriguing parallels exist with *Othello*. This is not to argue that the *Newes* was a source for the play; rather, it is merely to suggest that the play's original readers and viewers would not have been shocked if Iago were ultimately revealed to be some kind of male witch. Iago behaves in ways that at least one notorious male witch – Fian – had also behaved, and no one would have been surprised if Iago were accused of being a witch himself.

Male witches in and before
Shakespeare's era

Before exploring the idea of Iago as a male witch, however, it seems worth reviewing the abundant (but often neglected) evidence that males *could* be witches. In one excellent source, Lara Apps and Andrew Gow begin by noting a pervasive neglect of male witches (and even, in some cases, an inability to imagine male witches) in much modern research, including work by some very prominent scholars. Yet as Apps and Gow simultaneously assert and demonstrate, 'Early modern writers refer to male witches throughout the witch-hunting period.'

Apps and Gow note that 'Between roughly 1450 and 1750', various courts 'tried approximately 110,000 people' as alleged witches, 'executing around 60,000'. Among these victims, 20 to 25 per cent were men – a surprisingly high percentage since male witches rarely figure in popular (or even scholarly) conceptions of early modern witchcraft. Interestingly, the percentage of alleged male witches varied greatly depending on location, from as low as 5 per cent in Basel to 92 per cent in Iceland. In the county of Essex, in England, between 1560 and 1602 (in other words, in the decades just prior to the composition of *Othello*), 24 male witches were prosecuted out of a total of 158 – or 13 per cent. In Scotland between 1560 and 1709, 413 males were prosecuted out of 2,208 (or 16 per cent). In Venice between 1550 and 1650, 224 of the 714 witches prosecuted were men (or 24 per cent). In England's neighbour Normandy, a stunning 73 per cent of prosecuted witches were men. Likewise, in nearby Burgundy, 52 per cent of witches prosecuted between 1580 and 1642 were men. Thus, any assumption that Shakespeare and his contemporaries would have been unfamiliar with the possibility of male witches seems flawed.[4]

Apps and Gow also show that references to male witches were not uncommon in major treatises of the time:

Table 5.1: References to witches in demonological texts

Edition	Author	Text	Masculine	Feminine
1480	Nider	*Formicarius*, Bk 5	47	13
1487	Institoris & Sprenger	*Malleus maleficarum*	197	453
1489	Molitor	*De laniis*	35	44
1580	Bodin	*De la demonomanie des sorciers*	820	399
1581	Jacquier	*Flagellum haereticorum*	40	3
1581	Daneau	*De veneficis*	174	88
1591	Binsfeld	*Tractatus de confessionibus*	157	47
1595	Rémy	*Daemonolatreia*	30	40
1613	de Lancre	*Tableau de L'Inconstance*	335	296
1632	Spee	*Cautio criminalis*	41	258

Apps and Gow are careful not to overemphasize these data, cautioning that 'The use of masculine references in abstract discussions of witches was probably not intended to suggest that most witches were male.' But they think the table 'does indicate a readiness to represent witches as male without any need to justify or question such representations'. Turning to visual representations of witches, they find more proof that male witches could be (and were) easily imagined during this era, and they find further references to male witches in a wide variety of classical, biblical and medieval sources.[5]

Many claims made by Apps and Gow are substantiated and extended by other scholars, such as E. J. Kent. Kent has shown that male witches in Essex during Shakespeare's time (1) often possessed 'substantial' social status; that they (2) operated independently of women (not as mere followers of female witches); that they (3) were often considered educated and bookish; and that they (4) often had powerful social connections that gave them influence beyond an isolated local community. Iago exemplifies all the traits just mentioned, and, given the heavy emphasis on witchcraft as an explicit theme of *Othello*, it would have been easy for a reader or auditor to see Iago as a sort of male witch.[6]

Male witches in and before Shakespeare's era: Specific cases

One key source of information about actual accusations during the English Renaissance against witches – including many male witches – is Marion Gibson's *Early Modern Witches: Witchcraft Cases in Contemporary Writing*, which reproduces relevant English documents dating from 1566 to 1621.[7] Gibson conveniently names some – but not all – of the accused witches her book covers. Of these 96 persons, most are women, but 13 men are also listed. And Gibson's list actually omits, perhaps through mere oversight, some males mentioned later. If we add these omitted names, the number of male witches mentioned by Gibson rises to 16. Thus the percentage of men totals (appropriately enough) exactly 16.666 per cent of all those listed. This is even more than the 13 per cent of prosecuted witches Apps and Gow found for Essex between 1560 and 1602 and slightly over the 16 per cent they reported for Scotland between 1560 and 1709. Far more interesting, however, are some of the particular details Gibson records. She shows, for instance, that male witches were sometimes well-educated, well-respected and

significantly influential figures. Indeed, Catholic priests and
even popes were often suspected of witchcraft, especially by
Protestants.[8]

At one point Gibson introduces *A brief treatise* by Richard
Galis (1579), which describes his own victimization by a
witch. 'Galis's account' (Gibson notes) 'is the first of its kind
… by a comparatively wealthy and reasonably learned victim',
but she also notes that his treatise 'is the first expression of an
attitude which will [later] become common': his presentation
of a '*motiveless*' attack (emphasis added). Coleridge, of course,
once famously referred to Iago's 'motiveless malignity',[9] and
that idea has since become a commonplace in *Othello* criticism.
Thus it is especially intriguing when Gibson explains that while
records 'featuring victims of lower social status … continue to
tell the traditional stories of the witch revenging an injury',
the story 'of allegedly motiveless attack becomes increasingly
common in narrations by, or written on behalf of, influential
victims'.[10] *Othello* combines both kinds of accounts: Iago
thinks of himself as seeking personal revenge, but Othello,
Coleridge and many others have considered his viciousness so
extreme as to seem irrational or inexplicable. Othello's lofty
rank and great influence (Galis's treatise suggests) might make
him a natural target for a witch's 'motiveless malignity'.

In fact, Galis's detailed account of being tormented by
witchcraft may remind some readers of Othello's sufferings,
as when Galis describes himself as being 'sundry times
greevouslye vexed, troubled and tormented aswell in Body as
in Minde, some times in my raging fits detesting & abhorring
all Company'. He even feared (ironically, in light of what
happens in Shakespeare's play) that he might be 'strangled in
[his] bed'. Even more intriguing, in light of events in *Othello*,
is the moment when Galis, driven to desperation by years of
torment, heads off to confront a local male witch:

> I made me ready and girding my Skeane [dagger] about my
> middle with a good cudgill in my hande, I gate me to …
> father Roseman, whom furiously pulling out of his house

by head and shoulders I charged (not using any daliaunce
with me) to tell me my griefes. Who being agast at my
dealings, and fearing least that being not able to governe
mee in my fury I would strike of his head: Said, O Maister
you are bewitched, you are bewitched, wherefore looke to
your selfe, if not: in fine you wilbe destroyed ...[11]

This passage strangely (if coincidentally) foreshadows the
moment when Othello, tormented and enraged, confronts
Iago with 'waked wrath', threatens him, and angrily demands
'ocular proof' of Desdemona's alleged infidelity (3.3.362).[12]
Galis's attack on 'Father Roseman' is an oddly similar attack
by a 'comparatively wealthy and reasonably learned victim'
on a male witch in response to torments the victim can no
longer endure.

Various threads run consistently throughout Gibson's
contemporary accounts of witches, including male witches.
Gibson notes, for instance, that in one pamphlet from 1585,
all the stories of victimization by witches 'are presented as
revenges for specific, usually economic, injuries', thereby
typifying reports about witches' motives. In another pamphlet,
however – this one from 1592 – the victim seems 'entirely
innocent: the witch became irritated with him for reasons
beyond his control'. Thus the 'witch is presented as malicious
without just cause'. Gibson, therefore, notes that by the
1590s, two competing narratives of tormenting by witches
had developed: in one, witches were motivated by revenge; in
the other, they seemed full of motiveless malignity.[13]

Of the various accounts of witchcraft reprinted by Gibson
that seem, in odd ways, to prefigure incidents in *Othello*,
one of the oddest of all comes from 1595. A female witch
variously tormented a tanner named Newman. For instance,

Shee stole an handchercher from his wife and after five
dayes keeping it sent it backe againe by one of her neighbours. Who delivering it, faire, and white, to Newmans
mayd, presently there fell three dropps of bloud upon it one

after another, and the mayd amazed giving it to her mistris it became all over red as bloud most wonderfull.[14]

Such incidents, of course, are probably purely coincidental, but Gibson's book is nevertheless clearly relevant to *Othello* in various undeniable ways. First, Gibson shows that male witches were hardly unknown or unheard of in Shakespeare's England.[15] Second, Gibson's book shows that revenge was a main motive of contemporary witches, both females and males.[16] Third, some attacks by male witches could seem unprovoked or motiveless. Fourth, witches sometimes even used stolen articles of clothing to promote their schemes.[17] For present purposes, however, Gibson's book seems especially valuable simply in proving that male witches were hardly unknown in Shakespeare's England.

King James on witches and witchcraft

Further evidence that male witches were far from inconceivable in Shakespeare's era abounds in various legal and theoretical writings from that period. Indeed, the evidence is so extensive that there is no point in quoting it here in any great detail.[18] The 1563 Elizabethan statute on witches and witchcraft, for instance, explicitly assumes that witches could be male, and such language was also included in the even harsher 1604 statute on witchcraft enacted under King James.[19]

In fact, it was probably James himself, more than any other witchcraft theorist, whose opinions would have interested most English people in the first years of the seventeenth century, particularly in 1603, when James finally (as had long been expected) became king. Shakespeare, writing a play around this time dealing so explicitly with issues of witchcraft, might have been especially interested in the new monarch's views. James had expounded these in *Daemonologie*, first published in Scotland in 1597 and then reprinted twice in

England in 1603. Nothing in this treatise is especially original or distinctive, which is precisely why it is so valuable. It expresses very common opinions. *Daemonologie* is, for this and various other reasons, especially intriguing in light of its possible relevance to *Othello*.[20] Among those reasons are the following:

- James immediately makes it clear that he believes in 'Witches or enchaunters', whom he calls 'detestable slaues of the Deuill'.

- He almost as quickly makes it clear that he believes that males, as well as females, can be witches, since he mentions a 'German physician' named 'Wierus' who 'plainely bewrayes himselfe to haue bene one of that profession'.

- He asserts that 'Witches can, by the power of their Master, cure or cast on disseases'.

- He states that it is God who allows the devil, using witches, to afflict various persons. Yet while God does so for various commendable purposes (such as to punish evil, test patience, or otherwise bring good out of evil), the devil's hope is 'euer to perish [i.e., destroy], either the soule or the body, or both of them, that he is so permitted to deale with'.

- He contends that the existence of witchcraft can easily be proven by consulting scripture. Thus good Christians were not only permitted to believe in witches but were almost obliged to do so.

- He concedes that women are more likely than men to be witches, mainly because most women are 'frailer' than most men (as Satan's successful temptation of Eve demonstrated. Yet in the very act of maintaining that women were *more* likely than men to become witches, he implies that male witches were hardly unknown.

- He asserts that 'there is no kinde of persones so

subject to receiue harme of them [i.e. witches], as these that are of infirme and weake faith'.

- He declares that if any persons troubled by witches 'be penitent and confesse, God will not permit him to trouble them anie more'.

- He proclaims that God permits witches to torment certain persons in order to admonish 'the beholders, not to truste ouer much in themselues, since they are made of no better stuffe, and peraduenture blotted with no smaller sinnes'.[21]

All these claims can, in various ways, seem relevant to *Othello*. It seems striking, for instance, that Othello, who professes his Christianity very openly at the end of the play, never once turns to God to help him deal with his suffering. Instead, good man though he very much seems to be, he turns to Iago. Yet James notes that sometimes God permits even 'persones of the beste nature' to be troubled by witches 'for the tryall of their patience, and wakening vp of their zeale'.[22] Only at the very end of *Othello* does the title character seem to have glimmers of a spiritual (re)awakening, but then he mars that opportunity by committing suicide. Iago, if he can be seen as a kind of male witch, could not have asked for a better outcome.

I say 'a kind of male witch' because it is not my intention to argue that Iago '*is*' a male witch. Nor do I at all believe that James's *Daemonologie* was an actual 'source' for *Othello*. Rather, I only want to suggest that James's book is a very typical text that put into prominent circulation very common ideas about witches that many people of Shakespeare's day took very seriously. And, rather than claiming that Iago '*is*' a male witch, I only wish to argue that playgoers of Shakespeare's day had many good reasons, right up until the very end of the work (and perhaps thereafter) to suspect that he *might* be. Repeatedly, especially at the start of the play, Shakespeare raises the issue of witchcraft so prominently that

we are invited to see that theme as having some real relevance
to the developing drama.

Witchcraft in *Othello*

Although the witchcraft theme does not become especially
obvious in *Othello* until the play's second scene, aspects
of the first scene already set the stage for the theme's later
prominence. The fact that the opening scene takes place
outside and at night, for instance, already suggests an air of
both literal and figurative darkness, and the conspiratorial
conversation of Iago and Roderigo already implies that some
evil is afoot. Iago is explicitly associated with 'hate' before
six lines have passed (1.1.6), and such other motivations as
pride (1.1.10), jealousy (1.1.15–19), envy (1.1.26–30), deceit
(1.1.50), selfishness (1.1.50–4) and, above all, a desire for
revenge (1.1.33, 41) darken the symbolic atmosphere even
further. Revenge, after all, was a key motive attributed to
witches, and Iago's desire for revenge is also linked to his clear
sense that he has been denied a much-deserved promotion.
As James noted in *Daemonologie*, witches' two main motivations were 'thrist [sic] of revenge, for some tortes [injustices]
deeply apprehended: or greedie appetite of geare [possessions
or gain], caused through great pouerty'.[23] At this point, Iago's
yearning for vengeance may not seem extraordinary, but later
it will seem pathological and almost demonic.

Soon, in fact, we begin to suspect that Iago is unusually
malignant. His famous statement 'I am not what I am' (1.1.64)
not only implies his essential deceptiveness but also, more
significantly, begins to make him sound profane, ungodly and
anti-Christian. That statement, after all, clearly echoes and
inverts God's proclamation 'I am that I am' (Exod. 3.14), just
as it also reminds us of Paul's gratefulness to God for having
transformed his life, so that he no longer persecuted true
Christians (1 Cor. 15.10). Witches' tendency to pervert and

invert Christian phrasing and practices was well known, and James discusses it at great length.[24] Thus Iago's very obvious and quite sacrilegious allusion to two key passages of scripture might have alerted Shakespeare's first audiences that Iago was especially profane.

Before less than a hundred lines have passed, then, we have good reasons to think that Iago may be particularly evil and irreligious. His references to 'poison', 'Plague', 'flies' and 'fire' (1.1.67–75) only enhance his satanic associations, but it is the ways he tempts, corrupts and manipulates Roderigo – and later Brabantio – that begin to make him almost resemble an evil spirit or male witch. He stokes their malicious motives, especially their desire for revenge. Moreover, it seems particularly cunning, brazen and contemptuous of him to accuse Brabantio of behaving as if Brabantio 'will not serve God, if the devil bid you' (1.1.107–8). Already, here, we sense Iago's delight in his own audacious, sacrilegious wit. It is this bold wit, this self-satisfied cleverness, that helps make him seem so gruesomely fascinating and that helps make it easy for him to deceive not only Roderigo and Brabantio but practically everyone else. He tells Roderigo that he hates Othello as much as he hates 'hell-pains' (1.1.152), almost as if he doesn't mind being associated with hell and hellish motivations. No one would be surprised to learn, at this point, that Iago was a kind of demon or witch.

Yet it is Brabantio, of course, who first raises explicitly (and repeatedly) the possibility not only of witchcraft but of *male* witchcraft. And he does so even before the first scene ends. Worrying that Desdemona may in fact have been seduced by Othello's use of 'charms', he asks, 'Have you not read, Roderigo, / Of some such thing?' (1.1.169–72), thereby alluding not only to witchcraft but to the whole extensive literature on that subject. Shakespeare thus reminds us that belief in witches and evil magic was not just a folk super-stition but had been the topic of much recent sophisticated discussion, often by extremely learned and sometimes very powerful people (including James).

The stage, then, is set for the exceptionally heavy emphasis on witchcraft – and male witchcraft, at that – in the rest of Act 1. That emphasis is especially pronounced when Brabantio accuses Othello of having 'enchanted' Desdemona by using 'chains of magic' and 'foul charms'. He even suspects use of 'drugs or minerals', and he ends by calling Othello 'a practiser / Of arts inhibited' (1.2.62–79). Yet this speech brims with ironies. Thus it is Brabantio, not Desdemona, who has fallen under the spell of a deceiving male enchanter (Iago). It is Brabantio who has been metaphorically drugged by a figurative 'poison' (1.1.67) concocted by Iago. Only Iago, so far, has been an obvious and self-satisfied 'abuser of the world', and both Brabantio and Othello have already been equally his victims. Ironically, Brabantio resembles Othello (and Roderigo) far more than he realizes.

Significantly, neither Brabantio nor anyone else seems to doubt that a practitioner of witchcraft might be a male, and in fact *Othello* can be read as a major Renaissance text that simply takes for granted the possibility of male witches. Thus Brabantio, addressing Venice's assembled leaders, proclaims that his daughter has been 'corrupted / By spells and medicines bought of mountebanks' and perverted by Othello's 'witch-craft' (1.3.61–5). No one dismisses his allegations by arguing that only women could be witches. Instead, everyone – including Othello – takes the accusation of possible male witchcraft quite seriously. What ensues is a kind of witchcraft trial, in which Brabantio presents his (flimsy) evidence and in which Othello (unlike many accused witches) quickly and easily defends himself and is found not guilty. Yet the Venetian Duke, who seems so wise and thoughtful, does not immedi-ately dismiss the charges. Instead he asserts that even a man as important as Othello (indeed, even the Duke's own son) might suffer death if actually guilty of witchcraft (1.3.66–71). No one doubts the existence of possible male witchcraft in general, only its existence in this particular case.

Othello famously asserts his innocence, even slightly mocking the claim that he had to use 'drugs', 'charms', 'conjuration' or 'mighty magic' to win Desdemona (1.3.92–4). Brabantio responds that only 'cunning practices of hell', including, perhaps, some powerful 'dram' or drug, could have caused his daughter's defection (1.3.103–6). The Duke then cautions that certain proof, rather than 'modern seeming', is needed to support the accusation of witchcraft (1.3.110). Most editions gloss 'modern seeming' as meaning something like 'trivial' seeming (Signet), 'commonplace appearances' (Arden), 'superficial commonplaces' (Oxford), 'commonplace assumptions' (Cambridge, Bantam), 'ordinary … appearances' (Folger; Pelican) and/or 'daily supposition' (Cliffs),[25] and the Arden editor even wonders if the phrase could allude to Othello's race. Yet it is the word 'modern' that is especially intriguing. The *Oxford English Dictionary* notes that such meanings as 'Everyday, ordinary, commonplace' for this word are 'Frequent in Shakespeare', but by the beginning of the seventeenth century the word had long also come to have its 'modern' meaning of 'current', 'recent' or 'present'. Edward Pechter even suggests that 'modern seeming' may refer to 'fashionably new claims',[26] and one wonders if any of Shakespeare's original auditors or readers might have heard an echo, in this term, of the recent craze for accusations of witchcraft and the 'modern' fad for witchcraft trials.

In any case, many Renaissance writers about witchcraft prosecutions stressed the importance of firm proof. No one should be punished, especially with death, if such proof were lacking. One interlocutor in James's dialogue, for instance, insists that 'Iudges ought indeede to beware whome they condemne: For it is as great a crime (as SALOMON sayeth,) *To condemne the innocent, as to let the guiltie escape free*; neither ought the report of any one infamous person, be admitted for a sufficient proofe.'[27] The Duke, then, is acting exactly as he should (and exactly as even the harshest critics of witches would have advised) when he seeks certain proof.

When Othello is asked directly whether he did by 'indirect or forced courses / Subdue and poison' (a significant verb, as we shall see) Desdemona's affections (1.3.112–13), he summons the best proof possible: Desdemona herself and her own testimony. In the meantime, he traces the beginnings of their mutual love. He concludes, 'She loved me for the dangers I had passed / And I loved her that she did pity them. / This only is the witchcraft I have used' (1.3.168–70). By openly using the word 'witchcraft', he shows: (1) that he concedes the possibility that a male *might* be a witch; but (2) that he does not personally fear the accusation. His innocence, in fact, becomes apparent when Desdemona arrives and confirms his story by professing her freely chosen love for him. Her father immediately concedes defeat, and so none of the drawn-out complications of many witchcraft trials ensue.

Only later, when Iago is alone with Roderigo, do hints of witchcraft begin to re-emerge. Thus, Iago tells Roderigo that if he wishes to 'damn' himself, he should do so in a 'delicate' way, and then he explicitly links his own 'wits' with the 'tribe of hell' (1.3.354–8). His brazen speech implies his supreme self-confidence, partly because he assumes that Roderigo is too stupid – and too corrupt – to be troubled by such language. A different, more virtuous character than Roderigo might have responded differently to Iago's references to damnation and hell, perhaps by being shocked and even repenting of his own evil motives. Roderigo, however, is only interested in assuring himself (ironically) of Iago's loyalty. Yet Iago professes interest in pursuing his own 'revenge' against Othello (1.3.368) even while encouraging the same motive in Roderigo. In fact, it is by emphasizing vengeance that he seems most witch-like or satanic.

King James, for instance, wrote that the devil lured the poor to become witches by promising them wealth and lured the wealthy by playing on a 'desperat desire of reuenge' by offering to 'get their turne satisfied to their hartes contentment'. The devil, wrote James, 'either by a voyce, or in likenesse of a man inquires ... what troubles them: and promiseth them, a suddaine and certaine waie of remedie, vpon condition on the other parte, that they follow his advise'. 'At their thirde meeting', James continues (and this, by pure coincidence, is

the third meeting of Iago and Roderigo shown so far) 'he
makes a shew to be carefull to performe his promises, either
by teaching them waies howe to get themselues reuenged, if
they be of that sort: Or els by teaching them lessons, how by
moste vilde and vnlawfull meanes, they may obtaine gaine,
and worldlie commoditie, if they be of the other sorte.'[28] And,
just as Satan thus lured potential witches, so witches used the
same tactics against others. Hunger for revenge was almost
always the key motive that led witches to follow Satan and
that led others to seek and accept help from witches.

Iago himself soon claims another reason for seeking revenge
against Othello – the belief that Othello has slept with Iago's
wife (1.3.385–7). As Iago carefully plots vengeance, he further
resembles a witch by using – and perverting – his reason to
concoct a highly complicated plan. Merely killing Othello
will not be enough; instead, Iago devises complex schemes
designed to hurt as many innocent persons as possible. And
he succeeds, of course, mainly because he is reputed to be
an 'honest' man. This reputation has been stressed so often
that there is no need to demonstrate it here. Suffice it to say
that Iago's elaborate plots could never succeed if he were
not reputedly virtuous. Precisely because he is assumed to be
so good he can succeed in being so evil. James himself had
written that 'the Diuel is permitted at som-times to put himself
in the liknes of the Saintes', quoting 'the Scriptures, where it
is said, that *Sathan can trans-forme himselfe into an Angell
of light*'.[29] Paradoxically, Iago would be far less effective if he
were more obviously evil.

To say this, however, is not to make all the other characters
merely innocent victims of Iago's satanic machinations. After
all, Roderigo, Othello and even Emilia cooperate in their
own deceptions, and each is morally responsible, at least to
some degree, for the consequences they suffer. Admittedly,
playgoers and readers have a better, more explicit sense of
Iago's evil than most of the characters do, because he often
speaks to us directly, as when he says with self-satisfaction
that 'Hell and night / Must bring this monstrous birth to the

world's light' (1.3.402–3). We are better positioned to suspect
Iago's evil because he so often and so openly confesses to us.
Thus, we are also better positioned to catch the many ironies
in much of what he says, as when, joking with Desdemona,
he asserts that women are 'devils being offended' (2.1.11) – a
claim that applies only to himself at this point. Likewise, when
he jokingly says that he is an anti-Christian 'Turk' (2.1.115),
he speaks more truly than Desdemona realizes, just as she
speaks more accurately than she knows when she teasingly
calls him a 'slanderer' (2.1.114). It is partly because we
possess greater knowledge of Iago than any of the characters
do that the play is so excruciating, since we are in no position
to warn or intervene.

Iago's associations with evil and witchcraft become especially
obvious again when, in an aside, he tells us how he intends,
with a 'little ... web' to 'ensnare as great a fly as Cassio'
(2.1.168–9). James had argued that 'God will not permit
[Satan] so to deceiue his own: but only such, as first wilfully
deceiues them-selues, by running vnto him, whome God then
suffers to fall in their owne snares, and justlie permittes them
to be illuded with great efficacy of deceit, because they would
not beleeue the trueth'.[30] And this, of course, is precisely what
happens first to Roderigo and then to Othello: each cooperates
in his own corruption; each accepts Iago's assistance, although
both, as nominal Christians, should realize at some point
that his advice is evil. Roderigo, in particular, should suspect
Iago immediately, and certainly he should already be highly
suspicious when Iago tells him to 'let [his] soul be instructed'
(2.1.219), or when he ironically asks why Desdemona would
want to 'look on the devil' (2.1.224). At this point, Roderigo
is the only character who has real reason to think that he may
be looking on, if not the devil, then at least one of the devil's
underlings.

Likewise, by this point Roderigo should realize that it is
both Iago and himself, not Cassio, who are 'putting on the
mere form of civil and humane seeming' in order to achieve
corrupt goals (2.1.236–7). Similarly, Roderigo should realize

that it is Iago (and himself), rather than Cassio, who is operating as a 'devilish knave' (2.1.242). Iago's deception of the all-too-willing Roderigo is merely a dress-rehearsal for his later, very similar, deception of Othello, and in both cases Iago could not succeed without cooperative 'victims'. One reason Iago, like a witch, prospers is that his targets are all too predisposed to *be* seduced. They never turn to God for help. Instead they turn to Iago.

Iago as male witch: Further developments

Sometimes, of course, Iago does pursue innocent victims, including not only Desdemona but also Cassio. His plies Cassio with drink, for instance, knowing that for Cassio alcohol will be a kind of metaphorical poison or magic potion, making him easier to manipulate. Iago thinks he can almost literally poison Cassio with just 'one cup' (2.3.45), much as he later figuratively poisons Othello by pouring lies into his ears. He seeks to excite, in Cassio, the same hateful, vengeful motives that he later provokes in Othello. Once Cassio succumbs, Iago again uses irreligious double-talk, which makes him seem not just evil but also brazenly sacrilegious. Thus when Cassio drunkenly hopes to be saved, Iago sarcastically responds, 'And so do I, lieutenant' (2.3.104). Obviously, however, conventional Christian motives mean absolutely nothing to Iago. He not only implicitly mocks Cassio but brashly mocks God, both here and throughout.

Especially interesting, in terms of the witchcraft theme, are the conversations that end Act 2. Addressing Cassio, Iago repeatedly employs hidden irony and sarcasm, whether referring to God (2.3.257), to his own 'honesty' (2.3.263, 322) or to his supposed love for Casio (2.3.306, 323). Iago's dishonesty is emphasized by Cassio's sincere self-blame, but while Cassio repeatedly calls drink and drunkenness the 'devil' (2.3.279, 291, 303), he never suspects that Iago, not wine, has been the true devilish influence on his own recent conduct. Iago, as M. R. Ridley has noted, even ironically alludes to the idea of a witch's 'familiar' when he calls wine a 'good familiar creature, if it be well used.'[31]

Further irony appears when Iago says Desdemona can, if she wishes, make Othello 'renounce his baptism, [and] / All seals and symbols of redeemed sin' since 'His soul is so enfettered to her love' (2.3.338–40). It is Iago, of course, who will soon have these kinds of satanic effects, and indeed Iago now makes his own links with 'hell', 'devils' and 'blackest sins' completely explicit (2.3.345–6). His plan to 'pour ... pestilence' into Othello's 'ear' (2.3.351) sounds even more openly satanic, but the most obvious re-emphasis on witchcraft appears when he explicitly claims to work 'by wit and not by witchcraft' (2.3.367). But his wit, or perverted use of reason, *is* a kind of witchcraft. His power over others sometimes seems almost supernaturally effective. His contempt for Othello and others implies his contempt for God. Iago is no small-time villain; he is as close to a truly satanic figure as Shakespeare ever created. He doesn't simply *do* evil; instead, he takes pleasure in *being* evil. In Act 2, he incites widespread vengeful desires (the standard motives of witches) on Cyprus before turning his attention, in Act 3, to stoking such desires in Othello.

Iago's slow, steady corruption of Othello is Act 3 is so well known, and so obviously satanic, that there is no point in retracing its details here. But Iago once again reiterates the witchcraft theme when reminding Othello that Brabantio thought the Moor had used 'witchcraft' to seduce Desdemona (3.3.214). Yet it is Iago, of course, who himself uses a kind of witchcraft to seduce Othello. In fact, his impact often resembles the impact James attributes to Satan and to witches in *Daemonologie*. At one point, for instance, James explains that witches can make 'men or women to loue or hate'. Satan is a 'subtile spirite' who 'knowes well inough how to perswade the corrupted affection of them whom God will permit him so to deale with'. He 'knowes well inough what humor domines

most in anie of vs, and as a spirite hee can subtillie walken
[i.e. waken] vp the same, making it peccant, or to abounde, as
he thinkes meete for troubling of vs'.[32] All these words might
easily describe Iago's subtle, corrupting effect on Othello in
Acts 3 and 4.

Iago's manipulation of Othello is most striking when
he uses the famous handkerchief as 'ocular proof' of
Desdemona's unfaithfulness (3.3.363). The handkerchief, of
course, figures prominently in the Italian tale by Cinthio on
which Shakespeare's play is based, but how many original
spectators or readers, even among the most educated, could
have been expected to know this? Many were far more likely
to have heard of the bizarre recent efforts, already cited, of a
witch to use a handkerchief or other piece of linen to kill King
James. And some members of Shakespeare's audience, given
the play's exceptionally heavy stress on the handkerchief (it
is mentioned 28 separate times) may even have recalled the
single time a handkerchief appears in the Bible, by far the best-
known and most important text in Shakespeare's culture.[33]
In Acts 19.11–12, handkerchiefs associated with the Apostle
Paul are used to cure diseases and drive away 'evil spirits'.
Thus the one handkerchief ever mentioned in scripture has
precisely the opposite associations as the one employed in
Othello. In the play, an evil figure uses a handkerchief to
poison Othello mentally and spiritually; in the Bible, Paul's
handkerchiefs have exactly contrary effects.

In any case, it is soon clear that Othello is indeed infected
by the metaphorical 'poison' (3.3.328) Iago has been pouring
into his ear – 'poisons' (3.3.329) which 'Burn like the mines
of sulphur' (3.3.331–2). Othello himself now speaks again
and again of 'damnation' (3.3.375, 399, 401), but the clearest
indication that he is now himself becoming evil is when he
repeatedly desires 'revenge' and 'vengeance' (3.3.446, 450,
462). His pact with Iago – involving a perverse sort of mutual
'sacred vow' (3.3.464) – resembles the perversion of holy
rites for which witches were famous: both men kneel, and
Iago invokes a supernatural 'Witness' for his grim pledge of

allegiance (3.3.466). This bizarre episode, often described as a kind of perverted marriage, ends very ironically with language that reflects back on Othello himself and may foreshadow his own fate: 'Damn her ... O damn her, damn her!' (3.3.478) He brands Desdemona a 'devil' (3.3.479), but that term is now more fitting as self-description. Equally ironic, Othello designates Iago his 'lieutenant' (3.3.481) or subordinate, but the opposite is more plausibly true. And especially ironic is Iago's statement 'I am your own for ever' (3.3.482) – words that apply more to Othello's relationship with Iago than Othello realizes. In this episode, Iago – pretending righteous indignation at Desdemona's alleged sins – resembles James's description of Satan, who often pretended to resemble God as 'a protectour of euerie vertue, and a iust reuenger of the contrarie'. God, according to James, 'loued cleannes, hated vice, and impuritie, & appoynted punishmentes therefore', and Satan, to deceive those he intended to harm, often faked the same motives. Satan would even pollute 'Ceremonies and Prayers' to achieve his goals, much as Iago does here.[34]

Iago most resembles a kind of male witch, perhaps, when he finally lets Othello see (from a distance, of course) Cassio holding (and speaking about) the handkerchief. As James himself had written, 'it is no wonder, that the Deuill may delude our senses, since we see by common proofe, that simple juglars [i.e., magicians or tricksters] will make an hundreth thinges seeme both to our eies and eares otherwaies then they are'.[35] Othello, eventually deceived both in his eyes and his ears, descends into an epileptic fit that remarkably resembles demonic possession, and his last words are 'Confess! handkerchief! O devil!' The stage direction notes that he 'falls in a trance' (4.1.43). At this point, many of James's words about witchcraft might seem relevant. Thus James warned that Satan's servants 'can make folkes to becom phrenticque or Maniacque' and that 'they can make some to be possessed with spirites, & so to becom verie Dæmoniacques'.[36] Certainly Iago seems to have such an effect on Othello, and indeed he especially resembles a witch when he exclaims 'Work on, / My medicine, work!' (4.1.44–5). His kinds of poison and perverse 'medicine' are, of course, merely metaphorical, but James had reaffirmed the common belief that witches often used real potions: Satan had taught them to employ 'such stones or poulders, as will helpe to cure or cast on diseases: And to some he teacheth kindes of vncouthe [i.e., unknown] poysons, which Mediciners vnderstandes not'.[37] Iago, repeatedly associated with poison, increasingly resembles a witch or other evil spirit, and Shakespeare keeps the general ideas of demons, hell, poison, revenge, haunting and damnation constantly before us (4.1.70, 147, 178, 201, 204, 233, 239, 243; 4.2.13, 36–8, 40, 65, 94, 138; 4.3.76; 5.1.62; 5.2.74, 114, 127, 129, 131, 135, 176, 207, 219, 241, 272–3, 275, 277–8, 283–4, 313, 362, 366). If one combines all these references with all the related references to words or topics that are their opposites – such as God, heaven, salvation, etc. – the final acts of *Othello* emerge as some of the most religiously emphatic of all of Shakespeare's writings.

It is not surprising to learn, for instance, that the word 'witchcraft' appears far more often in *Othello* than in any other play by Shakespeare, and the same is true of the word 'damn'. Only *Henry V* uses the word 'damnation' (slightly) more than *Othello*, and the word 'damned' appears an extraordinary number of times in *Othello* (11 times – equalled only by *Hamlet*). Especially noteworthy is the fact that some version of the word 'devil' appears in *Othello* roughly thirty times (see Spevack, *Harvard Concordance*). Othello even suspects, briefly, that Iago may be a literal 'devil': he looks to see if his tormentor has cloven feet, sees that he does not, realizes that if Iago *were* an actual devil he could not be killed, and therefore stabs him, assuming that although Iago is evil he is not a devil in the strictest sense (5.2.283–4). Later, therefore, Shakespeare coins a brand new term for Iago: Othello calls him a 'demi-devil' (5.2.298) implying (in Honigmann's words) that 'Othello accepts that Iago bleeds, [and] therefore is not a proper devil'.[38] Yet if Iago is not a devil in the strictest sense of the word, then perhaps he would have been seen by many contemporaries of the playwright as a male witch – that is, as a human who, by seeking demonic powers, had placed himself in Satan's service. James had defined such persons as 'detestable slaues of the Deuill' and had called them 'Witches or enchaunters', and he thought they were particularly 'abounding' during his lifetime.[39] Seeking power over others, witches (by God's allowance) gave Satan power over themselves.

Few people, leaving an early performance of the play or finishing an early reading of it, would have been surprised by the idea that Iago, acting as an agent of Satan, might be a kind of witch. Certainly Othello would not have been incapable of thinking of Iago in this way. After all, Lodovico feels that Othello has 'Fallen in the practice of a cursed slave' (5.2.289), and Othello himself feels that Iago has 'ensnared' both his 'soul' and his 'body' (5.2.299). And James himself, describing Satan's impact on witches and, by extension, on their victims, had written that the devil 'oblices [i.e., obliges] himself in some trifles to them, that he may on the other part obteine the fruition of their body & soule, which is the onlie thing he huntes for'.[40]

Othello was written during a period when interest in witchcraft was especially strong in England, partly because the new monarch himself not only possessed an intense interest in the topic but had actually written about it at length. James himself had famously been the target of a plot against his life by Scottish witches using a handkerchief to promote their devilish conspiracy, and their leader had been a male witch whose deeds had been widely publicized both in Scotland and in England. When *Othello* was performed – apparently, for the first time, before King James in the royal palace of Whitehall in November 1604 – it would not have been surprising if James and others noted the play's many references to witchcraft and were inclined to perceive Iago as a kind of male witch using a handkerchief to seek the destruction and damnation of a good and noble man.

6

New Directions: Othello, the Turks and Cyprus

Raphael Falco[1]

More than forty years ago Emrys Jones argued that, like *Measure for Measure* and *Macbeth*, both probably written around the same time and 'intended to reflect James I's opinions and tastes', *Othello* 'was also designed as a work appropriate to the chief dramatist of the King's Men'.[2] In particular, Jones refers to James's fame as the poet of the *Lepanto*, suggesting that the subject matter of *Othello* acted as a kind of tribute to the new king's poetically documented attitude towards the Ottomans. If this were true, however, the tribute would be at best an ambiguous one. It might even be possible to see the play as quite the opposite of a tribute. The fact that the defender of Cyprus is driven mad and suicidal by a man named Iago – James, in Spanish, and forcibly reminiscent of Santiago Matamoros – certainly ought to put in doubt the question of this play as a thoroughgoing tribute to the new king, given what we know happened to Cyprus in the years following the action of the play. It is perhaps unthinkable to suggest that the politically careful Shakespeare, as playwright of the King's Men in 1604, could have ventured a subversive critique of the monarch or the monarch's motive. There is no need to press so controversial a speculation too far. Nevertheless, the relation of the Cyprus wars to Iago's vicious manipulations and Othello's fatal actions deserves more consideration than it has so far received.

The Cyprus wars, more specifically the sieges of Nicosia and Famagusta, introduce a peculiarly contradictory element into the historical background – and the so-called tribute – of *Othello*. The siege of Famagusta ended just before the Battle of Lepanto, and was notoriously fierce and grisly. What is perhaps more significant, however, is that the siege was successful. The Turkish invaders wrested Cyprus from Venice and kept it in their possession despite their naval defeat of 1571. When *Othello* was produced in 1604 Cyprus was a Turkish possession. If the action is meant to take place before the siege, then Iago's conduct and Othello's death would resonate with the subsequent loss of the island. If the action takes place any time after the siege, the fiction of Venetian defence and government would have been bitterly ironic since Venice (and the Christians) never regained possession of Cyprus.

The action of Shakespeare's main source for the tragedy, story seven in the third decade of Giraldi Cinthio's *Hecatommithi*, clearly occurs before the siege. Shakespeare added the dramatic urgency of a Turkish attack, an urgency swiftly and (and unhistorically) removed when the 'desperate tempest hath that so banged the Turk'.[3] We know the date and outcome of the Cyprus wars, and we know that Shakespeare's tragedy probably takes place before the notorious siege.[4] Therefore, we might ask why Shakespeare chose to show the collapse of the commander and, presumably, Venice's best hope for victory should the Turks refit their ships. We might also ask what it means that the once-mighty Othello is replaced as governor by Cassio. This final appointment not only complicates the notion of *Othello* as a tribute to James, but might also be seen as another kind of suicide, the true presage of Venetian defeats to come.

While a great deal of energy has been spent on establishing the date of *Othello*'s writing and production, much less scholarly effort seems to have gone into clarifying the time of the play's action. There would nonetheless be value in being able to say, with confidence, that Othello's expeditionary force reaches Cyprus in, say, the spring of 1570 – a few months before the Turkish sieges began. Or should we speculate that the action takes place much earlier? According to Lodovico, in the final speech of the play, Cassio accedes to the governorship once Othello dies: 'To you, lord governor / Remains the censure of this hellish villain, / The time, the place, the torture' (5.365-7). This could lead us to conclude Cassio will be installed to meet the inevitable Turkish threat in the future. If so, there is something discomfiting in this last moment of the play. Knowing the actual outcome of the Cyprus wars, we can't avoid a sense of foreboding, a sense that Shakespeare might be foreshadowing the disasters of the siege with the sudden accession of Cassio as the island's protector. Neither audience nor reader would be likely to forget that Cassio got drunk on guard duty, an offence for which he was rightly cashiered. Significantly, the drunkenness, what Montano calls Cassio's 'ingraft infirmity' (2.3.136), is Shakespeare's addition to the source: in Cinthio, the Capo di Squadra loses his rank because he raises his sword to a fellow soldier while on guard duty.[5] This is a serious enough infraction, and translates well to Iago's conniving aside to Roderigo: 'Away, I say, go out and cry a mutiny' (2.3.153). Mutiny at any time is punishable by death, and in time of war demands a commander's severest action. For this reason Iago tries to raise the alarm and inflate the ramifications of Cassio's drunken brawling. There is no such elaboration in Cinthio and when the Disdemona of the *Hecatommithi* entreats the Moor for the Capo's reinstatement, her arguments seem reasonably justified. The same cannot be said for the situation Shakespeare creates. Cassio's offence, though not expressly mutinous, is nevertheless one of the worst offences a soldier can commit, precisely because such conduct leaves comrades unprotected and a geographical position vulnerable. To abandon one's responsibilities while on guard duty – whether by falling asleep, getting drunk or leaving your post – incurs the severest censure. From that standpoint, Cassio's reputation deserves to be ruined.[6]

Further, we can surmise that Cassio, as the Italian source describes the Capo di Squadra, is 'no less adroit than brave' ('non meno accorto che valoroso').[7] 'Accorto' can mean 'shrewd' or 'astute' in addition to 'adroit', but Shakespeare's Cassio demonstrates little shrewdness, and therefore it is difficult to conjure up a future Cassio replete with leadership and governing qualities. He is vocally and emphatically repentant about his drunkenness on guard, but the episode is only days old when he is reinstated (not by his general) and given command of Cyprus. Lodovico seems to have confidence in his abilities, yet Iago's words from Act 2 echo ominously at the end of the play, casting doubt despite the patently corrupt nature of the speaker:

> I fear the trust Othello puts him in
> On some odd time of his infirmity
> Will shake this island. (2.3.122–4)

Cassio's 'infirmity' is his tendency to drink to excess and, unlike the stereotypical soldier, to be unable to hold his liquor. He fails expressly to follow Othello's orders to 'teach ourselves that honourable stop / Not to outsport discretion' (2.3.2–3). More critical to the Cyprus wars, however, is Iago's designation of an 'odd time' when Cassio's tendency 'will shake this island'. One wonders if that 'odd time' will be hastened along by Cassio's accession to the governorship of Cyprus, followed inexorably by the successful Turkish sieges of 1570 and 1571. If so, then the death of the Moor takes on more weight, raising it from a sordid domestic tragedy to a political disaster. The political implications also reformulate Iago's role, in his alter ego Santiago Matamoros, from petty conniving underling into the engineer, however unwitting, of the infamous conquest of Cyprus.

Conflating Cyprus and Lepanto

At no time in Shakespeare's professional life was Cyprus a Venetian possession. In fact, by the time Hieronimo, in Kyd's *Spanish Tragedy* (1592), casts his homicidal play-within-the play, saying to his protagonist/victim 'You must provide a Turkish cap, / A black mustachio and a fauchion' (4.1.144–5), the Ottomans had recovered from the disaster of Lepanto and were well on their way to conquering the Spanish (and therefore Christian) territories of the Mediterranean. After Lepanto, and beyond the play's fictional tempest, as Robert Appelbaum has noted, 'by 1572 – that is, within a year of losing the great battle – the Ottomans had already rebuilt their navy' and set about conquering half the Mediterranean: 'although the allied Christian forces certainly won a battle over the Ottoman armada in 1571, virtually wiping out the enemy fleet, they were very possibly on their way that day toward losing a century-long war'.[8] Appelbaum elaborates on this:

> In 1573 the Venetians, working independently of the [Holy] League, negotiated a separate peace with the Ottomans, ceding Cyprus and a large indemnity in return for the reestablishment of trade. Far from being a decisive victory in the campaign of Christianity against the infidel, the battle was a temporary triumph in a sequence of events which ended in a loss of territory, wealth, and prestige for Spain, Venice and the Christian confederacy alike.[9]

These would seem to be important facts in analysing *Othello*, and not merely in trying to set the time of the action on stage. Jones had speculated on the time of the action by suggesting that to Shakespeare's first audience everything would have seemed 'to be moving towards the naval action which culminated in Lepanto and which was fought over the same issue as that presented in the play: the possession

of Cyprus'; he added that the audience, hearing the line 'The
Turk with most mighty preparation makes for Cyprus', might
have expected the play to stick more closely to history.[10]
Othello, however, rejects the facts of the Turkish invasion of
Cyprus and moves into what Jones goes on to call 'an entirely
fictive realm'.

But I think we might ask if 'entirely fictive' isn't a misleading
characterization of the implications of Othello's death and
the apparent breakdown of his command. Presumably such
confusion in the leadership of the expeditionary force would,
at the very least, put Cyprus at risk. In the play, according to
Othello, 'our wars are done, the Turks are drowned' (2.1.201).
Yet, as is well known, no tempest drowned the Turks before
they attacked Cyprus and wrested it from Venice, beginning
in July 1570 and ending with the fall of Famagusta a year
later – only three months before Lepanto. It is difficult to
say how cognizant Shakespeare and his audience were of the
historical details, although in the intervening 30 years the fall
of Nicosia and the siege of Famagusta had been widely seen as
notorious instances of Ottoman barbarity. The horrors of the
interminable siege, the duplicity of the Ottoman commander
Lala Mustafa, and the disgusting tortures he inflicted on
Marcantonio Bragadino, the governor of Famagusta, were
rallying points for the Christian league that made up Don
John's victorious naval armada at the Battle of Lepanto.

Even King James, at the beginning of his *Lepanto*, writes
urgently about the Turkish conquest of Cyprus. His poem –
a thousand-line epic published and circulated in 1585, then
republished in 1591 and 1603, just as he took the throne and
a year before *Othello* – certainly encourages the conclusion
that, inspired by such outrages as occurred on Cyprus, the
Battle of Lepanto was joined. Like *Othello*, the poem begins
in Venice, what James calls 'this artificiall Towne' because it
doesn't stand on 'Ile nor ground' and the sea runs through the
streets. The Christian God, 'IEHOVA, whose nod doth make /
The heauens and moutaynes quake', initiates the action, when,
'from thundering throate' he commands: 'No more shall now

these Christians be / With Infidels opprest.'[11] He sends the angel Gabriel to Venice to agitate anonymously among men of spirit and to start a rumour of revenge. The rumour 'last of all ... comes vnto / The Duke and Senates eare' (B2r), and James underscores the oppressed atmosphere with a piece of vital information: 'The Turke had conquest Cyprus Ile, / And all their lands that lay / Without the bounds of Italie' (B2r).

According to the *Lepanto*, moreover, not only had the conquest of Cyprus 'moou'd each Christian King, / To make their Churches pray for their / Reliefe in euery thing' (B2r); incursions by the 'Mahometists' had also reduced the weeping Venetians to mirrors of both the sea and of their own streets. James's passage is affecting, if a bit strained:

pale distresse had banisht them,
    By sadde and sory cheare.
As Seas did compasse them about,
    As Seas the Streets did rin,
So Seas of teares did euer flowe,
    The houses all within.
As Seas within were ioyned with howles,
    So Seas without did rayre,
Their carefull cries to Heauen did mount,
    Resounding in the ayre. (B2v)

This extraordinary intermingling of salt tears with salt sea and salt-watery Venetian streets creates a unique image of imitative and synesthetic sorrow, while, opportunely, providing the author with an emotional moment for a traditional epic invocation. 'O stay, my Muse', he begs, and, on the heels of having established his *bona fides* as a poet, James relates the Venetian Senate's urgent pleas for alliance in their revenge: 'At last, support was graunted them, / The holy league was past, / Als long to stand, as twixt the Turkes / And Christians warre shoulde last' (B2v). The proximity in the poem of James's invocation to his muse and the passage describing the formation of the Holy League is very suggestive. It could be

seen as James's attempt – metaphorically and well after the fact
– to link himself to the group of Christian princes responsible
for the victory, thereby confirming his dual identities as poet
and anti-Ottoman king. This nostalgic, bifurcated identity,
while no doubt more pronounced when James ruled in
Scotland, continued to resonate after his accession to the
British throne.

As Shakespeare does in Act I, Scene 3 of *Othello*, James
uses Cyprus as a spur to action among the Venetians, possibly
leading readers to infer that the subsequent Christian victory
retook the island and returned it to 'the bounds of Italie'
(or, in the case of Shakespeare's audience, that the island
remained a Venetian possession). This conflation of the status
of Cyprus and the Battle of Lepanto became widespread,
at least in part because James's sense of Cyprus's role as a
motivating factor among the Holy League participants was
in all likelihood accurate. According to Andrew Wheatcroft,
during the formation and marshalling of Don John's armada,
'Every Venetian in the fleet knew the Ottomans were besieging
the town of Famagusta in Cyprus.'[12] They knew too of the
Ottoman reputation for barbarous cruelty, and their practice
of massacring or enslaving those whom they conquered.

James suggests as much in the *Lepanto* when Don John
exhorts the armada before the battle, rowing among his ships
and calling on the names of special men 'with louing speech …
Remembring them how righteous was / Their quarrell' (C2v).
He makes it abundantly clear that it is their responsibility to
uphold 'the glory of God in earth' (C2v), thereby preventing
the inevitable enslavement of Christians 'From cruell Pagans
hands' (C2v). The ominous warning comes in a personal appeal
to his men from the hero of *Lepanto*: 'if the Enemie triumphe
/ Of them and of their fame, / In millions men to bondage
would, / Professing IESVS name' (C2v). References to 'cruell
Pagans hands', as well as the danger of having 'millions men to
bondage' sent in the event of a loss, highlight the barbarity of
what James later calls the 'Turkish yoke prophane' (D4v). The
'iust reliefe of Christian soules' no doubt includes, or targets,

the rescue of recently besieged and slaughtered inhabitants of Nicosia and Famagusta. In the words of the Archangel Gabriel, as he stirs up the Venetian populace:

> What doe we all? me thinke we sleepe:
>   Are we not day by day
> By cruell Turks and infidels
>   Most spitefullie opprest?
> They kill our Knights, they brash our forts,
>   They let vs neuer rest. (B1v)

Killing knights and 'brashing' forts is meant perhaps to bring to mind Bragadino's vicious treatment by the treacherous Lala Mustafa near the walls of Famagusta. The fall of Nicosia in 1570 and the subsequent massacres of the conquered inhabitants of the city were widely known by the summer of 1571. However, not until 4–5 October 1571, when a small craft heading from Crete to Venice brought the unwelcome tidings, did the Holy League learn the news of Famagusta's fall in August; at the same time they no doubt learned of the treachery of the Ottoman commander. Coincidentally, on those two days, the Christian fleet was weathering a tempest, 'battened down, riding out the storm' that prevented Don John from advancing on the Turkish ships.[13] Unlike *Othello*'s Turks, however, the Holy League ships pulled through.

An ambiance of sources

In reviewing Emrys Jones's essay, Paul Jorgensen long ago pointed out that, 'Unfortunately, as Jones admits, Shakespeare seems … to have had no direct indebtedness to King James, and there was a much clearer indebtedness to Richard Knolles's *Generall Historie of the Turks*'.[14] Jorgensen is referring especially to the 'prominence of the Cyprus wars', which are not found in Giraldi Cinthio's tale of the Moor, Shakespeare's main source of the plot. Still, despite the absence of direct verbal echoes, it is difficult not to associate the *Lepanto*'s opening scenes in Venice with the panicky realizations in *Othello* Act 1, Scene 3, when the Duke and Senators gather to interpret the news delivered by the sailor and the messenger. Moreover, the conflation of Bragadino's humiliation with Don John's subsequent victory is understandable, particularly in light of Knolles's elaborate description of the wrongs inflicted on the Christian governor by Lala Mustafa.

Knolles begins his author's induction by saying that 'the long and still declining state of the Christian commonweale, with the utter ruine and subversion of the Empire of the East' never can be 'fully lamented'.[15] If, in fact, Shakespeare was familiar with Knolles's history, then he couldn't have missed the tone of defeat and loss from the first pages: forced submission, obeisance and bloody conquest come to the Christians in every encounter with Solyman's generals and the Turkish janissaries. His account of the attack on Cyprus is no exception, and in fact begins with a tactical discussion pertinent to the Turkish threat in *Othello*:

> Now all the hope of the Christians was to have kept the Turkes from landing, which they should with all their strength and power have done; neither was it a matter of any great difficultie: for had the defendants but kept the shore, and from the drie and firme land valiantly repulsed their enemies, they might undoubtedly with their shot and weapons have kept them from landing, or else have done them greater harme: knowing in the meane time, that in all the island was no good harbour for them to put into, and that riding in the open rode, subject to all wind and weather, they could not long without danger of shipwracke ride it out.[16]

Knolles's description of the preparations, fortifications, and potential defensive alternatives are sound military advice. More to the point for *Othello*, however, is the last sentence quoted above, from which the exchange between Montano

and the Second Gentleman, prior to Othello's arrival, might
well have been drawn:

> MONTANO
> Methinks the wind hath spoke aloud at land,
> A fuller blast ne'er shook our battlements:
> If it hath ruffianed so upon the sea
> What ribs of oak, when mountains melt on them,
> Can hold the mortise? What shall we hear of this?
> SECOND GENTLEMAN
> A segregation of the Turkish fleet:
> For do but stand upon the foaming shore,
> The chidden billow seems to pelt the clouds,
> The wind-shaked surge, with high and monstrous mane,
> Seems to cast water on the burning bear
> And quench the guard of th'ever-fired pole.
> I never did like molestation view
> On the enchafed flood.
> MONTANO
> If that the Turkish fleet
> Be not ensheltered and embayed, they are drowned.
> It is impossible to bear it out. (2.1.5–19)

I quote this passage for two reasons: first, to demonstrate
how Shakespeare might have borrowed from Knolles but,
if so, how he used the tactical information to set his action
earlier than the successful conquest of the island; and, second,
to suggest that the conflation of victory at Lepanto and the
miracle of 'our wars are done' in *Othello* (2.1.201), despite
being a cause for relaxation and celebration, foreshadows in
the play what Knolles calls the 'utter ruine and subversion of
the Empire of the East'.

Shakespeare had other precedents for storms. Turks
and tempests were regularly linked in the literature of the
period, probably because climatic natural disaster proved the
Christian deity was taking a hand in dismantling the Muslim
empire. For instance, in Giovanni Canevari's 1572 Neo-Latin

poem *In Mustafam* (*On Mustafa*), the poet describes the
return of Mustapha by sea with the spoils of his conquest.
Not sparing the vitriol, Canevari catalogues Mustafa's crimes
and betrayals in a series of questions and answers: 'Mustafa,
how could you dare snuff out so many men in a death they
did not deserve ... in violation of the trust we offered and the
treaty we sealed?' ('Ergo tot heroas ... adversus pactamque
fidem foedusque receptum / ausus es indigna, Mustafa,
extiguere morte?'[17]) He castigates Mustafa as a killer of
unarmed men, a 'natural-born thief' ('ingenuo ... latroni', l.
32), and a man who spurns Christ. He asks, significantly, if
Mustafa is worried about Nemesis: 'Are you not afraid that
Nemesis or chance that turns all things, or the vicissitude of
Fortune, will requite you in kind?' ('Non veritus Nemesim
versantemque omnia sortem, Fortunaeque vicem, ac eadem
tibi posse ripendi?' ll. 31–2.)

Inevitably, Canevari answers his own question and describes
retribution worthy of Nemesis himself. In the inveterate
tradition of humanist poetry, he uses the Greek pantheon,
rather than the Christian god, to effect Mustafa's punishment.
Nereus covers Salamis with a wave to protect it from the
contagion of Famagusta's atrocities; and the Nile retreated
so as not to come in contact with Cyprus's waters. Most
important, however, the winds attacked Mustafa's laden ships,
creating a tempest that sank them:

> Aeolus indecorum referentia carbasa praedam
> infamesque duces Boreali turbine adortus
> non tulit insonti temeratum sanguine foedus,
> sed fremitu horrendum increpitans et murmure saevo
> contorsit, repulit, totum disiecta per aquor
> allisit scopulis infestisque obruit undis. (ll. 49–54)

[Aeolus attacked the ships carrying these infamous leaders
and their unseemly spoils with the gusts of Boreas, for he
could not bear that they had broken the treaty with the
blood of the innocent. Roaring menacingly with thunder

and fierce cloudbursts, he tumbled and tossed them about on the water, wrecked them on the cliffs, and sank them in the perilous waves.]

Like Shakespeare's shipwreck of the Turks, Canevari's is more a matter of wishful thinking than historical fact. Daniel J. Vitkus, for instance, compares the fantasy storm in *Othello* to 'the providential storms that protected the English from Spanish armadas'. He notes that 'The idea of a tempest sent by God against the invading fleet of an evil empire is found in providentialist propaganda directed against the Spanish and Turkish powers ... Cyprus was like England in being a "beleaguered isle" victimized by an "Eastern" foe bent on the extirpation of Christian rule.'[18] The geographical distance between England and Cyprus, rather than polarizing the two cultures, allows for a conflation of moral and ethical values, a conflation Shakespeare exploits throughout the play in Othello's changeability and Iago's innuendoes regarding his general's Moorish allegiances. And Shakespeare too adds an ominous reference when Desdemona, protesting before the Duke and her father, exclaims: 'That I did love the Moor to live with him, / My downright violence and storm of fortunes / May trumpet to the world' (1.3.249–51). By the play's end the 'downright violence' and 'storm of fortunes' that begins as a description of fierce devotion will be linked, as if by a kind of cruel depolarization, both to the tempest that frees Cyprus and to Desdemona's own horrid end.

Though we can never prove it, perhaps the conflation of the two islands that Vitkus suggests, as well as the imaginary redirection of the storms, were meant to conceal the fate of Famagusta and Nicosia and the subsequent encroachment of the Ottomans on Europe. Unfortunately, the truth of the tempests following Lepanto was much less encouraging for the Christians than the 'providentialist propaganda'. As the editors of the I Tatti volume observe, 'Reality would prove more Machiavellian than miraculous. Winter storms, exhausted troops and rowers, as well as lingering mistrust among ostensible allies prevented the coalition fleet from liberating Cyprus or attacking Constantinople.'[19] James, Gascoigne, Knolles, Canevari and myriad others recorded and aestheticized the legend of Lepanto until it was replete with historical conflations and admonitory revisions.

It must be emphasized, however, that there is no such conflation in Knolles's history. His account of the siege of Famagusta, which spares no detail of Bragadino's humiliation, the execution of his officers and the destruction of the town, never implies that Lepanto or a post-Famagusta storm like Canevari's avenges the victims. Yet there is a connection between Shakespeare and Knolles's description of the events leading up to Famagusta's fall. Moreover, the source of the Moor's tale in Cinthio seems to be interwoven with Knolles's as well. Several things stand out. First, in the *Hecatommithi* there is no urgency about sending the Moor to Cyprus. On the contrary, the Senators select the Moor in what seems to be a routine changing-of-the guard, however prestigious the appointment is for the Moor: 'It happened that the Venetian lords made a change in the armed forces that they used to maintain in Cyprus, and they elected the Moor as captain of the soldiers they sent there' ('Occorse, che i Signori Ventiani fecero mutatione delle genti d'arme, ch'essi sogliono tenere in Cipri, & eleseno per Capitano de soldati, che là mandavano').[20] The comparable passage in *Othello* incorporates the idea of replacing the present administration in Cyprus because of the imminence of a Turkish attack: 'The Turk with a most mighty preparation makes for Cyprus. Othello, the fortitude of the place is best known to you, and, though we have there a substitute of most allowed sufficiency, yet opinion, sovereign mistress of effects, throws a more safer voice on you' (1.3.222–6). In both the *Hecatommithi* and *Othello*, the ensuing discussion centres round the Moor's and Disdemona/Desdemona's reluctance to be parted (in Cinthio they've been married for more than one night). Desdemona's insistence to go with her husband rather than be left behind like a 'moth of peace' (1.3.257) demonstrates spousal loyalty and her pluck in speaking up. It also, however, shows her to be a disloyal daughter. And, more significantly, her accompanying Othello to Cyprus proves systematically disastrous – not only because she and Othello die miserable deaths, but also because Othello's death leaves Cyprus relatively unprotected.

In Knolles, as in *Othello* if not in Cinthio's story, the urgency to rescue Famagusta produces a scene much more akin to that in the play when the Duke says, 'Valiant Othello, we must straight employ you / Against the general enemy Ottoman' (1.3.49–50). Knolles records the story that Governor Bragadino of Famagusta entreated a bishop, Hieronimus Ragazonius, to sail with a Venetian nobleman to Venice to inform the Senate of the Turkish incursions. At first 'very unwilling to go, as loth in so great danger to leave his flock', the bishop finally consented to carry the plea:

> After four dayes sayling he came to Crete and so to Venice: where … unto the Senat he declared the dangerous estate of the citie, the strength of the enemie, the weakenesse of the defendants against so great a multitude, and the want of many things needfull for the holding out of the siege: and to be briefe, that except they sent speedie reliefe, the citie could not be kept.[21]

The man the Senators decided to send, Antonius Quirinus, turns out to be an excellent complement to the Moor of the *Hecatommithi*, and possibly another model for Shakespeare's Moor. Cinthio says 'There was already in Venice a very brave Moor, who, for being personally valiant, and having given sign [proof] of great prudence and lively ingenuity in things of war, was very dear to these lords' ('Fù già in Venetia un Moro, molto valoroso, il quale, per essere prò della persona, & per haver dato segno, nelle cose della guerra, di gran prudenza, & di vivace ingengno, era molto caro a que' signori').[22] Knolles describes Quirinus in notably comparable terms: 'This *Quirinus* was a most valiant and expert captain, meanly discended, but by service growne to be a man both of great reputation and wealth.'²³ Both Othello and Quirinus are appointed to rescue Venice from a pressing Ottoman threat; Othello, a Moor, is an outsider in the country, while Quirinus is an outsider in terms of class. There is a curious link here. While Othello may not be 'meanly discended' as is Quirinus, his claim 'I fetch my life and being / From men of royal siege' (1.2.21–2) makes rare and tantalizing use of the word 'siege'. An allusion to Famagusta does not seem entirely impossible.

George Gascoigne's 'devise of a maske'

Although histories like that of Knolles or William Malim's *The true report of all the successe of Famagosta* (1572) do not in fact conflate Famagusta and Lepanto – in Knolles Famagusta represents another example of the erosion of empire – Christian authors might nonetheless have felt a kind of obligation to endorse the conventional belief that Don John avenged Ottoman depredations. It would have been forgivable to assume that such an apparently conclusive sea battle, the subject of hundreds of poems and songs across Europe and commemorated by an annual holiday, had effected both the appropriate vengeance for Bragadino's humiliation and the recapture of Cyprus. George Gascoigne seems to have felt this way. In 1573, only two years after the Turks took Cyprus, he published his *'devise of a maske for the right honorable Viscount Mountacute'*, which conflates the siege of Famagusta with the triumph of Lepanto, allowing the audience to infer that the latter resolved the former. He got his information on the siege from Malim's *The true report*, a translation of Nestor Montinengo's Italian account of the Turkish assault. Malim offers Montinengo's graphic version of the deprivations of the siege, as when he notes how

virtually no food remained, 'our company having eaten up
their horse, asses, and cattes, for lacke of other victualls'.[24]
The writer, a nobleman close to the governor, also relates
with horror the betrayal by Mustafa after the surrender, the
subsequent slaying of the Venetian officers, and Bragadino's
drawn-out punishment. According to Malim, in a story often
repeated, Mustafa invited the governor and his nobleman
to his tent as part of an unheard-of truce from an Ottoman
commander. The Christians were asked to lay down their
arms, and, after a few polite words, Mustafa conceived an
insult; disingenuously indignant, according to Malim, he
charged Bragadino with breaking the truce by executing
his Turkish slaves. A quarrel ensued, and Mustafa had the
Christians bound, after which they were led 'one by one into
the market place, before hys Pavilion, being presently cutte
and hewen in sunder in his presence, and last of all from that
worthy and noble *Bragadino* (who being bound as the rest,
and being commanded twise or thrise to stretch forth his
necke, as though he should have bene beheaded, the which
most boldly he without any sparke of feare) hys eares were
cut of, and causing him to be stretched out most vilely upon
the ground, *Mustafa* talking with hym, and blaspheming the
holy name of our Saviour, demaunding hym, where is now
thy Christ'.[25] The details of Bragadino's maiming, torture
and death became indelible reminders of Ottoman cruelty,
inspiring the kind of righteous, vengeful anger necessary not
only to the Holy League at Lepanto but to anti-Muslim sentiments long after the battle. As G. W. Pigman notes, Richard
Hakluyt included *The true report* in his 1598 edition of *The
Principal Navigations, etc. [...] of the English Nation*, and
this late reappearance of the details of the siege, however
distorted, might easily have come into Shakespeare's hand.[26]

Gascoigne's masque is peculiar in its emphases. It was
written for a double wedding, and, as Robert Cawley put
it, the 'devise consists in having a fictitious relative of the
Mountacutes return from the siege of Famagusta where his
roving father had been killed and where he himself, taken

captive by the Turks, had been liberated by a group of noble
Venetians, happily Mountacutes also, who had escorted him
to his native England'.[27] The English Mountacutes were in
fact the family of Anthony Browne, first Viscount Montagu,
and the masque includes a reference to the 'ancient grutch'
between the Italian Montagus and Capulets.[28] In an imaginative genealogical fantasy Gascoigne not only links a
dispossessed English Mountacute to his distinguished Italian
kin, who in fact restore him to his land and wealth, but also
manages to associate an English knight with the defeat of the
Turks. Viscount Montagu was that rarity, a trusted Catholic
under Elizabeth, and, papist associations notwithstanding,
Gascoigne's linking of a fictional relative to the Holy League is
no more unusual than the Protestant monarch writing an epic
poem about the victory at Lepanto.

The boy supposedly relating the story in fact has come
directly from the battle. In the opening words of the masque,
the 'trucheman', or presenter, explains 'that his father being
slayne at the last warres against the Turke, and he there taken,
he was recovered by the Venetians in their last victorie, and
with them sayling toward Venice, they were driven by tempest
uppon these coasts' (0.25–8). That was quite a tempest to drive
a ship on its way to Venice all the way to England – almost as
bad, perhaps, as the one that 'so banged the Turks' (2.1.21).[29]
In any case, in the spirit of Sinbadian romance, Gascoigne then
treats the guests to a recounting of Famagusta and Lepanto.

The *Turke* that tirant he, with siege had girt the walls,
Of famous *Famagosta* then and sought to make them
thrals. (81–2)

The boy's father approaches by sea, but the Turks overcome
him and his crew. The father is killed and the boy is spared
and taken prisoner 'Like a slave before the Gates' (152).
His description of the governor Bragadino's humiliation
Gascoigne would have found in Malim's translation, as
quoted above:

There did I see such sights as yet my hart do pricke,
I saw the noble *Bragadine*, when he was fleyd quick.
First like a slave enforst to beare in every breach,
Two baskets laden full with earth *Mustafa* did him teach.
By whome he might not passes before he kyst the ground,
[...]
His eares cut from his head, they set him in a chaire,
And from a main yard hoisted him alofte into the aire.
(155–610)

Already in 1573, the flaying and facial mutilation of Bragadino,
like Mustapha's breaking of the treaty understanding, had
become sufficiently legendary for Gascoigne to weave them
into the mythopoesis of his romantic 'devise'. Ironically, as
if compelled by generic criteria, the narrator of Gascoigne's
masque escapes from Mustapha's janissaries by being taken as
a slave onto a Turkish galley. The boy's luck holds:

To see that cruell Turke whiche helde me as his slave
By happie hande of Christians his payment thus to have:
His head from shoulders cut, upon a pyke did stand,
The whiche *Don John* of *Austrye* helde in his triumphant
hande. (219–23)

Apparently Gascoigne confused his admirals, substituting
Prelybassa (actually Piali Pasha) for the Turkish admiral, Ali
Pasha, who led the fleet at Lepanto and who was beheaded.
Yet that mistake is negligible. More important, it seems to
me, is the smooth transition from enslavement at Famagusta
to victory and eventual freedom at the Battle of Lepanto. This
transition, by linking the escape from the siege to the triumph
of the Turkish admiral's head on a pike, might have allowed
readers to infer that the battle led to a reversal of the situation
on Cyprus – as would James's implication in the *Lepanto*.
This impulse to use Lepanto as a kind of equalizer led authors
besides James to conflate Cyprus and Lepanto.[30] Such a
conflation, though, tended to conceal the fate of Famagusta

and the success of the Ottomans in the years following their naval defeat.

It may be that Shakespeare never read Gascoigne, or, having read him, also conflated Lepanto with the liberation of Cyprus (but then why have the Turks destroyed by a tempest?). It seems odd that critics have not felt impelled to question Shakespeare's knowledge of the true situation on Cyprus. For if *Othello* is meant to take place before 1570, as does Cinthio's tale, then Iago's action might be seen as abetting the Turkish conquest of the island. If the play takes place any time after 1571, then there is a thick layer of irony in the pretence that Cyprus is saved by a 'desperate tempest' (2.1.21) and a 'segregation of the Turkish fleet' (2.1.10). For this does not sound like Lepanto either. The weather was good, if breezy after the mist lifted, on 7 October 1571.

The defence of Cyprus

The conflation of Famagusta and Lepanto carries over to the conflation of King James with Iago. Santiago (Saint James) was the patron saint of Spain and his name was often heard as an anti-Protestant epithet on the English stage. Moreover, Santiago's surname was Matamoros – Moor-killer – a name appropriate for Iago (and perhaps also for the author of the *Lepanto*).[31] Laurie Maguire has argued that Iago's role in the plot is cued by his name: 'we might validly blame Shakespeare for giving the unnamed ensign of the source the name Iago … Iago's role, as destroyer of Othello, the Moor of Venice, is thus cued by his name; word matches thing, his behaviour supports the sign.'[32] But the ramifications of this 'cuing', in light of the historical events surrounding the Ottoman conquest of Cyprus, are less than flattering if we identify Iago with King James. Whether he's a descendant of the Vice figure of the medieval cycles or Shakespeare's idea of a cunning Satan incarnate, Iago bears a name that does not appear in the source of this play, and that was associated on the Jacobean stage with Moor-killing. Santiago Matamoros was a heroic figure of the church militant, but, in the wake of the Armada and other Spanish threats, 'the name Iago', as G. N. Murphy suggested, 'would strike an important dissonance' in the ears of an English audience: 'At minimum Iago's name would stir English resentment, and Iago's personal duplicity would be reinforced by memories of what the English considered national – almost racial – duplicity.'[33] The myth of the Moor-killing Christian saviour clashes with the fractious Spanish–English relationship in Iago's name, and, consequently, in Iago's engagement with Othello. Not surprisingly, Shakespeare distorts both myths to complicate the action. In *Othello*, Shakespeare's Iago is undeniably responsible for the Moor's death; even if he does not kill him by his own hand, his lies and malevolent tricks bring it about. He fails to kill Cassio, but his plan seems to succeed in that Desdemona and Othello lie dead at the end of the play. He may be improvisatory along the way in his tactics, but he does not waver in his aim until he achieves his (Pyrrhic?) victory.

The island of Cyprus, rich in resources and strategically located, remained a jewel in the crown of Turkish military victories. This fact has been overlooked, perhaps because Muslims did not commemorate victories as did the Christians with civilian holidays or victory parades. Moreover, if contemporary reports are to be believed, when the news of Lepanto reached Constantinople the grand vizier Mehmed Sokullu told the Venetian emissary that Lepanto was meaningless:

I would have you know the difference between your loss and ours. In wresting Cyprus from you, we deprived you of an arm; in defeating our fleet, you have only shaved our beard. An arm when cut off cannot grow again; but a shorn beard will grow all the better for the razor.[34]

There are several striking aspects to this passage. The 'shorn beard' has significance in the Islamic religion, and its tendency to grow 'all the better for the razor' would be an apt and prophetic metaphor for the spread of an empire guided by the Muslim deity. Of more interest in regard to *Othello* is the reference to the amputated arm. Although Shakespeare could not possibly have seen the Venetian emissary's text, the echo in the play is uncanny. Compare two scenes, one in which Othello's authority is palpable:

> Zounds, if I once stir,
> Or do but lift this arm, the best of you
> Shall sink in my rebuke. (2.3.203–5)

And this one, from Act 5, echoing the earlier lines but showing Othello weakened and even emasculated:

> I have seen the day
> That with this little arm and this good sword
> I have made my way through more impediments
> Than twenty times your stop: but, O vain boast,
> Who can control his fate? (5.2.259–66)

Othello's vain boast might well be the boast of the *Lepanto* and the scores of similar songs and chronicles. But, as Shakespeare might well have known, Cyprus could not control its fate and even came to represent the resurgence of Ottoman strength. Therefore, if Iago's destruction of the Moor in the play is reimagined in a historical setting, then he (and his counterpart King James Matamoros) did incalculable harm by leaving Cyprus unprotected.

Unless we think of *Othello* as an allegory of some kind, which it patently is not, then Iago orchestrates the death of a Christianized Moor whose loyalties are to the Venetian Republic. His homicidal malice, which fuels his undoing of the defender of Venice, might be seen as a subversive political act (which can hardly be construed as a tribute to James). Yet even if James was regularly associated with Santiago Matamoros in the public mind – or in the minds of the Globe Theatregoers

– his association with Iago does not necessarily follow. The links between the names Santiago Matamoros and James, and between James and Iago, might indeed be plausible and might continue to raise puzzling questions, especially when set beside the conflation of Lepanto with the true historical fate of Cyprus as recounted in Knolles's, Malim's and Gascoigne's accounts of the siege of Famagusta. But, as I said above, it is unlikely that the leading dramatist of the King's Men would risk associating James with such subversive politics – which in itself would be subversion.

Yet it would be difficult to prove Shakespeare was *not* aware of what became a virtually conventional approach to the Cyprus Wars. His use of conflations involving both history and proper names provides a more productive way to complicate the play's hermeneutic possibilities. We can see in Iago/James and Lepanto/Famagusta parallel manifestations of unease. This very real unease with the contemporary Ottoman advance in the Mediterranean became merged (and mixed up) with a prevalent cultural unease about the effectiveness of Christian armed forces against their Turkish counterparts, and, inevitably, of the Christian god against the 'Mohammedan' god. Shakespeare's and others' ambiguous conflations help to express the inexpressible – that is, that there could ever be a crisis of faith in the Christian Church militant. But, to borrow one of George Lukács's terms, tragedy above all other genres expresses the 'possible consciousness' of such a crisis of faith. In linking silence to Moor-killing when, at the end of the play, Iago refuses to speak, Shakespeare seems to reveal this possible consciousness of crisis. 'Demand me nothing', Iago says, 'What you know, you know. / From this time forth I never will speak word' (5.2.300–1). Iago's adamancy has been interpreted in many ways, but it is Lodovico's answer that is most telling in regard to the tragic situation: 'What, not to pray?' he asks, with apparent innocence (5.2.302). He obviously expresses his astonishment that Iago seeks nothing from the deity. Yet his short question can have terrifying ramifications: it can reveal the possible consciousness of crisis in the authority of the entire cultural belief system.

What, however, is Iago speaking for, or refusing to speak for? Scholars and audiences have conjectured everything from a criminal's base pragmatism to self-satisfaction to tacit satanic glee. But in the shadow of Lodovico's appalled remark, Iago's silence – precisely because it is silence – suggests there is nothing to pray for, or no deity to pray to. Like all the other conflations in the play, this murderer's silence permits conflation with a more significant silence, the silence of fate or ill fortune confronting the Venetians as they (under the unreliable Cassio) prepare to hold off the soon-to-be-returning Turks. The conflation allows hope and victory to flicker like a guttered candled in the dark knowledge of future defeat. An audience can ask for no more powerful glimpse of the abyss.

7

New Directions: Othello and His Brothers

Lisa Hopkins

The Caroline dramatist John Ford engaged so extensively with the plays of Shakespeare that he has some claim to be considered Shakespeare's first literary critic. *'Tis Pity She's a Whore* ingeniously rewrites *Romeo and Juliet* to make its lovers not inappropriately divided by family but inappropriately united by it; *The Lover's Melancholy* equally creatively combines elements of *King Lear* and *Twelfth Night*; and *Perkin Warbeck* revisits the narrative substance of *Richard III* in the style of *Richard II*. Most insistently, though, Ford revisits *Othello*. There are echoes of it as well as of *Romeo and Juliet* in *'Tis Pity She's a Whore*, in the shape of Soranzo's murderous jealousy, and the debt is unmistakable in two other plays, *Love's Sacrifice* and *The Lady's Trial*.

In the first of these, both the Italian setting and the basic plot premise of *Othello* are reprised as Philippo Caraffa, the Duke of Pavia, goaded into suspecting that his wife is having an affair with his closest friend, murders them both. The Iago character, Roderico D'Avolos, has names which echo both the actual name of Roderigo and the supposed diabolism of

Iago; the Desdemona character, the Duchess Bianca, has a
name which echoes that of the courtesan who loves Cassio.
The Duke doubly recalls the language of Othello himself
when he says 'I am a monarch of felicity, / Proud in a pair
of jewels rich and beautiful',[1] recalling both Othello's initial
happiness – 'I cannot speak enough of this content' – and his
subsequent comparison of Desdemona to a pearl and to a
chrysolite;[2] D'Avolos's interpretation of what he takes Bianca
and Fernando to be saying recalls Iago's similar glossing of
Cassio's alleged dream (2.3.53ff.); Fernando clearly shares
Cassio's scale of values when he reacts with lightning speed
to a perceived threat to his reputation: 'How's that? My
reputation? Lay aside / Superfluous ceremony. Speak, what
is't?' (I.i.213–14), just as Cassio regards his reputation as
'the immortal part of myself' (2.3.259–60). Bianca proposes
to intercede for Roseilli (1.2.171–5) and later for Mauruccio
(4.1.122–3) as Desdemona does for Cassio (3.3.45–51); and
the Abbot of Monaco, who is Bianca's uncle and arrives on
a visit, echoes Lodovico. Also as in *Othello* there are games
played with the audience's sense of time: Bianca says at
2.1.141 that this is the third time Fernando has told her he
loves her, but it is the first such declaration that we have seen.
We also experience as preternaturally short the time elapsing
between the revelation of Julia's, Colona's and Morona's
pregnancies and their entrance each with a baby in her arms.
Ford's final rewriting of *Othello* comes in his last play, *The
Lady's Trial*, which is also set in Italy (this time in Genoa),
and here the parallels are even closer in that the hero Auria
first wars against the Turks and is subsequently sent to govern
the island of Corsica. Again, too, it is the hero's friend and
most trusted counsellor who assures him that his wife is
unfaithful, and again the warrior husband is older than his
wife.

Nor is Ford the only writer of the period to revisit *Othello*.
Shakespeare himself does so, twice. The first time is in
Cymbeline, where the hero Posthumus, convinced that his
wife Imogen is unfaithful to him, orders his servant Pisanio

to kill her; the second is in *The Winter's Tale*, where Leontes, similarly convinced, similarly orders the deaths of his wife and his friend. A rather different play written a couple of years after *The Winter's Tale*, Elizabeth Cary's *The Tragedy of Mariam*, also has features in common with *Othello* (indeed there is a Longman volume which pairs editions of the two).[3] Herod resolves that 'Thou shalt not liue faire fiend to cozen more, / With heauy semblance, as thou cousnedst mee';[4] he feels that 'I had but one inestimable Iewell, / Yet one I had no monarch had the like' (sig. H3v); and the Arabian king, like Cassio, is badly wounded in the leg as a result of another man's belief (in this case justified) that he is having an affair with his wife (sig. D3v). For all the marked similarities, though, each of these plays also has equally marked differences from *Othello*. In this essay, I want to consider those differences and ask what they can tell us about Shakespeare's play and about contemporary perceptions of what were the crucial issues raised in it.

When the raw materials of *Othello* are reused in these reworkings, some of them are kept and some are jettisoned. An element that only some of these retellings have in common is an age difference between the husband and the wife: the Duke in *Love's Sacrifice* is older than the lovers (5.1.68), and Bianca reproaches him with it; Auria is older than Spinella. This is, however, not the case in either *The Winter's Tale* or *Cymbeline*, or at least not obviously so.

One aspect of the original story which nearly all subsequent versions dispense with is Cyprus, setting for four of the five acts of *Othello* (the single exception is *The Tragedy of Mariam*, and even there it is glanced at only obliquely, when Mariam mentions 'beauties Goddesse Paphos Queene' [sig. G4r]). While *The Lady's Trial*, *Love's Sacrifice*, *Cymbeline* and *The Winter's Tale* either retain or at least visit the Italian setting (*The Lady's Trial* is set in Genoa, *Love's Sacrifice* in Pavia, *The Winter's Tale* partly in Sicily, and *Cymbeline* contains two scenes in Rome), none of them has the faintest interest in Cyprus. This suggests that whatever ironic overtones may be generated by the fact that Cyprus is traditionally associated with Venus, goddess of love, are essentially incidental, and certainly not worth making an effort to retain. But Cyprus also had other overtones for a Renaissance audience, and ones that seem to have been of rather greater interest: it was the stake in the Battle of Lepanto, a crucial conflict between Christian and Turkish forces over who should control the lands and seas of the eastern Mediterranean. *The Lady's Trial* too is interested in that question – the hero Auria departs to fight a successful battle against the Turks and is subsequently rewarded with the governorship of Corsica – and *Cymbeline* is interested in questions of colonial power and national expansion more generally, for both it and *The Tragedy of Mariam* show a world in which a proud indigenous nation is pitted against the rapidly advancing shadow of Rome. Even *The Winter's Tale*, as I have argued elsewhere,[5] can be seen as touching on issues pertinent to the developing English colonial enterprise.

A concomitant of this is that two of Othello's closest analogues, in *The Lady's Trial* and in *Cymbeline*, are also soldiers, as are a number of other characters in their respective plays. The Duke stabs Bianca himself, and we can clearly see very conflicted views on how soldiers are likely to behave when they return home from the wars. On the one hand, it seems that if they do not have a war to fight outside the house, they are likely to fight one in it. At the same time, though, it is also firmly indicated that soldiers are acutely aware of a code of conduct that governs when and in what circumstances they may and may not fight. In *Mariam*, Constabarus, husband of Herod's wayward sister Salome, declares that 'I'm apt enough to fight in any case, / But yet for Salome I will not fight' (sig. D2v). Constabarus is not, he assures his opponent, a coward, and indeed he is quick enough to leap into action when his opponent ventures to doubt this assertion, and subsequently triumphs in their encounter with impressive ease; but his unfaithful wife is not, it seems, a worthy cause for a quarrel. A similar reluctance to fight marks the tetchy first encounter between Aurio and Aurelio in *The Lady's Trial* after the latter has accused the former's wife of adultery: when Aurio draws his sword, Aurelio at first refuses to be provoked, and by the time he eventually is so it is Auria who is ready to temporize (3.3.125–40). Ford is typically reticent in this play about his characters' motivations and psychology, but later events suggest that Auria is from the outset inclined to an instinctive faith in Spinella's innocence but is also aware that it will be hugely difficult to rehabilitate her reputation once it has been called into question, so he is unwilling at this stage to commit himself by either fighting his friend or by deliberately and pointedly refusing to do so. We might also notice in *Love's Sacrifice* the trouble that Bianca – who is positively eager to die – has in provoking her husband into killing her. This may perhaps explain what might otherwise seem a bizarre and puzzling feature of *Othello*, which is Othello's willingness to let Iago arrange the death of Cassio rather than challenge and fight him. If Desdemona is unfaithful she is not worth fighting for, and perhaps too he still hopes to conceal what he has done, less I think out of cowardice than from abhorrence at being publicly revealed as a cuckold: certainly when he hears Emilia coming, he says, 'Let me the curtains draw' (5.2.103), pretends not to hear Desdemona groan (5.2.117), and asks disingenuously, 'Why, how should she be murdered?' (5.2.124).

One of the most noticeable and to our eyes significant differences comes in the treatment of race. Apart from the fact that Ford's *Love's Sacrifice* twice mentions the Moorish-derived form of the morris dance (1.2.73 and 1.2.229) and that Libya is mentioned briefly in *The Winter's Tale*, when Florizel attempts to pass Perdita off as the daughter of its king, no other text telling the story of Othello's brothers registers any awareness of Africa, and none even hints at any form of racial difference between the hero and hero's wife or the rest of those around him. But surely *Othello* is centrally interested in race?

I have suggested elsewhere that *Othello* reproduces some of the concerns and emotions generated by Black Virgins,[6] statues or images of the Virgin Mary showing her with a dark skin, either because an originally paler image had been darkened by candle smoke or as an acknowledgement of the fact that as a first-century inhabitant of Palestine she was likely to have been darker rather than fairer. This is an idea that might just conceivably be supported by a definite link between black man and black virgin in Jan Jansz Mostaert's *Portrait of an African Man,* c. 1525–30 wearing a hat badge that commemorates a visit to the Black Madonna of Hal in Belgium. While some of the concerns activated by Black Madonnas were about race, many others were not, and in this context, it is worth noting that *Othello* is not the only play in which *Love's Sacrifice* is interested. Fiormonda's unsuccessful courtship of Fernando (1.1.140ff.) is very obviously modelled on the Duchess of Malfi's of Antonio. The chess game in Act 2, Scene 3 recalls *Women Beware Women* (there too the heroine is named Bianca). Perhaps most notably, Roseilli's opening question 'Depart the court?' (1.1.1) recalls *The White Devil*, which has a black / white pattern denoting abstract polarities rather than actual ethnicity, and whose secondary heroine Isabella de' Medici was based on a real woman of that name whose body was displayed after her murder and was said to be 'black in its upper half, but completely white below'.[7] Roseilli's subsequent disguise as a fool equally obviously recalls *The Changeling*, where a similar contrast underlies the dual identity of Beatrice-Joanna, whose hyphenated name, Sara Eaton suggests, recalls both the spiritual guide Beatrice and Gehenna, hell.[8] The presence of such a pattern is also a marked feature of *The Tragedy of Mariam*, where despite the fact that none of the characters is actually black, metaphorical blackening is laid on with a liberal hand, particularly onto the women. Kim F. Hall has powerfully argued that in early modern discourse blackness is a relative rather than an absolute term;[9] Dympna Callaghan, in an illuminating recent discussion, has similarly suggested that 'what allows whiteness to be represented at all is a certain conceptualization of sexual difference', and she further argues for the inherent instability and contingency of whiteness in her point that '[o]n stage, whiteface was probably the primary way of signifying femininity. It was an impersonation, just like blackface.'[10] Even the whitest of women can thus be seen as always already black, and this certainly seems to be the case in *The Tragedy of Mariam*. When Herod comes to believe that Mariam has planned to kill him, he rages,

> Now doe I know thy falshood, painted Diuill
> Thou white Inchantres. Oh thou art so foule,
> That Ysop cannot clense thee worst of euill. (sig. F2v)

When he vacillates, Mariam becomes white again:

> Here take her to her death Come backe, come backe,
> What ment I to depriue the world of light:
> To muffle Iury in the foulest blacke,
> That euer was an opposite to white. (sig. F3v)

It is Salome, by contrast, who is now blackened as Herod tells her that 'You are to her a Sun burnt Blackamore' (sig. G2v). Herod is speaking solely in terms of appearance, falling back on the standard opposition between beauty and blackness, but his former wife adduces a rather different sense when she tells Mariam, 'Your soule is blacke and spotted, full of sinne' (sig. G4v). Blackness, for Doris, is the opposite not of beauty but of virtue, but what is really apparent here is the extent to which it is the schematic and associative potential of blackness which is being mobilized rather than an essentially racialized understanding of it.

Collectively, the various retellings of *Othello* thus suggest that what happens to Othello is not, to misquote Ali G, cos he is black,[11] but because he is different, as in the 1997 Washington Shakespeare Theatre production starring Patrick

Stewart as an Othello who is the only white member of an otherwise all-black cast. In other words, the stories of Othello's brothers would suggest that for Shakespeare's contemporaries Othello's own behaviour is to be understood not in terms of a racialized concept of human identity, but of the insidious impact of the cultural construction of difference: he is less black than marked as 'black', with all the implications of the cultural baggage which that trailed for an English audience. The distinction is no mere abstraction but one central to the crucial philosophical difference between the both still influential but mutually contradictory official praxes of New Historicism and Cultural Materialism, in that the one (New Historicism) perceives all protest as fundamentally futile and always already structurally contained and the other (Cultural Materialism) regards it as capable of effecting genuine and meaningful change. Fundamentally, this impacts on the question of what this play is actually saying to its readers and audiences. For Thomas Rymer, the moral of the play was that wives should look well to their linen. If Othello's actions are dictated by the colour of his skin, it is scarcely less reductive. If, however, they are a response to a culturally constructed imposition of essentially arbitrary ideas of difference, then we have something that we can learn.

If Othello's behaviour is not conditioned by his skin colour, might Iago's be equally independent of its apparent determinants? In fact these plays do not always find an Iago-figure necessary at all – Leontes acts as his own, and Iachimo in *Cymbeline* is motivated largely by financial considerations and is happy to confirm Imogen's innocence at the close. Aurelio in *The Lady's Trial* is more intriguing because his motive for exposing what he takes to be Spinella's infidelity is on the face of it prompted both by genuine cause for suspicion and real concern for his friend. Nevertheless both Auria and Spinella are inclined to read his actions rather differently. Spinella sees him as motivated by a desire to ingratiate himself with Auria and as prompted by a sense of her as a threat to their relationship:

> Whiles you, belike,
> Are furnished with some news for entertainement
> Which must become your friendship, to be knit
> More fast betwixt your souls by my removal
> Both from his heart and memory. (2.3.79–80)

Even Auria is not particularly grateful to him, and it is notable that when Auria chooses a husband for Spinella's sister, the perfectly virtuous Castanna, it is not the conspicuously righteous Aurelio whom he picks but the flawed but penitent Adurni, whose unsuccessful attempt to seduce Spinella caused all the trouble in the first place. Aurelio himself attributes his motive to 'curiosity': 'You will pardon / A rash and over-busy curiosity' (5.3.176–7). This is a word that Ford is fond of, and the meaning that seems cumulatively to emerge from his uses of it is of an almost pathologically close investigation into other things and people that seems primarily to be prompted by a sense of edginess and uncertainty about the enquirer's own position, giving rise to an unhealthy interest in the behaviour of one's neighbours of the sort that motivates Angelo in *Measure for Measure* and Malvolio in *Twelfth Night*. Equally striking is the fact that two of the Iago figures are female. In *Love's Sacrifice*, D'Avolos does catch the Duke's attention by muttering, 'Beshrew my heart, but that's not so good' (3.2.5), but he does not play with him as Iago does with Othello – soon he is telling him straight out, 'In short, my lord, and plain discovery, you are a cuckold' (3.3.38–9). In effect he splits the role with Fiormonda, who slightly recalls Bianca in *Othello* in that she loves Fernando, but like Salome in *The Tragedy of Mariam* is clearly motivated primarily by jealousy of the beauty of her brother's wife, widely reckoned to be superior to her own. If these characters were to be seen as collectively offering a 'reading' of *Othello*, the explanation of Iago's behaviour that they would implicitly be endorsing is his resentment of the fact that Cassio 'hath a daily beauty in his life / That makes me ugly' (5.1.19–20).

The stories of Othello's brothers also turn the spotlight at least obliquely onto Desdemona as well as onto Othello and Iago, for collectively they raise the question of what female infidelity actually *is*. Is it the mere physical fact of a woman having sex with a man other than her husband? Certainly this is what seems to be at the heart of the pervasive Renaissance obsession with cuckoldry: a visceral fear, in an age before paternity tests, of inadvertently bequeathing one's property to an infant not biologically one's own. But the stories of Othello's brothers suggest that something rather different from and rather subtler than this might be at stake. In the first place, it is notable that in almost all these plays there is what one might well feel to be a positively pointed avoidance of the question of parenthood in all these plays, with the solitary exception of *The Winter's Tale*. Although Caraffa speaks of the possibility that Bianca might be pregnant (5.1.61–4), and Ford is certainly not above staging the murder of a pregnant woman (he does it in *'Tis Pity She's a Whore*), there is no other indication that this might be so; no one raises the question of whether Spinella might be pregnant; Posthumus never thinks of it in relation to Imogen; and Herod's conviction that Mariam has been serially unfaithful to him does not result in any doubts about the paternity of her son. In the case of Othello himself contemporary controversies about the role of the respective parents in determining the racial characteristics of babies would mean that the play is virtually crying out for the introduction of such a motif; and yet Shakespeare, it seems, has no interest in it. Instead, attention is dislocated onto a very different question: not what difference adultery itself makes, but what difference *knowing about it* makes. Othello asks,

> What sense had I of her stolen hours of lust?
> I saw't not, thought it not, it harmed not me,
> I slept the next night well, fed well, was free and merry;
> I found not Cassio's kisses on her lips;

He that is robbed, not wanting what is stolen,
Let him not know't, and he's not robbed at all. (3.3.341–6)

Leontes too draws attention to the (supposed) discovery of the
act rather than to the act itself when he says 'I have drunk, and
seen the spider', as does Herod when he says 'I would I were
like any begger poore, / So for I for false my Mariam did not
know' (sig. F3r).

This in turn resonates on two separate levels. First, there is
the question from passing from innocence to experience, and
while discovery of a partner's adultery might be a particularly
powerful and emotive instance of this, it is of course merely
one among many, and is a symptom of something much
more deeply rooted and troubling than itself. That there is,
however, no simple binary divide between innocence and
experience is suggested by the games *Othello* plays with time.
In *Mariam*, the closing Chorus draws attention to the fact that
the action has occupied only a single day; in *The Lady's Trial*
and *Cymbeline*, characters make sea journeys, and in *The
Winter's Tale*, extraordinarily, we are explicitly told that 16
years have passed between the two halves of the story; but no
one can confidently say how long the action of *Othello* takes
to unfold. Perhaps Ford was sensitive to the force of this, for
he too blurs the time scheme in both *The Lady's Tragedy* and
Love's Sacrifice, and couples this with a marked oscillation
of attitude on the part of both the Othello figures, Auria and
Caraffa, as though for them the boundary between innocence
and experience has been rendered permeable.

Second, we are made acutely aware that the fact of knowing
raises the question of what to do about it, because it is
symptomatic of all these plays that the discovery or apparent
discovery of adultery is almost invariably not a private
but a distressingly, damagingly public affair. Posthumus,
Auria, Othello himself and the Duke of Pavia all have this
in common: that they do not *discover* their partners' alleged
adultery but are *told* of it, with the inevitable concomitant
that it then becomes incumbent on their sense of their public

self to do something about it (in the case of Pavia, this is exacerbated by the fact that his sister Fiormonda is also party to the revelation of Bianca's secret meetings with Fernando, and the situation is of course further inflected by the fact that, as she knows, these really have occurred). Leontes is the exception here, since he is famously his own Iago, and it is therefore particularly noteworthy that his virtually instant reaction is to publicize it anyway, even though Camillo is both an unwilling and an incredulous recipient of his confidences. It is clear that the actual or apparent adultery of a wife thus has public as well as private consequences for a husband, for in order not to lose face and credibility he must be seen to react, and react in a way commensurate with the expectations of his peer group and culture (while English gentlemen don't on the whole kill their wives, unless perhaps by the occasional display of conspicuous kindness, Italians definitely do).

This public aspect of infidelity complicates still further the already vexed question of *Othello*'s genre, and here too the stories of Othello's brothers have something to say about the matter. It has often been suggested that *Othello* has less in common with tragedy of state, the genre so securely inhabited by *Hamlet*, *Macbeth* and *King Lear*, and more with the quieter, rather differently configured one of domestic tragedy. The inclusion of actual domestic details such as the handkerchief, the pillow and the wedding sheets that Desdemona orders to be placed on the bridal bed would seem to support this, as would the fact that Othello, alone of the 'big four' tragic heroes, is neither head of state himself nor heir to that position, so that what happens in his private household has no repercussions in the community as a whole. To throw the spotlight onto the extent to which others know of his predicament, though, offers a different perspective, forcing us to notice not only that the climax takes place in a bedroom but also that it is a bedroom which has essentially lost its private character as more and more of the characters crowd into it; it makes *Othello* seem less like a domestic tragedy than like a domestic tragedy *manqué*.

More probingly, though, some at least of these plays raise the possibility that infidelity is something more, and more significant, than a mere physical act: it is, as adultery is so often felt to be, a betrayal, and as such it is more a product of, and more damaging to, the spirit than the mind. In *Love's Sacrifice*, Bianca draws a sharp and, many critics have felt, essentially quite arbitrary distinction between *wanting* to commit adultery and actually *doing* it. She loves Fernando; she has no hesitation in letting her husband know this, and abusing him to his face for being old and ugly; she even offers Fernando her body, but with the proviso that she will kill herself immediately if he accepts. In her own eyes she thus remains innocent, and what is really surprising is that so many of the other characters, most notably her husband, accept her at her own estimation: as soon as Caraffa is assured that she has not actually slept with Fernando he apparently forgets all the wounding things she said, immediately acclaims her as a wronged martyr whom he has murdered without cause, and kills himself in remorse. Despite attempts to read this in the light of Queen Henrietta Maria's interest in Platonic love,[12] there has been no shortage of critics who have felt there is something deeply distasteful about this fetishizing of the mere fact of physical contact, and that Bianca's supposed innocence is a pure technicality which ignores the fact that she has undoubtedly lusted after Fernando and thus committed what we might well classify as adultery in her heart.

Shakespeare himself takes the question to precisely the opposite extreme in *Cymbeline*, when Posthumus apostrophizes a piece of material stained with what he takes to be Imogen's blood:

Yea, bloody cloth, I'll keep thee: for I wish'd
Thou shouldst be colour'd thus. You married ones,
If each of you should take this course, how many
Must murder wives much better than themselves
For wrying but a little?[13]

The reference to a 'bloody cloth' clearly invites us to compare this piece of cloth with the handkerchief in *Othello*, and to register the astonishing difference in attitude between Othello himself and Posthumus, who alone among husbands in Renaissance drama forgives his wife while still believing her to be guilty, on the grounds that her supposed adultery with Iachimo is in fact only a small flaw in an otherwise admirable character. Sexual fidelity thus becomes not the be-all and end-all of a relationship but a component within it. Seeing Othello as the midpoint between these two positions may perhaps help us to notice the extent to which he kills Desdemona only partly because of the damage she has done to him and also because of the damage she has done to herself, or at least to his own image of her perfection.

An inevitable and concomitant part of this interest in when and what one knows is an interest in *how* one knows. This is a concern so strongly marked that it would not be far-fetched to see these plays as collectively engaged in a species of sustained epistemological enquiry. I have argued elsewhere that in an *Othello*-informed play, *'Tis Pity She's a Whore*, Ford is fascinated by the question of how one knows.[14] There are also clear signs of such an interest in *The Lady's Trial*, for paradoxically, it is only when Spinella faints that Auria declares 'Spinella, / Regent of my affections, thou hast conquered'.[15] It is true that there have been hints before this that he has never really believed Aurelio's insinuations, but he has certainly seemed less than sure of how he should publicly manage the fact that they have been made in the first place, and unwilling to risk simply ignoring them. In his delicate attempt to finesse a conclusion that will leave everyone's reputation retrievable and forestall any potential disasters, in an atmosphere in which one misplaced word could precipitate a problem, Spinella's sudden descent into wordlessness affords the perfect opportunity for him to pre-empt any alternative interpretations and ensure the supremacy of his own construction of events. It is a moment that recalls the parallel manoeuvre of the Friar in *Much Ado About Nothing* when he imposes a reading of Hero's faint as manifesting innocence rather than guilt, but that also reprises Iago's sleight-of-hand in persuading Othello to accept his glossing of the exchange between Cassio and Bianca, when he effectively overwrites subtitles onto a scene otherwise perceived only as dumbshow. There is also a similar moment in *Love's Sacrifice*, again involving a character named Bianca and another whose role closely echoes that of Cassio, when D'Avolos spies on a meeting between Bianca and Fernando and supplies a running commentary which implies that he either cannot hear what they are saying or simply disbelieves it. In both these instances the audience is acutely conscious of the extent to which meaning is being made rather than revealed and of the provisional and uncertain nature of what is being accepted as evidence.

A central question in *Othello* is the nature of proof and the extent to which 'Trifles light as air / Are to the jealous confirmations strong / As proofs of holy writ' (3.3.325–7), for Shakespeare too is interested in the question of how we know what we know, but he treats it rather differently. For Leontes, it takes the form of a sudden intuition. Of particular note is the striking irony that it is Posthumus who is given arguably the strongest reason to make him doubt his wife, and yet it is he who is quickest to forgive: here, as in Auria's interpretation of Spinella's faint, there seems to be a directly inverse correlation between the ostensible weight of the evidence and the belief afforded to it, almost as if it is only the perverse and the occluded that truly carry conviction, and this is I think certainly the case in *Othello*, where it is remarkable how much of Iago's attack on Othello consists not in the providing of actual evidence but in persuading his victim of a supposedly right way to interpret such evidence as there is.[16] As Hermione says in *The Winter's Tale* and as the stories of all Othello's brothers confirm, the lives of women stand in the level of men's dreams.

Women are not quite powerless, though, for in all the stories of Othello's brothers, the voice of the wife is important. In *The Lady's Trial*, Auria seems both genuinely to want to

know what Spinella will say and also to be acutely aware that
the public rebuttal of the accusation is a crucial component of
his strategy not only to face up to the situation but actively to
defuse and recuperate it, and what she does eventually say is
particularly striking in that not only does she declare that the
accusation is unfounded but she also implies that the question
should never have been asked because of the lack of faith it
implies: 'You can suspect, / So reconciliation then is needless'
(5.2.136–7). In *The Winter's Tale*, though Leontes may not
want to know Hermione's response to his accusation, the
audience certainly does, for it rarely fails to provide an electri-
fying moment in the theatre:

> Since what I am to say, must be but that
> Which contradicts my accusation, and
> The testimony on my part, no other
> But what comes from myself, it shall scarce boot me
> To say 'not guilty': mine integrity,
> Being counted falsehood, shall, as I express it,
> Be so receiv'd. (3.2.22–8)

Imogen's protestation of her innocence is equally striking:

> False to his bed? What is it to be false?
> To lie in watch there, and to think on him?
> To weep 'twixt clock and clock? If sleep charge Nature,
> To break it with a fearful dream of him,
> And cry myself awake? That's false to's bed, is it? (3.4.41–5)

Even Bianca, who one might well feel does not really have a
leg to stand on, manages to stop insulting her husband just
long enough to inform him that he is mistaken. Separately and
collectively, these women make Desdemona look ineffectual
and inarticulate, and Shakespeare himself seems to have felt
that he had flattened the women's perspective unduly, because
he revised the part of the play that dealt with it, developing
significantly the dialogue between Desdemona and Emilia.

However, a slightly different perspective on events is offered by *The Tragedy of Mariam*, because Mariam does speak out, and that is exposed as having negative consequences of a rather different sort. Even Sohemus, who is well-disposed towards her, regards it as a blot on an otherwise admirable character – 'Vnbridled speech is Mariams worst disgrace' (sig. E3r) – and the Chorus is even more condemnatory:

> Tis not enough for one that is a wife
> To keepe her spotles from an act of ill:
> But from suspition she should free her life,
> And bare her selfe of power as well as will.
> Tis not so glorious for her to be free,
> As by her proper self restrain'd to bee. (sig. E4v)

Worst of all, Herod reads her willingness to speak her opinion as *prima facie* evidence of adultery: 'shee's vnchaste, / Her mouth will ope to eu'ry strangers eare' (sig. G2v). This suggests that ultimately it makes no difference whether the woman speaks or is silent, since either can be equally damning, and it may help to make us more alert to the double-bind that keeps Desdemona so fatally silent.

One final and rather unexpected feature of the stories of Othello and his brothers is the extent to which they all, albeit in rather different ways, intertwine a discourse of the sacred with that of the personal relationship which in each case lies at the heart of the narrative. In *Love's Sacrifice* the fact that the final scene takes place in front of Bianca's tomb makes a certain amount of religious atmosphere inevitable, but does not wholly account for the full panoply of the ceremony and the odour of sanctity that develop around what increasingly comes to seem like a shrine rather than simply a grave. In *The Tragedy of Mariam*, religion is made always already implicit by the fact that this is a story about Herod, a figure famous primarily in the context of the biblical narrative of Jesus' birth. In *The Lady's Trial* Auria says of the reconciliation between himself and Spinella, 'Our holy day / Deserves

the calendar' (5.2.221–2); in *Cymbeline* Posthumus is visited
in sleep by the god Jove himself, and in *The Winter's Tale*
Paulina refers to the location of Hermione's statue as a chapel
and adjures her hearers that 'It is requir'd / You do awake your
faith' (5.3.94–5). In *Othello* itself the narrative of Othello's
relationship with Desdemona is subtly counterpointed by the
narrative of his commitment to Christianity, apparently as a
result of conversion, and the possibility that this might now
falter, for one reason or another. Iago declares that it would be
easy for Desdemona 'To win the Moor, were't to renounce his
baptism' (2.3.338). Othello does not do that, but he does fall
into the deeply un-Christian position of committing the sin of
despair, as he apostrophizes the dead Desdemona:

> When we shall meet at compt
> This look of thine will hurl my soul from heaven
> And fiends will snatch at it. (5.2.271–3)

And in the very act of dying he paradoxically manages both to
affirm his Christianity and yet simultaneously collapse it into
its own opposite:

> in Aleppo once,
> Where a malignant and a turbanned Turk
> Beat a Venetian and traduc'd the state,
> I took by th'throat the circumcised dog
> And smote him – thus! (5.2.350–4)

In this context it is notable that Othello should twice mention
his parents in connection with the handkerchief (3.4.56–77,
5.2.214–15), for as far as this narrative of salvation and
damnation is concerned Othello's closest brother is in fact that
first father Adam, betrayed (not in a sexual sense but nonetheless
devastatingly) by that first mother, Eve, for like Adam he has
passed from innocence to experience and like Adam he finds
the way back barred by a beautiful, terrible, judging face
and a bright, fatal sword. These echoes are reinforced by the

obvious parallel between Iago's jealousy of the more favoured
Cassio and Cain's of the more favoured Abel, and this is a
concern even more marked if there are indeed resonances
between the play and the phenomenon of Black Virgins for
the metaphorical meanings of blackness which they were so
often seen to evoke remind us again of how little this play's
story has to do with the carnal concept of sexual knowledge
and how much it has to do with other forms of knowledge
and belief. Adultery is thus confirmed not as something solely
corporeal and contingent but as centrally constitutive of the
spiritual condition and ultimate eschatological destiny of the
spouse who is or believes themselves wronged, as if husband
and wife were indeed one flesh and the corruption of one part
of that composite body irredeemably tainted the other. 'Not
fierce Othello in so loud a strain / Roar'd for the Handkerchief
that caus'd his pain', wrote Pope mischievously; but the
stories of Othello's brothers show that the handkerchief (itself
connected to religion insofar as it resembles a Veronica's
veil)[17] is no trifle but the outward sign of a cataclysm, and
its whiteness marks not a blankness but something whose
magnitude defies inscription.

8

Teaching *Othello*: Materials and Approaches

Alison V. Scott

As one of the most adapted and appropriated of Shakespeare's works in recent times, *Othello* can be and is the subject of whole literature courses. The majority of undergraduate students, however, probably still encounter the play at least initially in a survey course; either a multi-author renaissance literature course, or a course dedicated to Shakespeare's canon. While courses focused thematically on race, or dedicated to exploring the Othello story across time and space, will naturally emerge from a particular pedagogical approach, the challenge for many teachers dealing with *Othello* in a larger survey course is often the obvious one – where to begin. The resources and possibilities for teaching the play constitute an endlessly evolving embarrassment of riches that can seem overwhelming, even as it is also energizing and inspiring, testament to the play's inexhaustibility in the classroom. Accordingly, my aim here is not to attempt to survey materials for and approaches to teaching *Othello* in any comprehensive way, for that would be a fool's mission, but rather to survey where scholars are currently at in terms of engaging with and teaching the play. What are some of the most up-to-date approaches emerging from current scholarship, and which are the most indispensable materials – old and new, critical, historical, theoretical – we might draw on to make *Othello* matter for our students today? Naturally, my selections reflect some of my own biases. However, taking my cue from some of the most important recent critical treatments of *Othello*, which seem to me particularly pedagogically suggestive, I outline five distinct but very broad ways teachers might choose to approach *Othello* in the classroom today, and supplement that with a select, annotated list of resources.[1]

Textual matters

Othello is by all accounts textually unstable. Assumed by many scholars to have been written in 1601–2, and certainly complete by early 1603, the play was published four times in relatively quick succession in the first half of the seventeenth century, the first quarto appearing in 1622, followed by the first folio in 1623. The relationship of these two texts has provoked intense critical debate, but while modern editors routinely consult and refer to both texts, they almost uniformly favour the folio and in doing so tacitly affirm its textual superiority. Yet the critical debate has only recently translated to the classroom, and it is surely still the case that students are far less likely to consider the textual variants of *Othello* than those of *King Lear* or *Doctor Faustus*. Textual problems might seem less immediately relevant to students than the questions of race, gender and sexuality that the tragedy so famously and richly engages; they tend to be reserved for small-group and advanced teaching. Perhaps this is a missed opportunity.

Lois Potter's reading of editorial cuts in Desdemona's part as an extension of the silencing of women in the play, for example, suggests how problems of gender might be directly engaged through a textual material approach. In 'The Two Texts of "Othello" and Early Modern Constructions of Race', meanwhile, Leah Marcus insists on the dynamic relation between textual history and the play's treatment of racial difference, arguing that the folio is more 'racist' than the quarto. Picking up that point, Douglas A. Brooks demonstrates its significant implications for classroom teaching. By putting the question 'which text?' at the centre rather than the margins of classroom discussion, Brooks finds a new way into historicist teaching. Yet the value of this text-focused approach extends beyond the new historicist project in which Brooks is obviously invested; there are diverse benefits of approaching the 'play' through the 'text' in the classroom (2005). A comparative reading of quarto and folio versions of the conversation between Iago and Roderigo in 1.1, for instance, presents opportunities to think about the play in its historical contexts, and about the political nature of textual cutting and modern editorial processes, but it also has the advantage of presenting students with a 'real' problem – why is the folio more racist than the quarto? – through which to negotiate more abstract questions of meaning and interpretation. In the other scene substantially different in the folio text, the willow scene, as Michael Warren discusses, the question shifts somewhat. The value of comparative study here rests with the question of what is lost in cutting the song in the willow scene; or, conversely, what might have been gained in the folio addition.

While such study is hampered somewhat by the absence of a parallel text edition, most modern critical editions draw attention to the folio additions and variations in some way, especially to the most substantial ones, which occur in the opening scene and the 'willow scene' (4.3). Comparative study is also aided by Scott McMillin fine edition of the quarto and E. A. G. Honigmann's comprehensive study of the play's textual history in *The Texts of 'Othello' and Shakespearian Revision* (1996).

In adaptation

The first recorded performance of *Othello* took place in the banqueting hall at Whitehall by the King's Men in 1604, and it was staged again at Oxford in 1610, where spectator Henry Jackson praised Desdemona's performance in begging the pity of the audience on her deathbed with her facial expression alone. Although the play has a long history of cut performances, designed in the eighteenth century at least to preserve decorum and avoid upsetting the delicate sensibilities of women, its popularity has never waned and it continues to be one of the most adapted and variously appropriated of Shakespeare's works. Dated as the approach may be, utilizing film adaptations of the play to support its close reading 'scene by scene and speech by speech', to borrow Maynard Mack's phrasing, is still useful. The 1981 BBC film version, for example, deliberately muffles the conversation between Iago and Cassio (4.1) that Othello is positioned to watch, so that the viewer fleetingly sees things from Othello's distorted perspective, even as she is aware of Iago's plot. In considering this choice, we must interrogate if Othello can hear the conversation or merely 'see' it, and why that question matters. This is an interesting way into the problem of credulity in the play, and one that accesses related issues of perception and its manifold distortion. Perhaps above any other, however, the death scene is fruitfully supported by film in the classroom, not least because in reading the text alone students can mistake Desdemona's action – her refusal to name Othello as her murderer – for mere subjection. Feminist criticism has opened the possibility of a Desdemona who fights back and comparative considerations of passive and post-feminist Desdemonas on film – and the film *Stage Beauty* is particularly useful in this respect – can demonstrate the significance of that reading in immediately accessible ways.

   Thinking about *Othello* from the perspective of adaptation studies, however, can take us back as well as forward from the play's own time. Almost all critical editions discuss the play's debts to various contemporary works, from early 'domestic' tragedies, to historical works like John Leo's *A Geographical Historie of Africa*, translated by John Pory in 1600; and many reprint its main source, a tale from Cinthio's *Hecatommithi*, to enable comparative study. Considering Shakespeare's work alongside its sources invariably helps students to appraise the play's innovations. It is clear, for example, that the decision to have Othello, not the ensign, murder Desdemona, is absolutely crucial to the play's tragic effect and to the highly fraught ways we relate to and are alienated by Othello. Approaching the play through its source texts on the one hand and its adaptation history on the other, however, presents other and dynamic possibilities. For example, in considering what Dympna Callaghan memorably called the play's 'embarrassingly domestic' focus, Cinthio's text, so literally preoccupied with the bedchamber and its destruction, can highlight Shakespeare's far more sophisticated treatment, not merely of place, but, as Emma Smith discusses, of space, containment, penetration and infection. Coupling that approach with Miller's 1981 BBC production (with its complete absence of exterior shots) can help students to grasp the play's claustrophobic proportions, while close attention to Othello's difficulties in speaking a private language of love and in adapting to his domestic environ once the Turks are defeated highlights the human vulnerability Iago exploits. Moving beyond film adaptations, Paula Vogel's feminist reworking of Desdemona's story in her 1994 play *Desdemona: A Play about a Handkerchief* can encourage students to think about what Shelia T. Cavanagh terms the 'counternarrative' (beyond the play's interior spaces) from which Desdemona is largely absent, as well as to give closer consideration of the treatment of female sexuality and pragmatism in the source that they will often overlook on first reading.

Generic expectations

The generic approach to *Othello* is as old as Thomas Rymer's infamous complaints that the play did not measure up as a tragedy due to its obsession with such a trivial object as a handkerchief. Mid- to late-twentieth-century criticism also thoroughly explored the play's various intersections with comic themes and topoi, especially with the domestic focus assumed to distinguish *Othello* from other major tragedies. Following Susan Snyder's observation that the first act of Othello is essentially a comedy in miniature, the climax of which is the scene in which Desdemona and Othello reunite in Cyprus, and out of which the play's tragedy emerges, many commentators have approached the work as an inverted comedy. Exploring the play from this perspective, thinking about its resemblances to the comedies, and considering the various effects of comic themes and patterns on its high tragedy, helps students to think critically about the place of *Othello* in Shakespeare's canon. Recently, however, scholarly interest in the tensions between comic and tragic visions in the play has opened up to encompass larger questions and relations of genre and these offer fresh possibilities for teaching.

François Laroque is especially noteworthy. He presents the play as a perverted comedy more properly understood as fantasy, and he explores its rich interaction with the imaginative structures of festive traditions. His reading of the opening scene provides an interesting way of framing classroom discussion, suggesting as it does how the scene affects a kind of festive misrule that illuminates the far-reaching disruptions to the ordinary sexual, social and linguistic order of things throughout the rest of the play. Laroque is not alone in considering *Othello*'s interconnections with fantasy. Following Stephen Greenblatt, historicist scholars have explored the play's engagement with travel books popular in medieval and early modern culture, a literature on which Shakespeare draws to craft Othello's wondrous, pitiful biographical history. Notably, Jean Howard takes this one step further in an essay on teaching *Othello* as adventure play. Reading *Othello* in relation to that subgenre (by positioning it alongside plays including George Peele's *The Battle of Alcazar*, Thomas Heywood's *Fair Maid of the West, Part 1*, and the co-authored

A Christian Turned Turk), she shows how it inverts and trans-
forms adventure play conventions. The European adventurer
to Africa becomes the African adventurer to Europe with
all the attendant pressures of negotiating Othello's cultural
difference. The play thus becomes a 'profound exploration
of the perils and possibilities of crossing boundaries between
cultures, religions, and races', and students can engage with
the problem of race in the play in a way more immediately
relevant to them than the issue of miscegenation.

Beyond new historicism

Related to innovations in genre, and among the most
suggestive critical developments for classroom teaching, is the
push beyond the new historicist agenda in recent historicized
readings of the play. Michael Neill's extensive work, gathered
in the volume *Putting History to the Question* and under-
pinning his excellent introduction to the Oxford edition, has
usefully posited the play as a tragedy of displacement as well
as providing detailed early modern contexts for understanding
racial difference in *Othello*. Virginia Mason Vaughan's study
shows that the play capitalizes on contemporary cultural
stereotypes vilifying Islam, which were in reality fairly complicated. Unsettling assumptions that *Othello* is a play about
race, meanwhile, Sasha Roberts discusses the extent to which
early moderns were likely indifferent to racial difference in
the play; while Emily Bartels corrects a long-standing anachronism of 'post-colonial' readings of race, suggesting why
we should ask students to take seriously Othello's status as a
Moor *of* Venice, not merely *in* Venice, even as they negotiate
the obvious ways in which he is alienated within and exploited
by that culture. The implications of this body of work are
far-reaching, but perhaps nowhere clearer in the classroom
than in close consideration of Othello's final speech. There,
Othello's tragic recognition of himself pitifully involves a

simultaneous performance of multiple and conflicting roles – the criminal Moor and the Venetian judge and executioner. Taken in conjunction with studies of Othello's fragmenting identity and language – James Calderwood's essay 'Speech and Self in *Othello*' is particularly noteworthy – the most recent and carefully historicized considerations of racial difference in the work compel us to take account of this layered, nuanced self-division and cultural alienation.

Equally important in this regard is Daniel Vitkus's counter-imperialist reading of the play, which argues convincingly for the tragedy as a drama of conversion. Othello's fears about female sexuality are shown to be purposefully and powerfully connected to racial and cultural anxieties about the Turks and their power to convert Christians in Shakespeare's England, and Othello's transformation and degradation is thereby understood in the context of early modern conversion narratives which connected Islam too with sexual transgression: the 'frustrated male violence' which the opening scenes gather and set against 'the Islamic Other is turned on the feminine Other'; the Turks are vanquished, so instead of the tragedy moving out to the drama of Christian purity, it closes in around the now-connected problem of female sexual purity.

Stage properties

Performance-oriented approaches to teaching Shakespeare are now a mainstay not only of high school classrooms, but also of university instruction. Recent trends in dramaturgical research and in material criticism of the play suggest quite focused manageable classroom strategies for aiding interpretation. The Globe's practical research experiment 'Unpinning Desdemona', originating in a scholarly essay by Denise Walen, is a good example. Taking the very different versions of the 'willow scene' from the Quarto and Folio texts, this experiment uses performance, complete with historically authentic costumes and stage properties, to test the viability of each version. Watching the videos that record the experiment gives students valuable information about the material conditions in which the play would have been staged. More particularly, by engaging a real textual problem and detailing how performance and attention to historical detail can illuminate it, the experiment can dynamically introduce a scene pivotal to understanding the play's treatment of gender and sexuality.

Surely few undergraduate classes on *Othello* will conclude without some debate about the meaning of the play's famous handkerchief. Yet, as Jonathan Gil Harris astutely and provocatively suggests in a recent study, the real question may be not what the handkerchief means but what it does or what is done with it. Considering the handkerchief in this way usefully calls attention back to textual details. When is the handkerchief first mentioned? When does it first appear? How many characters touch it? How do they use it? Pursuing the handkerchief in this way, students can begin to map crucial exchanges, substitutions and disjunctions.

This is in essence Janelle Jenstad's approach. She details a highly effective strategy for encouraging students to make the standard critical connections between Desdemona's body, the wedding sheets and the handkerchief – originally made by Lynda E. Boose in 1975 – for themselves. Where Harris argues convincingly for the handkerchief as palimpsest, Jenstad picks up the theme of textual instability and, by coupling Desdemona's linens with Dinesen's 'blank page', focuses the woman's text and its vulnerabilities in the play. Teachers may find it difficult to ask their students 'what does the handkerchief look like?' without remembering Harry Berger's playfully ironic essay enquiring after its size, but Jenstad demonstrates that this material approach is critically and pedagogically sharp. In light of Ian Smith's recent challenge to the long-standing critical assumption that the handkerchief is white and thus a metonym for Desdemona's sexuality, however, it might be time to draw race as well as gender into classroom discussion about *Othello*'s linen. Certainly, Smith's point, that the handkerchief might be black and thus a metonym for Othello's rather than Desdemona's story, is likely to be newly galvanizing in the classroom, highlighting for students the incongruity of a 'magic' handkerchief styled in English white lace even if we can't finally imagine it coloured otherwise.

Current complete works editions

The Arden Shakespeare Complete Works. Eds Ann Thompson, David Scott Kastan and Richard Proudfoot, rev. edn (London: Bloomsbury, 2010).

The Complete Pelican Shakespeare. Eds Stephen Orgel and A. R. Braunmuller (New York: Viking, 2002).

The Complete Works of Shakespeare. Ed. David Bevington, 7th edn (New York: Longman, 2013).

The Norton Shakespeare (based on the Oxford edition). Eds Stephen Greenblatt et al., 2nd edn (New York: W. W. Norton, 2008).

The Oxford Shakespeare: The Complete Works. Eds Stanley Wells et al., 2nd edn (Oxford: Oxford University Press, 2005).

Current single text editions

Honigmann, E. A. J., ed. *Othello*, Arden 3rd series (1997).
    A thoroughly annotated edition favoured by instructors, offering an accessible comprehensive and illustrated introduction to the play, its textual problems, performance history, historical and cultural contexts, and critical tradition. Like the comparable Oxford edition, it includes a useful appendix discussing the play's sources and generic debts and reprinting a modern translation of the play's main source, Giraldi Cinthio's *Gli Hecatommithi* (1565), which enables comparative consideration of Shakespeare's innovations in character and plot development.

Kernan, Alvin, ed. *Othello*, Signet Classic Edition, revised and updated (New York, 1998).
    Originally published in 1963 this budget edition, including its

helpful bibliography, was updated in 1998. It includes select nineteenth- and twentieth-century commentaries on the play, along with several essays focused on its performance history.

McMillin, Scott. *The First Quarto of Othello* (Cambridge, 2001). An excellent critical edition of the 1622 Quarto text, including a substantial introduction focused on the play's textual history and scholarship.

Muir, Kenneth, ed. *Othello*, New Penguin (Harmondsworth, 2005). Annotated edition of the play featuring a detailed consideration of its performance history up to 2004. Explanatory notes appear at the end of the text rather than page by page. A substantial textual introduction by Tom McAlindon offers students a useful summation of some the most influential readings of Othello (T. S. Eliot and F. R. Leavis) and Iago (Coleridge) as it argues the limitations of conceiving the play as either a tragedy of jealousy or as domestic tragedy.

Neill, Michael, ed. *Othello*, Oxford (New York, 2006). An excellent modern-spelling, critical edition favoured by instructors and comparable to the Arden 3rd series edition in its accessibility, layout and supplementary material. The substantial introduction is thematically focused, paying particular attention to race and gender, and its rich discussion of performance history is illuminated by modern production photographs.

Pechter, Edward, ed. *Othello*, Norton Critical Editions (New York, 2004). A valuable modern edition set apart by its inclusion of 17 critical essays, from early commentators on the play including Samuel Johnson and William Hazlitt through to influential essays of the twentieth century and to recent readings by Mark Rose and Patricia Parker. A select and annotated bibliography is also included, along with a translation of Cinthio's novella.

Sanders, Norman, ed. *Othello*, New Cambridge Edition, 2nd edn (Cambridge, 2003). Features a substantial, illustrated introduction, integrated notes on the page plus longer supplementary notes at the end of the text, a valuable and impressively clear discussion of textual problems and the history of editorial decision making around the Quarto and Folio texts of the play. Includes a reading list not substantially updated from the first edition.

Selected critical essays

Bach, Rebecca Ann. 'Seventeenth- and Eighteenth-Century Othello
    and Desdemona: Race and Emerging Heterosexuality', in
    Feminisms and Early Modern Texts: Essays for Phyllis Rackin
    (Selinsgrove, PA: Susquehanna University Press, 2010), 81–98.
    Considers seventeenth- and eighteenth-century performances of
    Othello in relation to the long eighteenth-century's 'emerging
    heterosexual imaginary'.
Bartels, Emily C. 'Othello and Africa: Postcolonialism
    Reconsidered', *The William and Mary Quarterly*, 3rd series,
    54.1 (1997): 45–64.
    Detailed historical reading that considers the difficulties of
    negotiating race as distinct from racism in the play. Explores the
    displacement of Africa from new world discourses of domination
    and argues that Othello is more integrated into Venetian society
    than a postcolonial perspective can acknowledge.
—'The "stranger of here and everywhere": *Othello* and the Moor
    of Venice', in *Speaking of the Moor from Alcazar to Othello*
    (Philadelphia: University of Pennsylvania Press, 2008).
    Builds on the 1997 essay above to argue that the idea that
    Othello is a Moor not merely *in* but *of* Venice contributes to the
    defining tension of the play.
Bayley, John. 'Tragedy and Consciousness: *Othello*', in *Shakespeare
    and Tragedy* (London: Routledge & Kegan Paul, 1981),
    200–20.
    Classic reading of the tension between comedy and tragedy
    in the play, specifically in the treatment of the theme of love,
    this essay presents *Othello* as a universal tragedy of privacy
    according neither with the comic nor the tragic worldview.
Berger, Harry Jr. 'Impertinent Trifling: Desdemona's Handkerchief',
    Shakespeare Quarterly 47.3 (1996): 235–50. Reprinted in
    Othello, ed. Lena Cowen Orlin (London: Palgrave Macmillan,
    2004), 103–25.
    Glancing at Thomas Rymer's infamous complaint against the
    fact that the tragedy of *Othello* proceeds from a trifle, Berger
    sidesteps the symbolic meaning of the handkerchief to pose the
    question of its size, and from thence explore the way in which it
    functions as fetishized object.

Berry, Edward. '*Othello*'s Alienation', *Studies in English Literature, 1500–1900* 30.2 (1990): 315–33.
Argues that Othello cannot be understood as an everyman (as Robert B. Heilman proposed), nor as a noble savage. Rather, we must recognize the complexity of his cultural difference, which breaks the boundaries of contemporary racial stereotypes. Othello's race is constructed in simultaneously negative and positive terms; ultimately it makes him a double victim, alienated from Venetian society, and from his own self.

Bevington, David. '*Othello*: Portrait of a Marriage', in *Othello: New Critical Essays*, ed. Philip C. Kolin (New York: Routledge, 2002), 221–31.
Explores the role of male anxiety and possessiveness in the collapse of Othello and Desdemona's marriage and the ensuing tragic action of the play.

Boose, Lynda E. '*Othello*'s Handkerchief: "The Recognizance and Pledge of Love"', *English Literary Renaissance* 5 (1975): 360–74.
Landmark essay establishing the metonymic relation of Desdemona's white handkerchief embroidered with strawberries and the wedding sheets that become her shroud. Recently challenged by Ian Smith (see below).

—'"Let it be Hid": The Pornographic Aesthetic of Shakespeare's *Othello*', in *Othello: Contemporary Critical Essays*, ed. Lena Cowen Orlin (Basingstoke: Palgrave Macmillan, 2004), 22–48.
Exploration of the pornographic elements of Iago's imagination and its alluring effects on Othello and on the audience.

Bradshaw, Graham. 'Obeying The Time in *Othello*: A Myth and the Mess it Made', *English Studies* 73.3 (1992): 211–28.
Explodes the theory (or myth) of *Othello*'s 'double time', arguing that no dramatic trick is required for the fiction of a long relation between Cassio and Desdemona to appear plausible – it can be assigned to the period of Othello's courtship of Desdemona, rather than to the too-short period of marriage.

Brooks, Douglas A. 'The Play and the Text: Book History and the Undergraduate Class', *Pacific Coast Philology* 40.2 (2005): 10–20.
Astute pedagogical essay presenting a convincing case for why teachers of *Othello* should emphasize the textual instabilities of the play; builds on Marcus's 2004 essay (see below) to provide

practical guidance on approaching the question of racism in the play through comparison of the quarto and folio texts.

Callaghan, Dympna. '"Othello was a White Man": Properties of Race on Shakespeare's Stage', *Shakespeare Without Women: Representing Gender and Race on the Renaissance Stage* (London: Routledge, 2002), 75–97.
While the implications of casting a black or a white actor in the play's main role typically preoccupy critics and students today, this essay is valuable for its close consideration of the play's representation of racial difference in a culture in which the roles of both Othello and Desdemona would have been played by white men.

Calderwood, James L. 'Speech and Self in *Othello*', *Shakespeare Quarterly* 38.3 (1987): 293–303.
Compelling exploration of the relation between Othello's failure of language and his fragmenting self. Revised and republished as 'Signs, Speech, and Self', in *The Properties of Othello* (Amherst: University of Massachusetts Press, 1989), 53–67.

Cartwright, Kent. 'Audience Response and the Denouement of *Othello*', in *Othello: New Perspectives*, eds Virginia Vaughan and Kent Cartwright (Madison: Fairleigh Dickinson University Press, 1991), 160–76.
Performance-critical exploration of the play's demand that the audience respond empathetically to Othello even as they are alienated by his choices; reads Othello's final speech as exemplary of that double response.

Cavell, Stanley. 'Othello and the Stake of the Other', in *Disowning Knowledge in Seven Plays of Shakespeare* (Cambridge: Cambridge University Press, 1987), 125–42.
In a world in which Othello substitutes Desdemona for God – 'my life upon her faith' – this influential essay explores the consequences of the sceptical doubt Iago too easily weaves.

Eagleton, Terry. '"Nothing": *Othello, Hamlet, Coriolanus*', in *William Shakespeare* (Oxford: Wiley-Blackwell, 1986), 64–75.
Provocative reading of the play that emerges from the observation that 'nothing' could refer to the female genitalia. Iago knows Othello is predisposed to find an appalling something in his blank, white space, and the tragedy unfurls from this paranoid over-reading of Desdemona's sweet and yet terrifying 'nothing'.

Empson, William. 'Honest in *Othello*', in *The Structure of Complex Words* (London: Chatto & Windus, 1951), 218–49.
Influential mid-century account of Othello's unusual and shifting 52 uses of 'honest' and honesty'.

Fineman, Joel. 'The Sound of "O" in *Othello*: The Real Tragedy of Desire', *October* 45 (1998): 76–96.
Famously observes that Othello's name sounds like the Greek for 'will' or 'desire', making *Othello* a tragedy of desire. Explores why Shakespeare calls his moor 'will' or 'desire', and why the story of a moor named desire should be tragic and not rather comic or romantic.

Garber, Marjorie. '*Othello*', in *Shakespeare After All* (New York: Random House, 2004), 588–616.
Valuable essay for introducing students to the play; offers a detailed exploration of the limitations of reason in the play, the binary oppositions emerging in part from its appropriation of the Venus and Mars myth, and its preoccupation with visual proofs and distractions.

Genster, Julia. 'Lieutenancy, Standing in, and *Othello*', *English Literary History* 57.4 (1990): 785–809.
Examines the corrosive structures of lieutenancy (or standing in) in the play and their effect on competing structures – military, marital and linguistic.

Greenblatt, Stephen. 'The Improvisation of Power', in *Renaissance Self-Fashioning: From More to Shakespeare* (Chicago: Chicago University Press, 1980), 222–54.
Landmark new historicist reading of *Othello* exploring processes of submission to narrative self-fashioning in the play; focused on the improvised nature of Iago's plotting.

Gross, Kenneth. 'Slander and Skepticism in *Othello*', *English Literary History* 56.4 (1989): 819–52.
Responding to Stanley Cavell's exploration of the consequences of scepticism in the play, reads *Othello* as an exploration of defamation, enabled by 'honest' Iago's rhetorical art of lying merely through the power of suggestion.

Harris, Jonathan Gil. 'Crumpled Handkerchiefs: William Shakespeare's and Michael Serres' Palimpsested Time', in *Untimely Matter in the Time of Shakespeare* (Philadelphia: University of Pennsylvania Press, 2009), 169–88.
Putting the interpretative question of the handkerchief's meaning

to one side, explores an arguably more pressing question –
what does it do? Introduced carefully, Harris's idea that the
handkerchief is a palimpsest, binding together people, meanings
and time, could help students to appreciate the contested nature
of texts/language in the play.

Hirsh, James. '*Othello* and Perception', in *Othello: New
Perspectives*, pp. 135–59.
Discusses the tragedy as unfolding from interrelated challenges
to perception – Othello's perception of Desdemona, and our
perception of Othello.

Knight, G. Wilson. 'The Othello Music', in *The Wheel of Fire:
Interpretations of Shakespearean Tragedy, with Three New
Essays* (London: Methuen, 1949), 97–119.
The first critical interpretation of the play to emphasize what
is now considered a key component of its tragic appeal – its
affective musicality.

Laroque, François. '*Othello* and the Festive Traditions', in
*Shakespeare's Festive World: Elizabethan Seasonal Entertainment
and the Professional Stage* (Cambridge: Cambridge University
Press, 1991), 282–302.
Reads the play in relation to contemporary European festive
traditions to conclude that the 'tragic loading' at its end
resonates simultaneously as tragic effect and as comic perversion.

Leggatt, Alexander. '*Othello*: I took you for a cunning whore of
Venice', in *Shakespeare's Tragedies: Violation and Identity*
(Cambridge: Cambridge University Press, 2005), 114–44.
Explores the conflicting readings in the play of the marriage of
Othello and Desdemona, arguing that Iago's cynical reading of
the union as violation becomes in itself a violation and finally a
means with which to violate Othello's own thought.

Loomba, Ania. '*Othello* and the Racial Question', in *Shakespeare,
Race, and Colonialism* (Oxford: Oxford University Press, 2002),
91–111.
A useful introductory essay on the historical and cultural
contexts of 'race' in the play.

Mack, Maynard. '"Speak of me as I am": *Othello*', in *Everybody's
Shakespeare: Reflections Chiefly on the Tragedies* (Lincoln:
University of Nebraska Press, 1993), 129–50.
An insightful and accessible 'speech by speech and scene by
scene' (130) analysis of *Othello*, this essay argues that the

tragedy pivots on the failure (under the exertion of Iago's villainous pressure) of a humanistic dream of a world in which polar opposites coexist harmoniously.

Marcus, Leah S. 'The Two Texts of "*Othello*" and Early Modern Constructions of Race', in *Textual Performances: The Modern Reproduction of Shakespeare's Drama*, eds Lukas Erne and Margaret Jane Kidnie (Cambridge: Cambridge University Press, 2004), 21–36.
Argues that the quarto and folio texts of the play construct race and female sexuality in significantly different terms; understands the folio text to amplify the 'racism' of the play.

Minear, Erin. 'Music and the Crisis of Meaning in *Othello*', *Studies in English Literature, 1500–1900* 49.2 (2009): 355–70.
One of the most recent contributions to a substantial body of scholarship focused on music in *Othello*, this essay explores the relation between the verbal music and the actual music of the play. It argues that the confusion of the two generates an interpretative crisis, forcing the play's opposing 'noise' and 'poetry' into the same space.

Moisan, Thomas. 'Repetition and Interrogation in *Othello*: "What needs this iterance?" or "Can anything be made of this?"' in *Othello: New Perspectives*, ed. Philip C. Kolin (New York: Routledge, 2002), 48–73.
Explores the purpose and rhetorical effects of recurrent questions in the play, and the role of repetition in the tragedy.

Neely, Carol Thomas. 'Women and Men in *Othello*: "What should such a fool / Do with so good a woman?"' *Shakespeare Studies* 10 (1978): 133–58.
Critics of the play tend to mirror Othello's romanticism or Iago's cynicism, and both misrepresent the women of the play, demeaning or else idealizing Desdemona. To correct that, this insightful feminist essay adopts the more objective position of Emilia to read the play as a conflict of men and women. Revised and reprinted in *The Woman's Part: Feminist Criticism of Shakespeare*, eds Carolyn Ruth Swift Lenz, Gayle Greene and Carol Thomas Neely (Urbana: University of Illinois Press, 1980), 211–39.

Neill, Michael. 'Changing Places in *Othello*', *Shakespeare Survey* 37 (1984): 115–31.
Reads the play as a tragedy of displacement.

'Unproper Beds: Race, Adultery, and the Hideous in *Othello*', *Shakespeare Quarterly* 40 (1989): 313–412.
Approaching the play through its interconnected scenes of darkness and obscenity, Neill argues that tragedy emerges out of the play's unusual conflation of psychological events and offstage action.

—'"Mulattos", "Blacks", and "Indian Moors"': *Othello* and the Early Modern Constructions of Human Difference', *Shakespeare Quarterly* 49.4 (1998): 361–74.
Erudite reading of the dramatic action of the play as the process by which Iago exploits and reveals the contradictions of the play's full title and Othello's hybrid racial identity – the 'Moor of Venice'.

Newman, Karen. '"And wash the Ethiop white": Femininity and the Monstrous in *Othello*', in *Fashioning Femininity and English Renaissance Drama* (Chicago: University of Chicago Press, 1991), 71–94.
Reads *Othello* as a product of racist, sexist and colonialist discourses of the time, and as a drama that represents its central characters in ways that are open to and enabling of interpretations that resist hegemonic ideologies of race and gender.

Nuttall, A. D. 'An Expert Makes a Man: *Othello*', in *Shakespeare the Thinker* (New Haven: Yale University Press, 2007), 277–84.
In his final claim that he is not easily jealous, is Othello entirely deluded? Not necessarily. Rather, he has been transformed by Iago's plastic art, which does not merely stimulate jealousy but creates it from insecurity.

Parker, Patricia. 'Shakespeare and Rhetoric: "dilation" and "delation" in *Othello*', in *Shakespeare and the Question of Theory*, ed. Patricia Parker and Geoffrey Hartman (New York: Methuen, 1985), 54–74.
Explores the 'close dilations' of the play in relation to three available meanings of the idea, namely amplification (in the rhetorical tradition), accusation and delay.

Pechter, Edward. 'Discomfirmation', in *Othello and Interpretative Traditions* (Iowa City: University of Iowa Press, 1999), 30–53.
A useful resource in the classroom, this chapter focuses intently on the opening scenes to show how in constructing the matter of the play we are forced to rely on Iago, ensuring that the play works against the free thinking of 'discomfirmation'.

Potter, Lois. 'Editing Desdemona', in *In Arden: Editing Shakespeare, Essays in Honour of Richard Proudfoot*, eds Ann Thompson and Gordon McMullan (London: Arden Shakespeare, 2003), 81–94.
Valuable essay for introducing students to the textual history of the play; shows how modern editions of *Othello* often repeat the silencing of the female voice that the play tragically enacts.

Pye, Christopher. '"To throw out our eyes for brave Othello': Shakespeare and Aesthetic Ideology', *Shakespeare Quarterly* 60.4 (1990): 425–47.
Through a series of theorized close readings, suggests the value of reading the play through concepts rather than historical contexts. Othello is a meta-aesthetic hero advancing towards a moment of self-recognition, which is tragic in the sense that it is inevitably performative.

Roberts, Sasha. 'Shakespeare's Tragedies of Love', in *A Companion to Shakespeare's Works: The Tragedies* (Oxford: Blackwell, 2003), 108–33.
Explores how *Othello* was read and transmitted in early modern England; focuses in particular on contemporary indifference to Othello's blackness and to the theme of racial difference emphasized in recent criticism.

Smith, Ian. 'Othello's Black Handkerchief', *Shakespeare Quarterly* 64.1 (2013): 1–25.
Contests the dominant critical reading of the handkerchief that originates with Boose's 1975 article (see above), by arguing that it was likely black rather than white, and thus represents and constructs Othello's story rather than Desdemona's.

Snyder, Susan. '*Othello* and the Conventions of Romantic Comedy', in *Shakespeare: A Wayward Journey* (Newark: University of Delaware Press, 2002), 29–45.
First published in the late 1970s, famously reads the first act of the play as a comedy 'in miniature', and the tragedy as developing from a contestation of comic assumptions, embodied by Iago.

Thompson, Ayanna. 'Unmooring the Moor: Research and Teaching on YouTube', *Shakespeare Quarterly* 61.3 (2010): 337–56.
Analyses three classroom-inspired YouTube videos in order to explore the opportunities the YouTube platform presents for teaching Shakespeare, specifically *Titus Andronicus* and *Othello*.

Raises pertinent questions about the status of student adaptations
as criticism; challenges teachers subscribing to performance-
based pedagogy to consider the meanings and uses of such texts.

Vitkus, Daniel J. 'Turning Turk in *Othello*: The Conversion and
Damnation of the Moor', *Shakespeare Quarterly* 48.2 (1997):
145–67.

Contending with historicist readings of *Othello* as the product
of a colonial and proto-imperial culture, argues convincingly
for the play as a reflection of English anxiety about the Turkish
threat to Christendom, and thus as a drama of conversion.

Walen, Denise A. 'Unpinning Desdemona', *Shakespeare Quarterly*
58.4 (2007): 487–508.

Explores the striking textual variation in the treatment of the
willow scene (4.3) in the quarto (1622) and First Folio (1623),
arguing that the longer folio version was necessary to the
material conditions of its original performance at the Globe,
but more dispensable at Blackfriars and later indoor stages.
This scholarship was the subject of a Globe Education practical
research experiment in 2008–9, for which video footage is
available online via The Capital Centre at the University of
Warwick (see below) and The Globe Theatre.

Selected critical guides

Erickson, Peter and Maurice Hunt, eds. *Approaches to Teaching
Shakespeare's Othello* (New York: MLA, 2005).

A fine collection of essays exploring materials for and
approaches to teaching *Othello* at the undergraduate level. In
addition to rich sections on race and gender, the volume offers
insightful considerations of genre, notably Jean Howard's
reading of the tragedy as an adventure play and Douglas
Bruster's consideration of the play's comic-tragic tensions; of
performance-based teaching, where the standout contribution is
probably Virginia Mason Vaughan's essay on 'Teaching Richard
Burbage's Othello'; and of comparative contexts, notably Sheila
T. Cavanagh's examination of the play in relation to several
well-known adaptive texts, and Janelle Jenstad's account of how
she uses Isak Dinesen's 'The Blank Page' as a creative entry point

into classroom discussion about the intersection of texts and textiles in the play.

Hadfield, Andrew, ed. *William Shakespeare's Othello: A Sourcebook* (London: Routledge, 2003).
A useful resource for contextualizing the play, this sourcebook includes contemporary documents, early critical texts, a selection of influential modern essays, and discussion of key scenes.

Hampton-Reeves, Stuart. *Othello, The Shakespeare Handbooks* (London: Palgrave Macmillan, 2011).
An introductory guide to the play's textual, performance and critical history. Particularly useful for its overview of screen adaptations and case studies of key stage productions.

Kolin, Philip C. 'Blackness Made Visible: A Survey of *Othello* in Criticism, on Stage, and on Screen', in *Othello: New Critical Essays*, ed. Philip C. Kolin (New York: Routledge, 2002), 1–88.
Comprehensive and insightful survey of responses to race and racism in the play in criticism, performance and adaptation; the lead essay in a valuable edited collection.

Potter, Lois. *Shakespeare in Performance: Othello* (Manchester: Manchester University Press, 2002).
Provides a detailed discussion of the play's performance history, divided into two parts, the first concerned with the period before the performance of an American black Othello (Paul Robeson) in a major theatre, and the second focused on the legacy of that performance through the second half of the twentieth century, in the UK, USA and Central Europe.

Potter, Nicholas. *William Shakespeare: Othello* (New York: Columbia University Press, 2000).
This Columbia Critical Guide surveys six key periods in the critical tradition of the play, focusing in each case on two or three influential voices. Beginning in the Restoration with Thomas Rymer, it concludes in postmodernity with Valerie Traub, Leonard Tennenhouse and Stanley Cavell.

Smith, Emma. *William Shakespeare: Othello* (Devon: Northcote House, 2005).
An excellent starting point for students of the play, this extended essay explores *Othello*'s thematic, generic and linguistic doubleness. The focus is on close textual readings and theatrical interpretation.

Vaughan, Virginia Mason. *Othello: A Contextual History* (Cambridge: Cambridge University Press, 1996).

Invaluable historicist study, first of the play in relation to its Jacobean contexts, and second of the cultural contexts of the play's performances from the restoration period through to its adaptation on film in the twentieth century.

Other print resources

Bullough, Geoffrey. *Narrative and Dramatic Sources of Shakesepeare*, Vol. 7: *Major Tragedies* (London: Routledge & Kegan Paul, 1975).
Contains the full text of Giraldi Cinthio's *Gli Hecatommithi* (1565) in English translation.

Hall, Kim F., ed. *Othello: Texts and Contexts*, The Bedford Shakespeare Library (New York: Bedford, 2007).
Reprints the Bevington edition of *Othello* and supplements it with dozens of contemporary documents and excerpted works that deepen contextual understanding in key thematic areas – Race and Religion, Cultural Geography, Marriage and the Household, Masculinity and Military Life, and the Passions – and enable different historical approaches to the play.

Hankey, Julia. *Othello: Shakespeare in Production*, 2nd edn (Cambridge: Cambridge University Press, 2005).
In addition to a full text of the play, complete with production annotations and notes on the cuts and variations made in particular performances, this volume includes a full list of productions and a substantial introduction to the play in performance.

Honigmann, E. A. J. *The Texts of 'Othello' and Shakespearian Revision* (New York: Routledge, 1996).
Definitive guide to the history of the quarto and folio texts and a detailed comparative reading of the two versions of '*Othello*'. In the absence of a parallel text edition of the play, a particularly valuable resource.

Jones, James Earl. *Othello*, Actors on Shakespeare (London: Faber and Faber, 2003).
Jones played Othello seven times and is considered by some to be the best American Othello. His personal reflection on the meaning of *Othello* provides a useful means of suggesting to

students why the play matters today. With its opening claim
that Iago is the most complex of all Shakespeare's characters,
the section on 'The Tragedy of Iago' is a great starting point for
classroom discussion.

Othello: A Concordance to the Text of the First Folio, ed. T. H.
Howard-Hill (Oxford: Clarendon Press, 1971).

McDonald, Russ. *The Bedford Companion to Shakespeare: An
Introduction with Documents*, 2nd edn (Boston: Bedford/St
Martin's, 2001).
Includes a wealth of historical information and documentation
designed to support teaching and learning in Shakespeare. The
section on 'Men and Women: Gender, Family, and Society'
introduces students to structures of early modern patriarchy; the
excerpt from *An Homily of the State of Matrimony* (pp. 285–90)
can serve both to contextualize and problematize Othello's
striking of Desdemona.

Rymer, Thomas. *A Short View of Tragedy* (London, 1693).
In which Rymer expressed his infamous complaint against the
trifling tragedy of the play, posing the question 'Why was not
this call'd the *Tragedy of the Handkerchief*?'

Vogel, Paula. *Desdemona: A Play about a Handkerchief* reprinted
in *Adaptations of Shakespeare: A Critical Anthology of Plays
from the Seventeenth Century to the Present*, eds Daniel
Fischlin and Mark Fortier (London: Routledge, 2000),
233–55.
Among many modern texts that appropriate and adapt the
Othello story, this feminist play featuring a bawdy Desdemona
compelling the audience with her tales of sexual conquest is
especially noteworthy.

Internet resources

The British Library. http://www.bl.uk/treasures/shakespeare/othello.
html
Provides access to Shakespeare's sources for *Othello* and to the
full Quarto editions, with detailed bibliographic notes.

The Capital Centre, University of Warwick. http://www2.warwick.
ac.uk/fac/cross_fac/capital/

Features 'Unpinning Desdemona' and is especially useful to students and teachers of *Othello* at undergraduate level. This online video records a practical research experiment conducted at Shakespeare's Globe in partnership with Globe Education and in conjunction with Professor Carol Rutter (University of Warwick) in 2008–9, exploring variations between Q1 and F1 in the willow scene (4.3). It concludes that the Quarto is not an actors' text, showing how dramaturgy can illuminate textual and interpretative problems.

The Folger Library Shakespeare Library. http://www.folger.edu. Provides online access to the Folger Digital Edition of *Othello*: http://www.folgerdigitaltexts.org

Hosts its own YouTube channel featuring numerous short videos relevant to the study of *Othello*: http://www.youtube.com/user/FolgerLibrary

Of particular note is 'Insider's Guide: Language in *Othello*' with resident dramaturg Michelle Osherow, which provides a basic introduction to the rhetorical power of language in the play.

Open Source Shakespeare. http://www.opensourceshakespeare.org/concordance/

An online concordance of Shakespeare's works.

Shakespeare's Globe. http://www.shakespearesglobe.com/education. Features a range of useful educational resources and web links to articles, databases and online resources.

Selected audiovisual materials

O. Directed by Tim Blake Nelson, starring Mekhi Phifer, Josh Hartnett and Julia Stiles (2001).
A modern update loosely based on Shakespeare's tragedy. Set in an American high school where Othello becomes 'OJ', the only African-American student and star basketball player for the school.

Otello. Directed by Franco Zeffirelli, libretto by Arrigo Boito, starring Placido Domingo, Katia Ricciardelli and Justino Díaz (1986). Acclaimed film version of Verdi's operatic adaptation of the play, frequently criticized for its unusual cuts, notably in the willow scene.

Othello. Directed by Stuart Burge, starring Laurence Olivier, Maggie Smith and Frank Finlay (1965).
A film version of the 1965 production released on DVD by Warner Home Video in 2007. Olivier's blackface performance makes this film adaptation a difficult object of study, but since it makes *Othello* a play about race in a way so disturbing for postmodern sensibilities, it is a valuable tool for exploring racial difference as a theme, and especially for considering the play's particular resonance with contemporary racial politics.

Othello. Directed by Jonathan Miller, starring Anthony Hopkins, Penelope Wilton and Bob Hoskins (1981). Released on DVD/video by BBC Time-Life Films, 1981.
The last BBC production to feature a white actor in the role of Othello, Miller's somewhat long and lacklustre adaptation is useful to teachers on several counts: exquisite sets inspired by sixteenth-century European paintings, a standout performance by Rosemary Leach as Emilia, and (though this could be a drawback for some) an assiduously faithful rendition of the text.

Othello. Directed by Trevor Nunn, starring Willard White, Imogen Stubbs and Ian McKellen (1990). Released on DVD/Video by Primetime, 1990.
Television version of the Royal Shakespeare Company's production from the 1989 season, the text is almost entirely uncut but the setting is relocated to the late nineteenth century, with military costumes evoking the American Civil War. McKellen is an exceptional Iago and White's opera training enables him to bring the 'Othello music' impressively to life.

Othello. Directed by Oliver Parker, starring Laurence Fishburne, Irène Jacob and Kenneth Branagh (1995). Released on DVD by Warner Home Video in 2001.
This was the first film adaptation of the play to star an African-American Othello. Branagh's 'alarmingly human' Iago (*New York Times*, 14 December 1995) won critical acclaim.

Othello. Directed by Janet Suzman, starring John Kani, Joanna Weinberg and Richard Haddon Haines (1988). Released on DVD by Arthouse Theatre, 2005.
Acclaimed film version of the Market Theatre production (1987) in Johannesburg, staged before the collapse of apartheid as a political protest against that regime.

Othello. Directed by Orson Welles, starring Orson Welles, Suzanne
Cloutier and Micheál MacLiammóir (1952). The restored cut
was released on DVD by Marceau Films / United Artists in
1992. The original cut has been made available for educational
purposes on YouTube.
Like Olivier, Welles used makeup to play a black Othello, but
race is not the focus of this adaptation as it is in Burge's; instead,
it is far more concerned with sexual jealousy. Cinematically
beautiful, the film's textual cuts can illuminate Shakespeare's
dramatic technique for students. What is lost in cutting Iago's
soliloquies, for example, or in downscaling Emilia's role? Is
Shakespeare's Desdemona really that innocent?

Shakespeare's Pronunciation. CD released in 2012 by The British
Library featuring an introduction by leading historical linguist
David Crystal and actor Ben Crystal and 28 readings from
Shakespeare's works in original early modern pronunciation.
The twenty-sixth reading is a section from Act 4 of *Othello*
(Desdemona and Emilia) that might usefully support classroom
teaching on language and gender in the play.

Stage Beauty. Directed by Richard Eyre (2004), screenplay by
Jeffrey Hatcher, starring Billy Crudup, Claire Danes and Rupert
Everett. Released on DVD by Lions Gate in 2005.
Adapting Jeffrey Hatcher's play of the same name, this film
dramatizes a decisive moment in stage history enabled by
Othello, namely Margaret Hughes' 1660 performance in the
role of Desdemona, the first occasion on which a female actress
legally acted on stage. The film provides a lively introduction
to the material conditions of restoration theatre, but its intense
preoccupation with questions of gender and the violent eroticism
of the death scene make it especially useful to teachers adopting
performance-based approaches to the play.

NOTES

Introduction

1 In preparing this overview of reactions to *Othello*, I have relied on numerous major modern editions, especially the ones published at various times, under various editors, as volumes in the 'Arden' series and the ones issued by Oxford and Cambridge University Presses.

Chapter 1

1 Brian Vickers, *Shakespeare: The Critical Heritage*, Vol. 2 (London: Routledge & Kegan Paul, 1974), 2: 27–8.

2 Vickers, 2: 51, 52, 28.

3 Vickers, 2: 34.

4 Vickers, 2: 74, 79, 85.

5 Russ McDonald, ed. *Othello* (London: Penguin, 2001), xxxvii.

6 These comments are from Johnson's 1765 edition of Shakespeare and are taken from Edward Pechter's Norton Critical Edition (*NCE*) of the play (New York: Norton, 2004), 216–17. All quotations from *Othello* itself in this chapter will be from the Arden edition (third series), ed. E. A. J. Honigmann (Walton-on-Thames: Nelson, 1997).

7 *Samuel Johnson on Shakespeare*, ed. W. K. Wimsatt (New York: Hill & Wang, 1960), 114–15.

8 From *An Essay of Dramatick Poesie* in Vickers, 1: 138.

9 'Reading Othello's Skin Color: Contexts and Pretexts', *Philological Quarterly* 87 (2008), 299.

10 *Othello: The New Variorum Edition*, ed. Horace Howard
Furness (Mineola, NY: Dover Publications, 2000; originally
published 1886), 389–90.

11 'On the Tragedies of Shakespeare. Considered with Reference
to Their Fitness for Stage Representation', in *Othello*, ed.
Edward Pechter, *NCE*, 221.

12 Furness, 390.

13 For a particularly vivid description of the English slave trade
see Andrea Stuart, *Sugar in the Blood: A Family's Story of
Slavery and Empire* (New York: Knopf, 2013).

14 Furness, 394.

15 Michael Neill, ed., *Othello, the Moor of Venice* (Oxford:
Oxford University Press, 2006), 44.

16 Furness, 395. Not much is known about Mary Preston;
examining the few facts that are available, Ann Thompson and
Sasha Roberts suggest that her sympathies in the Civil War
appear to have been with the Confederacy (*Women Reading
Shakespeare 1600–1900)* [Manchester: Manchester University
Press, 1997], 126).

17 Furness, 395, 394.

18 *NCE*, 241, 242.

19 *Othello, the Moor of Venice*, 49.

20 Quoted in Neill, 117.

21 Neill, 119.

22 G. K. Hunter, 'Othello and Colour Prejudice', in Pechter, *NCE*,
248–62; see esp. 255, 256.

23 Hunter, 259–60, 262. See Eliot's essay, 'Shakespeare and
the Stoicism of Seneca', in his *Selected Essays* (New York:
Harcourt, Brace and World, 1932), 111.

24 *Shakespeare Quarterly* 38 (1987), 188.

25 *Black Face, Maligned Race: The Representation of Black
in English Drama from Shakespeare to Southerne* (Baton
Rouge: LSU Press, 1999), 160, 161. Meredith Anne Skura,
however, denies that Othello is essentially similar to the
characteristics of other black dramatic figures discussed by
Barthelemy: 'what Barthelemy means by stage stereotype is

a combination of Aaron in *Titus Andronicus and Eleazar in Lust's Dominion*, without [in *Othello*] "the usual desire for sexual gratification and power", in other words, a stereotype without its usual defining characteristics' ('Reading Othello's Skin', 305–6).

26 'Othello and the Problem of Blackness', in *A Companion to Shakespeare's Works*, ed. Richard Dutton and Jean E. Howard (Malden: Blackwell, 2006), 370.

27 J. Duke Pesta, 'C. S. Lewis's Lost *Othello* Manuscript and the Re-Presentations of Race', *Journal of the Wooden O Symposium* 1 (2001): 36–41. Pesta says that 'all citations of this brief, unpublished essay are from the same transcription made of the original by Michael W. Price'.

28 'Othello, Racism, and Despair', *Understanding Racial Issues in Shakespeare's* Othello *and* Titus Andronicus: *Selected Critical Essays*, ed. Solomon O. Iyasere and Maria W. Iyasere (Albany, NY: Whitston Publishing Company, 2008), 137.

29 *Myriad-minded Shakespeare* (New York: St Martin's Press, 1998), 69–72.

30 *Othello, the Moor of Venice*, 125.

31 See Pechter, ed., *NCE*, 222–3, 228–9.

32 See Pechter, ed., *NCE*, 231.

33 See Pechter, ed., *NCE*, 220.

34 *Shakespearean Tragedy* (London: Macmillan, 1937), 233, 209, 231.

35 Summaries of all these articles can be found in the useful volume of *Othello* criticism edited by Margaret Lael Mikesell and Virginia Mason Vaughan, *Othello: An Annotated Bibliography* (New York: Garland, 1990). The articles described in this paragraph are bibliographic items 95, 133, 347, 399, and 750 and 754.

36 *Shakespeare the Thinker* (New Haven: Yale University Press, 2007), 281–2.

37 *Shakespeare and the Allegory of Evil* (New York: Columbia University Press, 1958), 55.

38 'Morality, Ethics and the Failure of Love in Shakespeare's

Othello', in Philip Kolin, ed. *Othello: New Critical Essays* (New York: Routledge, 2002), 262, 269.

39 'Blasphemous Preacher: Iago and the Reformation', *Shakespeare and the Culture of Christianity in Early Modern England* (New York: Fordham University Press, 2003), 385, 386, 387, 404.

40 'Iago the Essayist: Florio Between Montaigne and Shakespeare', *Renaissance Go-betweens: Cultural Exchange in Early Modern Europe*, eds Andreas Höfele et al. (Berlin: Spectrum Literaturwissenshcaft, 2005), 264.

41 'Iago as Deconstructionist', *The Philological Review* 16 (1990), 77, 64.

42 'Iago as Villain in *Othello*', *Publications of the Arkansas Philological Association* 21 (1995), 21.

43 Mikesell and Vaughan, item #997.

44 *The New Cambridge Companion to Shakespeare*, eds Magreta de Grazia and Stanley Wells 2nd edn (Cambridge: Cambridge University Press, 2010), 337 fn.

45 See Pechter, ed. *NCE*, 235, 236, 238, 239.

46 See Pechter, ed., *NCE*, 239. See also Bradley's *Shakespearean Tragedy*, 175–6.

47 *Othello: An Historical and Comparative Study* (1915; rpt, New York: Haskell House, 1964).

48 'Diabolic Intellect and the Noble Hero', in *Othello: A Casebook*, ed. John Wain (London: Macmillan, 1994), 126, 131–2.

49 *Myriad-minded Shakespeare*, 69.

50 *Myriad-minded Shakespeare*, 72.

51 'The Noble Moor', *Interpretations of Shakespeare*, ed. Kenneth Muir (Oxford: Oxford University Press, 1985), 172, 170.

52 'The Improvisation of Power', in *Modern Critical Interpretations: William Shakespeare's Othello*, ed. Harold Bloom (New York: Chelsea House Publishers, 1987), 55.

53 Greenblatt, 'Improvisation', 47.

54 *City of God*, trans. Philip Levine; The Loeb Classical Library

(Cambridge: Harvard University Press, 1966), 4: 386–7 [Book 14 of the *City of God*].

55 *The Body and Society: Men, Women and Sexual Renunciation in Early Christianity* (New York: Columbia University Press, 1988), 402–3.

56 St Thomas Aquinas is in *Summa Theologica*, II–II, Q. 153, Reply Obj. 2, trans. by the Fathers of the English Dominican Province (London: Burns, Oates & Washbourne, 1920).

57 Convenient summaries of all of these articles may be found in the Mikesell and Vaughan bibliography: Ribner #387, Millward #1379 and Morris #1381.

58 'Othello', in Bloom, 141.

59 '"Exchange Me for a Goat": Iago's Ewes and Rams, Othello's Goats and Monkeys, and Matthew 25.31–45', *Cithara* 46 (2007), 3.

60 *Staging Reform, Reforming the Stage: Protestantism and Popular Theater in Early Modern England* (Ithaca: Cornell University Press, 1997), 125–55.

61 '*Othello* as Protestant Propaganda', in *Religion and Culture in Renaissance England*, eds Claire McEachern and Debora Shuger (Cambridge: Cambridge University Press, 1997), 235.

62 '"Black but Beautiful": *Othello* and the Cult of the Black Madonna', *Marian Moments in Early Modern British Drama*, eds Regina Buccola and Lisa Hopkins (Burlington: Ashgate, 2007), 75–6.

63 'Intercession, Detraction, and Just Judgment in *Othello*', *Comparative Drama* 35.1 (2001): 43–68; see 49–50, 57.

64 'Keeping Faith: Water Imagery and Religious Diversity in *Othello*', in *Othello: New Critical Essays*, ed. Philip Kolin (New York: Routledge, 2002), 278, 282, 290.

65 'Predestination and the Heresy of Merit in *Othello*', *Comparative Drama* 30 (2006): 346–76.

66 'Protestant Epistemology and Othello's Consciousness', *Renascence* 64 (summer 2013), 269.

67 'The Problem of Inartificial Proof: Othello Peers into Bacon's Universe', *Ben Jonson Journal* 10 (2003): 175, 173.

68 '*Othello*: Portrait of a Marriage', in Kolin, ed., *Othello: New Critical Essays*, 221–2.

69 'Love and Lies: Marital Truth-Telling, Catholic Casuistry, and *Othello*', in *Shakespeare and the Culture of Christianity in Early Modern England*, eds Dennis Taylor and David N. Beauregard (New York: Fordham University Press, 2003), 417–19, 430.

70 This article is summarized in the Mikesell and Vaughan bibliography, item #1220.

71 Bloom, 81, 87, 89, 90, 97, 103.

72 *Shakespeare* (New York: New York Review of Books, 2005; originally published 1939), 192–203.

73 *All of Shakespeare* (New York: Columbia University Press, 1993), 255.

74 *Shakespeare After All* (New York: Random House, 2005), 589, 602.

75 Nuttall, 279. Reference here is to the Riverside edition of Shakespeare's plays (Boston: Houghton Mifflin, 1997).

76 'Shakespeare: The Tragedies', *Teaching Shakespeare and Early Modern Dramatists*, ed. Andrew Hiscock and Lisa Hopkins (Houndmills, Basingstoke: Palgrave Macmillan, 2007), 70, 71.

77 'Motivating Iago', *Approaches to Teaching Shakespeare's Othello*, eds Peter Erickson and Maurice Hunt (New York: MLA, 2005), 125, 128.

78 'Friendship in Shakespeare's *Othello*', *Ben Jonson Journal* 6 (1999), 111–12.

79 'Flattery in Shakespeare's *Othello*: The Relevance of Plutarch and Sir Thomas Elyot', *Comparative Drama* 35 (2001), 2, 17.

80 'The Curse of Cush: Othello's Judaic Ancestry', in Kolin, ed., *Othello: New Critical Essays*, 170, 172.

81 Newark, DE: University of Delaware Press, 1990.

82 Kolin, ed., *New Critical Essays*, 391–400; 399.

83 Discussed in *Nichomachean Ethics*, 4.4.3.

84 Halio, 395.

Chapter 2

1 Unless otherwise noted, all citations to the play are to *Othello: The Arden Shakespeare*, 3rd series, ed. E. A. J. Honigmann (Walton-on-Thames: Nelson, 1997).

2 Quoted in Virginia Mason Vaughan, *Othello: A Contextual History* (Cambridge: Cambridge University Press, 1994), 151.

3 Thomas Rymer, *A Short View of Tragedy* [1693] (New York: AMS Press, 1970), 135.

4 Two useful essays on audience response to the play are Hugh M. Richmond, 'The Audience's Role in *Othello*', in Philip C. Kolin, ed., *Othello: New Critical Essays* (New York: Routledge, 2002), 89–101, and Kent Cartwright, 'Audience Response and the Denouement of *Othello*', in Virginia Mason Vaughan and Kent Cartwright, eds, *Othello: New Perspectives* (Madison, NJ: Fairleigh Dickinson University Press, 1991), 160–76.

5 Quoted in Edward Pechter, *Othello and Interpretive Traditions* (Iowa City: University of Iowa Press, 1999), 13.

6 Quoted in Pechter, 11.

7 Marvin Rosenberg, *The Masks of Othello* (Newark: University of Delaware Press, 1992), 1.

8 Hugh Quarshie, *Second Thoughts About Othello* (Chipping Camden, England: International Shakespeare Association, 1999), 7.

9 A. C. Bradley vigorously attacked this view of Othello in his essay on the play in *Shakespearean Tragedy* (New York: Meridian Books, 1955), 152–3. Nevertheless, even in modern productions Othello often enters Desdemona's bedchamber clad in Eastern rather than European dress, intimating a certain atavistic quality to her murder.

10 Martin Holmes, *Shakespeare and Burbage* (London: Phillimore, 1978), 170–1. I follow here Andrew Gurr's distinction between the acting styles of Alleyn and Burbage, which has been challenged by R. A. Foakes; see Foakes's discussion in his 'Shakespeare's Elizabethan Stages', in *Shakespeare: An Illustrated Stage History*, eds Jonathan Bate and Russell Jackson (Oxford: Oxford University Press, 1996), 15–16.

11   Quoted in C. C. Stopes, *Burbage and Shakespeare's Stage* (New
     York: Haskell House, 1970), 121.

12   Quoted in Michael Dobson, 'Improving on the Original:
     Actresses and Adaptations', in Bate and Jackson, 48.

13   On the Smock Alley promptbook, see G. Blakemore Evans,
     Shakespearean Promptbooks in the Seventeenth Century
     (Charlottesville: University of Virginia, 1980), Vol. 6; and
     Rosenberg, 20–4.

14   Quoted in Vaughan, 100.

15   Katherine Philips witnessed a Dublin production in 1662 in
     which 'the Doge of Venice and all his Senators came on the
     Stage with Feathers in their Hats, which was like to have
     chang'd the Tragedy into a Comedy' (quoted in George
     C. D. Odell, *Shakespeare from Betterton to Irving* (New York:
     Dover, 1966), 1: 206. See also Addison's *Spectator* 42 for an
     interesting description of contemporary costumes in which
     feathers figured prominently.

16   Rymer, 93, 120, 91, 113.

17   Steele, Sir Richard. *The Tatler*, ed. Lewis Gibb (London:
     Everyman's Library, 1953), 197.

18   Steele, 197.

19   Samuel Pepys, *The Diary of Samuel Pepys*, eds R. C. Latham
     and W. Matthews (Berkeley and Los Angeles: University of
     California Press, 1970), 1: 264; (11 October 1660).

20   Quoted in Vaughan, 119.

21   Vaughan, 115.

22   Quoted in Rosenberg, 45–6.

23   Quoted in Vaughan, 119.

24   Quoted in Rosenberg, 40.

25   Quoted in Peter Holland, 'The Age of Garrick', in Bate and
     Jackson, 71.

26   Quoted in Rosenberg, 51.

27   Quoted in Vaughan, 121.

28   Quoted in Rosenberg, 47.

29   It is difficult to avoid sensing a sexual charge in these

descriptions of uninhibited audience response; for fuller discussion of the sexual dimension of the play, see Valerie Traub, *Desire and Anxiety: Circulations of Sexuality in Shakespearean Drama* (New York: Routledge, 1992), 33–43.

30   Quoted in Nicholas Potter, ed. *Shakespeare: Othello* (New York: Columbia University Press, 2000), 72. In 1773, Herder had earlier captured this sense of organicism in a mechanical figure: 'In Othello, the Moor, what a world! What a whole! A *living history of the genesis, development, eruption, and sad end to the passion of this noble and unfortunate man!* And what complexity! All these different cogs turning within a single mechanism!' Johann Gottfried Herder, *Shakespeare*, trans. and ed. Gregory Moore (Princeton: Princeton University Press, 2008), 38.

31   *Inquiring Spirit: A Coleridge Reader*, ed. Kathleen Coburn (New York: Minerva Press, 1968), 294. Perhaps thinking of Kean's irregular life offstage, Coleridge then adds: 'I do not think him thorough-bred gentleman enough to play Othello.'

32   Quoted in Rosenberg, 62.

33   Quoted in Rosenberg, 63.

34   Quoted in Rosenberg, 65.

35   Quoted in Vaughan, 154.

36   Quoted in Rosenberg, 136.

37   Quoted in Catherine Clifton, *Fanny Kemble's Civil Wars* (New York: Simon & Schuster, 2000), 143.

38   Quoted in Rosenberg, 136.

39   Ellen Terry, 'Desdemona', in *Othello: Critical Essays*, ed. Susan Snyder (New York: Garland, 1988), 61.

40   Terry, 62, 64, 67, 65.

41   Quoted in Rosenberg, 113.

42   Quoted in Rosenberg, 115.

43   Quoted in Julie Hankey, ed. *Othello,*, 2nd edn (Cambridge: Cambridge University Press, 2005), 60.

44   Quoted in Stanley Wells, *Shakespeare in the Theatre: An Anthology of Criticism* (Oxford: Oxford University Press, 1997), 116.

45   Vaughan, 159.

46 Alex Ross, 'Othello's Daughter', *The New Yorker* (29 July 2013), 31.

47 Rosenberg, 118.

48 Quoted in Ross, 30.

49 Quoted in Hankey, 55.

50 Krystyna Kujawinska Courtney, 'Ira Aldridge, Shakespeare, and Color-Conscious Performances in Nineteenth-Century Europe', in *Colorblind Shakespeare: New Perspectives on Race and Performance*, ed. Ayanna Thompson (New York: Routledge, 2006), 114.

51 Quoted in Rosenberg, 152.

52 Quoted in Stuart Hampton-Reeves, *Othello* (New York: Palgrave Macmillan, 2011), 109.

53 Quoted in Vaughan, 190.

54 Quoted in Hankey, 71.

55 Quoted in Rosenberg, 152.

56 Vaughan, 193.

57 Quoted in Hankey, 70.

58 This film is available as a feature on the two-disc DVD of *O* (2001).

59 Douglas Brode, *Shakespeare in the Movies: From the Silent Era to Today* (New York: Berkley, 2001), 153.

60 Kenneth Rothwell, *A History of Shakespeare on Screen: A Century of Film and Television* (Cambridge: Cambridge University Press, 1999), 81.

61 Pamela Mason, 'Orson Welles and Filmed Shakespeare', in *The Cambridge Companion to Shakespeare on Film*, ed. Russell Jackson (Cambridge: Cambridge University Press, 2000), 189.

62 Samuel Crowl, *Shakespeare Observed: Studies in Performance on Stage and Screen* (Athens: Ohio University Press, 1992), 54.

63 Patricia Tatspaugh, 'The Tragedies of Love on Film', in Russell Jackson, 146.

64 Anthony Davies, 'Filming Othello', in *Shakespeare and the Moving Image: The Plays on Film and Television*, ed. Anthony Davies and Stanley Wells (Cambridge: Cambridge University Press, 1994), 209.

65 Laurence Olivier, *On Acting* (New York: Simon & Schuster, 1986), 151.

66 Olivier, 153.

67 Olivier, 158.

68 Quoted in Wells, 270.

69 Olivier, 148.

70 Quoted in Wells, 271.

71 Quoted in Susan Willis, *The BBC Shakespeare Plays: Making the Televised Canon* (Chapel Hill: University of North Carolina Press, 1991), 121.

72 Quarshie, 5.

73 James Earl Jones and Penelope Niven, *James Earl Jones: Voices and Silences* (New York: Scribner's, 1993), 157.

74 *Othello*, writ. William Shakespeare, dir. Janet Suzman, Arthaus Theatre, 1988, DVD.

75 Janet Suzman, 'Othello in South Africa', The Tanner Lectures on Human Values, Oxford University, 3–4 May 1995, 277 (accessed 17 December 2013), http://tannerlectures.utah.edu/_documents/a-to-z/s/Suzman96.pdf

76 Suzman, 'Othello in South Africa', 282.

77 Quoted in Hankey, 100.

78 Thomas Cartelli and Katherine Rowe, *New Wave Shakespeare on Screen* (Cambridge: Polity, 2007), 122.

79 *Othello*, writ. William Shakespeare, dir. Wilson Milam, Kultur, 2007, DVD.

80 Neil Forsythe, 'The Shakespeare Summer, 2007', *Early Modern Literary Studies*, 13.1 (May 2007), 16 December 2013, http://extra.shu.ac.uk/emls/13-1/forsshak.htm

Chapter 3

1 Maynard Mack, *King Lear in Our Time* (1965) (rpt London: Routledge, 2013), 86.

2 'Introduction', *Othello*, ed. E. A. J. Honigmann, Arden
   Shakespeare, 3rd edn (London: Thomas Nelson, 1997), 1.

3 Michael Neill, ed., *Othello* (New York: Oxford University
   Press, 2006), 1.

4 Edward Pechter, *Othello and Interpretive Traditions* (Iowa
   City: Iowa University Press, 1999), 2; Julie Hankey, ed.,
   Othello, 2nd edn (Cambridge: Cambridge University Press,
   2005), 1.

5 Eldred Jones, *Othello's Countrymen* (London: Oxford
   University Press, 1965); Ruth Cowhig, 'The Importance of
   Othello's Race', *Journal of Commonwealth Literature* 12.2
   (1977): 153–61; G. K. Hunter, *Dramatic Identities and
   Cultural Traditions* (New York: Barnes and Noble, 1978);
   Anthony Gerard Barthelemy, *Black Face, Maligned Race: The
   Representation of Blacks in English Drama from Shakespeare
   to Southerne* (Baton Rouge: Louisiana State University Press,
   1987); Karen Newman, '"And Wash the Ethiop White":
   Femininity and the Monstrous in *Othello*', in *Shakespeare
   Reproduced*, ed. Jean Howard, et al. (New York: Methuen,
   1987), 141–62; Martin Orkin, *Shakespeare Against Apartheid*
   (Craighill, South Africa: Ad Donker, 1987); Michael Neill,
   'Unproper Beds: Race, Adultery and the Hideous', *Shakespeare
   Quarterly* 40.4 (1989): 383–41; Ania Loomba, *Gender, Race,
   Renaissance Drama* (Manchester: Manchester University
   Press, 1989; Emily Bartels, 'Making More of the Moor:
   Renaissance Refashionings of Race', *Shakespeare Quarterly*
   41.4 (1990): 433–54; Joyce Green MacDonald, '"The Force
   of Imagination": The Subject of Blackness in Shakespeare,
   Jonson, and Ravenscroft', *Renaissance Papers* (1991): 53–74,
   'Sex, Race, and Empire in *Antony and Cleopatra*', *Literature
   and History* 5.1 (1996): 66–77, *Race, Ethnicity, and Power
   in the Renaissance*, ed. Joyce Green Macdonald (Madison,
   NJ: Associated University Press, 1997); *Women, Race, and
   Writing*, ed. Margo Hendricks and Patricia Parker (London:
   Routledge, 1994); Kim Hall, *Things of Darkness: Economies
   of Race and Gender in Early Modern England* (Ithaca: Cornell
   University Press, 1995); Jyotsna Singh, 'Othello's Identity,
   Postcolonial Theory, and Contemporary African Rewritings of
   Othello', in Hendricks and Parker, 287–99. In addition, from

2000 onwards, full-length studies of race in Shakespeare and his historical moment include: Imtiaz Habib, *Shakespeare and Race: Postcolonial Praxis in the Early Modern Period* (Lanham, MD: University Press of America, 2000) and *Black Lives in the English Archives: Imprints of the Invisible* (Burlington, VT: Ashgate, 2008); Catherine Alexander and Stanley Wells, eds, *Shakespeare and Race* (Cambridge: Cambridge University Press, 2000); Thomas Earle and K. J. P. Lowe, eds, *Africans in Renaissance Europe* (New York: Cambridge University Press, 2005); Mary Floyd-Wilson, *English Ethnicity and Race in Early Modern Drama* (Cambridge: Cambridge University Press, 2003); Ania Loomba and Jonathan Burton, *Race in Early Modern England: A Documentary Companion* (New York: Palgrave Macmillan, 2007).

6 Lena Orlin, ed., *New Casebooks: Othello* (New York: Palgrave Macmillan, 2004), 1.

7 Philip C. Kolin, 'Blackness Made Visible: A Survey of Othello in Criticism, On Stage, and on Screen', in Kolin, ed., *New Critical Essays on* Othello (London: Routledge, 2002), 1–88.

8 Peter Erickson and Maurice Hunt, eds, *Approaches to Teaching Shakespeare's Othello* (New York: Modern Language Association of America, 2005); 'Introduction', 10.

9 Erickson and Hunt, 'Introduction', 10–14.

10 'Images of White Identity in *Othello*', in Kolin, 133–46.

11 'White Faces, Blackface: The Production of "Race" in *Othello*', in Kolin, 103–33; see 103, and also 105. The proposition of this essay is reminiscent of Dympna Callaghan's essay 'Othello was a White Man' (*Alternative Shakespeare*, ed. Terence Hawkes, [London: Routledge, 1996], 192–215).

12 '"Black and White, and Dread All Over": The Shakespeare Theater's Photonegative *Othello* and the Body of Desdemona', in Orlin, 220–49; see 222.

13 Ian Smith, Review of Ayanna Thompson's *Colorblind Shakespeare* in *Shakespeare* Quarterly 59.3 (2008): 354–6; 354.

14 Virginia Vaughan, *Performing Blackness on English Stages, 1500–1800* (New York: Cambridge University Press, 2005), 105–6; 172.

15 Ayanna Thompson, ed., *Colorblind Shakespeare: New
    Perspectives on Race and Performance* (New York: Routledge,
    2006), 139.

16 *Passing Strange: Shakespeare, Race, and Contemporary
    America* (Oxford: Oxford University Press, 2011), 97; 102–3.
    This chapter first appeared as 'The Blackfaced Bard: Returning
    to Shakespeare or Leaving Him?', *Shakespeare Bulletin*, 27.3
    (2009): 437–56.

17 Joyce MacDonald, 'Acting Black: *Othello*, *Othello* Burlesques,
    and the Performance of Blackness', *Theatre Journal* 46 (1994):
    231–49.

18 James Andreas, 'The Curse of Cush: Othello's Judaic Ancestry',
    in Kolin, 169–88.

19 John Ford, '"Words and Performances": Roderigo and the
    Mixed Dramaturgy of Race and Gender in *Othello*', in Kolin,
    147–67; see 149.

20 Virginia Vaughan, *Othello: A Contextual History* (Cambridge:
    Cambridge University Press, 1994), 70); Michael Neil, '*Othello*
    and Race', in Erickson and Hunt, 37–52; see 51.

21 *Speaking of the Moor: From Alcazar to Othello* (Philadelphia:
    University of Pennsylvania Press, 2008), 2–4.

22 'Othello and the Problem of Blackness', in *A Companion to
    Shakespeare's Works, Volume I: The Tragedies*, eds Richard
    Dutton and Jean E. Howard (London: Blackwell, 2006),
    357–741; see 360 and 363.

23 Lara Bovilsky, *Barbarous Play: Race on the English
    Renaissance Stage* (Minneapolis: University of Minnesota
    Press), 2008; see 3.

24 Lisa Hopkins, '"Black but Beautiful": *Othello* and the Cult
    of the Black Madonna', in *Marian Moments in Early Modern
    British Drama*, ed. Regina Buccola, Lisa Hopkins and Arthur
    Marotti (Burlington, VT: Ashgate, 2007), 75–86.

25 Celia Daileader, *Racism, Misogyny, and the Othello* Myth:
    Inter-racial Couples from Shakespeare to Spike Lee
    (Cambridge: Cambridge University Press, 2005), 15.

26 Ian Smith, 'Othello's Black Handkerchief', *Shakespeare
    Quarterly* 64.1 (2013): 1–25; see 2, 3; Lynda E. Boose, 'Othello's

Handkerchief: "The Recognizance and Pledge of Love"', *English Literary Renaissance* 5 (1975): 360–74, esp. 362.

27 Sheila Cavanagh, 'Tales of a Pitiful Handkerchief: Verdi, Vogel, Cinthio, and Shakespeare Present *Othello*', and Janelle Jansted, 'Paper, Linen Sheets: Dinesen's "The Blank Page" and Desdemona's Handkerchief', in Erickson and Hunt, 187–93, and 194–201 respectively.

28 'Shakespeare's Moor', *Raritan* 21.4 (2002): 1–14.

29 Thomas Cartelli, *Repositioning Shakespeare: National Formations, Postcolonial Appropriations* (New York: Routledge, 1999); Imtiaz Habib, *Shakespeare and Race*; Arthur Little Jr, *Jungle Fever: National and Imperial Re-Visions of Race, Rape, and Sacrifice* (Stanford: Stanford University Press, 2000); Ania Loomba and Martin Orkin, eds, *Postcolonial Shakespeares* (London: Routledge, 1998); Lisa Hopkins, *Beginning Shakespeare* (Manchester: Manchester University Press, 2005), Chapters 1 and 4.

30 This natural linkage may interestingly have been hinted at by Shakespeare himself, who puts his most poignant protest of marginalization and oppression in almost identical terms in the mouths of a Jewish character and a white maid – Shylock in *the Merchant of Venice* and Emilia in *Othello*.

31 Lynda Boose, '"Let it be Hid": The Pornographic Aesthetic of Shakespeare's *Othello*', in Orlin, 22–47; see 25.

32 Emily Bartels, 'Improvisation and *Othello*: The Play of Race and Gender', in Erickson and Hunt, 72–9; see 75.

33 Cynthia Marshall, 'Orders of Fantasy in *Othello*', in Erickson and Hunt, 80–9; see 80–2.

34 Nicholas F. Radel, '"Your Own for Ever": Revealing Masculine Desire in *Othello*', in Erickson and Hunt, 62–71; see 63.

35 Daniel Boyarin, 'Othello's Penis: Or, Islam in the Closet', in *Shakesqueer: A Queer Companion to the Complete Works of Shakespeare*, ed. Madhavi Menon (Durham, NC: Duke University Press, 2011), 254–62; see 254–6, 275.

36 John Gronbeck-Tedesco, 'Morality, Ethics and the Failure of Love in Shakespeare's Othello', in Kolin, 255–70; see 256, 260, 269.

37   Eric S. Mallin, 'Othello, Marriage, Middle Age', in *Shakespeare and I*, eds William McKenzie et al. (London: Continuum, 2012), 40–60; see 43; David Bevington, 'Othello: Portrait of a Marriage', in Kolin, 221–32; see 222–3.

38   Sandra Logan, 'Domestic Disturbance and the Disordered State in Shakespeare's *Othello*', *Textual Practice* 18.3 (2004): 351–75; see 351; Theodore B. Leinwand, '*Coniugium Interruptum* in Shakespeare and Webster', *ELH* 72.1 (2005): 239–57; see 245–6.

39   Thomas Moisan, 'Relating Things to the State: "The State" and the Subject of *Othello*', in Kolin, 189–202; see 189–91; Bryan Reynolds and Joseph Fitzpatrick, 'Venetian Ideology or Transversal Power? Iago's Motives and the Means by which Othello Falls', in Kolin, 203–20.

40   Elizabeth Hansen, 'Brothers of the State: *Othello*, Bureaucracy, and Epistemological Crisis', in Orlin, 125–47; see 127–8.

41   Virginia Vaughan, 'Supersubtle Venetians: Richard Knolles and the Geopolitics of Shakespeare's Othello', in *Visions of Venice in Shakespeare*, eds Stanley Wells et al. (Burlington, VT: Ashgate, 2011), 19–32; see 19–20, 29, 30; Eugenie R. Freed, '"News on the Rialto": Shakespeare's Venice', *Shakespeare in Southern Africa* 21 (2009): 47–59; see 47; John Drakakis, 'Shakespeare and Venice', in *Italian Culture in the Drama of Shakespeare and His Contemporaries: Rewriting, Remaking, Refashioning*, ed. Michele Marrapodi (Burlington, VT: Ashgate, 2007), see 170, 169–86; Graham Holderness, *Shakespeare and Venice* (Burlington, VT: Ashgate, 2010), 8–10; Jonathan Burton, *Traffic and Turning: Islam and English Drama, 1579–1624* (Newark: University of Delaware Press, 2005), 53–60; Linda McJannet, *The Sultan Speaks: Dialogue in English Plays and Histories about the Ottoman Turks* (New York: Palgrave Macmillan, 2006), 64–5; Daniel Vitkus, *Turning Turk: English Theater and the Multicultural Mediterranean,1570–1630* (New York: Palgrave Macmillan, 2003), 3–10; and Peter Stallybrass, 'Marginal England: The View from Aleppo', in *Center or Margin: Revisions of the English Renaissance in Honor of Leeds Barroll*, ed. Lena Cowen Orlin (Susquehanna, PA: Susquehanna University Press, 2006), 27–39.

42 Joel Altman, *The Improbability of Othello: Rhetorical Anthropology and Shakespearean Selfhood* (Chicago: University of Chicago Press, 2010), 4; Alan Sinfield, 'Cultural Materialism, *Othello* and the Politics of Plausibility', in Orlin, 49–77.

43 Stefan Kellar, 'Combining Rhetoric and Pragmatics to Read Othello', *English Studies* 91.4 (2010): 398–411; see 400; Stephanie Chamberlain, 'Resolving Clandestine Disputes: Narrative Strategy and Competing Juridical Authority in Othello', *Explorations in Renaissance Culture* 31.2 (2005): 259–78.

44 Bernadette Andrea, 'The Ghost of Leo Africanus from the English to the Irish Renaissance', in *Postcolonial Moves: Medieval through Modern*, eds Patricia Clare Ingham and Michelle R. Warren (New York: Palgrave Macmillan, 2003), 195–215; Christopher Baker, 'Ovid, Othello, and the Pontic Scythians', in *A Search for Meaning: Critical Essays on Early Modern Literature*, ed. Paula Harms Payne (New York: Peter Lang, 2004), 61–80.

45 Karina Feliciano Attar, 'Genealogy of a Character', in *Visions of Venice in Shakespeare*, eds Stanley Wells, Laura Tosi and Shaul Bassi (Burlington, VT: Ashgate, 2013), 47–64.

46 '*Othello* as an Adventure Play', 'Teaching *Othello* as a Tragedy and Comedy', '"'Tis But a Man Gone": Teaching *Othello* as an (Anti) Revenge Play', all in Erickson and Hunt, 90–100; 100–7; 108–16, respectively.

47 Catherine Bates, 'Shakespeare's Tragedies of Love', in *The Cambridge Companion to Shakespearean Tragedy*, ed. Claire McEachern (Cambridge: Cambridge University Press, 2002), 182–203; John Bayley, *The Character of Love: A Study in the Literature of Personality* (London: Collier, 1963), 113–25.

48 Sean Benson, *Shakespeare, 'Othello' and Domestic Tragedy* (London: Continuum, 2011).

49 Enrique Cámara Arenas, 'Causal Attribution and the Analysis of Literary Characters: A. C. Bradley's Study of Iago and Othello', *Journal of Literary Semantics* 39.1 (2010): 43–66; see 45.

50 Nicola Borrelli and Tea Cammarota, 'Mental Illness and Sexual

Deviations in Shakespeare's *Othello*: A Freudian Perspective on the Cast Study of Iago', *Textus: English Studies in Italy* 20.3 (2007): 633–57; see 635.

51 Maurice Hunt, 'Motivating Iago', in Erickson and Hunt, 125–32.

52 Catherine Belsey, 'Iago the Essayist: Florio between Montaigne and Shakespeare', in *Renaissance Go-Betweens: Cultural Exchange in Early Modern Europe*, ed. Andreas Höfele and Werner von Koppenfels (Berlin: de Gruyter, 2005), 262–78. Curiously, Belsey does not mention James Calderwood's extended (admittedly New Critical) analysis of this very topic in the late 1980s in *The Properties of Othello* (Amherst, MA: University of Massachusetts Press, 1989.

53 Harry Berger Jr, 'Acts of Silence, Acts of Speech: How to Do Things with Othello and Desdemona', *Renaissance Drama*, 33 (2004): 3–35; see 7, 10.

54 Ken Jacobson, 'Iago's Art of War: The "Machiavellian Moment" in *Othello*', *Modern Philology* 106.3 (2009): 497–529; see 498–9. A spate of character studies focusing on Desdemona include Ronald J. Boling, 'Desdemona's Venetian Agency', *Philological Review* 34.1 (2008): 1–34; Christopher Clausen, 'Desdemona's Sacred Image: Shakespeare, Verdi and the Making of the Italian Woman', *Shakespeare-Jahrbuch* 138 (2002): 99–110; Sara Munson Deats, '"Truly, an Obedient Lady": Desdemona, Emilia, and the Doctrine of Obedience in Othello', in Kolin, 233–54; Igor Djordjevic, 'Goodnight Desdemona (Good Morning Juliet): From Shakespearean Tragedy to Postmodern Satyr Play', *Comparative Drama* 37.1 (2003): 89–115; Barbara L. Estrin, 'Coming into the Word: Desdemona's Story', in *Luce Irigaray and Premodern Culture: Thresholds of History*, eds Theresa Krier et al. (London: Routledge, 2004), 53–65; Elizabeth Gruber, 'Erotic Politics Reconsidered: Desdemona's Challenge to Othello', *Borrowers and Lenders: The Journal of Shakespeare and Appropriation* 3.2 (2008), http://www.borrowers.uga.edu/781790/display; Yong Li Lan, 'Ong Keng Sen's Desdemona, Ugliness, and the Intercultural Perfomative', *Theatre Journal* 56.2 (2004): 251–73; Louise Noble, 'The Fille Vierge as Pharmakon: The Therapeutic Value of Desdemona's Corpse', in *Disease, Diagnosis, and Cure on the Early Modern Stage*, eds Stephanie

Moss and Kaara L. Peterson (Burlington, VT: Ashgate, 2004),
135–50; Martha Ronk, 'Desdemona's Self-Presentation',
English Literary Renaissance 35.1 (2005): 52–72; Carol
Chillington Rutter, 'Unpinning Desdemona (Again) or "Who
Would Be Toll'd with Wenches in a Shew?"', *Shakespeare
Bulletin* 28.1 (2010): 111–32; Denise A. Walen, 'Unpinning
Desdemona', *Shakespeare Quarterly* 58.4 (2007): 487–508;
Lawrence Warner, 'Desdemona's Wooing: Towards a Pre-1538
Othello', in *Word and Self Estranged in English Texts,
1550–1660*, eds Philippa Kelly and L. E. Semler (Burlington,
VT: Ashgate, 2010), 121–34.

55 Karley K. Adney, 'Shaping Shakespeare, Reflecting History:
Adaptations of *Othello* for Children in 1990s Britain',
Pennsylvania Literary Journal 2.1 (2010): 81–113; see 84.

56 Jill L. Levenson, 'The Society of Women in the History of
Othello from Shakespeare to Verdi', *University of Toronto
Quarterly* 81.4 (2012): 850–9; Alexander Leggatt, 'Love and
Faith in *Othello* and *Otello*', *University of Toronto Quarterly*
81.4 (2012): 836–49.

57 Joyce Green MacDonald, 'Border Crossings: Women, Race, and
Othello in Gayl Jones's *Mosquito*', *Tulsa Studies in Women's
Literature* 28.2 (2009): 315–36.

58 *Othello*, ed. Russ McDonald (New York: Penguin, 2001);
Othello, The Moor of Venice, ed. Thomas Woodman
(Hyderabad, India: Orient Longmans, 2002); *Othello*, ed.
Norman Sanders (Cambridge: Cambridge University Press,
2003); *Othello*, ed. Edward Pechter (New York: Norton,
2003); Michael Neill, ed., *Othello* (already cited); *Othello*, eds
Barbara Mowatt and Paul Werstine (New York: Washington
Square Press, 2004); *William Shakespeare: Othello*, ed. Burton
Raffel (New Haven: Yale University Press, 2005); Bhattacharya,
ed., *Othello* (already cited); *Othello: Texts and Contexts*, ed.
Kim Hall (New York: Bedford/St. Martin's, 2007); *Othello*, eds
Jonathan Bate and Eric Rasmussen (Basingstoke, Hampshire
[UK]: Macmillan, 2009); *Othello*, ed. Adrian Coleman and
Shane Barnes (Elsternwick, Victoria, Australia: Insight, 2010);
*Shakespeare: Four Tragedies: Hamlet, King Lear, Othello,
Macbeth*, eds David Bevington and David Scott Kastan (New
York: Bantam Dell, 2004).

59 Nicholas Potter and Nicolas Tredell, eds, *William Shakespeare: Othello* (New York: Columbia University Press, 2000); Andrew Hadfield, ed., *A Routledge Literary Sourcebook on Shakespeare's Othello* (London: Routledge, 2003).

60 *William Shakespeare* Othello, ???? (Otillo), trans. Abul Quasem Khan Nasir al-malk (Nilofer 2007), and *William Shakespeare*, Othello ???? (Authilo), trans. Mohsin al-Khafiji (Darul Bahar, 2010).

61 Richard Proudfoot, 'Foreword', in E. A. J. Honigmann, *The Texts of* Othello *and Shakespearian Revision*, 1996 (rpt, London: Routledge, 2013), n.p.

62 'The Mystery of the Early *Othello* Texts', in Kolin, 401–24; see 420–1.

63 Leah Marcus, 'The Two Texts of *Othello* and the Early Modern Construction of Race', *Textual Performances: The Modern Reproduction of Shakespeare's Drama*, eds Lukas Erne and Margaret Jane Kidnie (Cambridge: Cambridge University Press, 2004), 21–36; see 22–3, 25, 32.

64 Gabriel Egan, *The Struggle for Shakespeare's Text: Twentieth-Century Editorial Theory and Practice* (Cambridge: Cambridge University Press, 2010).

65 *New Critical Essays*, 30–1.

66 'Introduction', *Screening Shakespeare in the Twenty-First Century*, ed. Mark Thornton Burnett and Ramona Wray (Edinburgh: Edinburgh University Press, 2006), 1.

67 Andrew Neiman, *Theater Mania*, 16 February 2000, http://www.theatermania.com/new-york-city-theater/reviews/02-2000/othello_230.html/?page=1 10.14.2013; D. J. R. Bruckner, 'THEATER REVIEW: New Clarity from a Colorblind "Othello"', *New York Times*, 17 February 2000.

68 Florianne Jiminez, internet essay at http://prezi.com/emugk0ep7pap/othello-in-film/, 11 October 2013; and Meghan Day, cited by Joel Worth in his electronic essay 'Watermarks: Othello and 20th-Century Race Consciousness', at http://www.llp.armstrong.edu/watermarks5/jw.html, 14 October 2013, respectively.

69 Laura Reitz-Wilson, 'Race and Othello in Film', *CLCWeb:*

Comparative Literature and Culture 6.1 (2004), http://dx.doi.
org/10.7771/1481-4374.1213

70 Charles Taylor, 'O', *The Salon.Com Reader's Guide to
Contemporary Authors*, 18 April 2002, quoted in Worth.

71 '"O" Movie Review', at http://movies.about.com/library/weekly/
aa083001a.htm. A negative view, on different grounds, was that
of James Welsh, who denounced the production's debasement of
Shakespeare's language; see 'Classic Demolition: Why Shakespeare
is Not Exactly "Our Contemporary" or, 'Dude, Where's My
Hankie?"', *Literature Film Quarterly* 30.2 (2002): 223–8.

72 Maitland McDonagh, 'Othello: Review', *TV Guide*, http://
movies.tvguide.com/othello/review/135918; Thomas Cartelli,
'Doing it Slant: Reconceiving Shakespeare in the Shakespeare
Aftermath', *Shakespeare Studies* 38 (2010): 26–36; see 21.

73 The *Guardian*, Saturday 26 May 2007.

74 'Othello', War Memorial Opera House, San Francisco, CA,
1 March 2002, http://www.criticaldance.com/reviews/2002/
sfb-othello_020301.html. The production was re-performed
by the Joffrey Ballet in Chicago's Auditorium Theater in April
2013, with Matthew Adamczyk and Valerie Robin as Othello
and Desdemona.

75 David Wiegand, 'PBS to show S. F. Ballet's "Othello"',
http://www.sfgate.com/entertainment/article/PBS-to-show-
S-F-Ballet-s-Othello-2,879,775php

76 http://www.imdb.com/search/text?realm=name&field=bio&q=
Eloise, 16 October 2013. The Australian film archives webpage
describes the plot as follows: 'Michael (Mark Jensen) and
Bruce (P J Parker) are the joint owners of a computer software
company that is the subject of a fierce takeover bid by a rival
corporation. Then Eloise (Melanie Holt), an inexperienced,
underqualified 22-year-old, applies for a job as Michael's
personal assistant. She's intelligent, has a sense of humour and
just happens to be good looking. Michael hires her on the spot.
But is Eloise all she claims to be? In fact, is anything what it
seems?' http://afcarchive.screenaustralia.gov.au/filmsandawards/
recentfilms/0304/feature_66.aspx, 16 October 2013.

77 A. O. Scott, 'Upstaged by the King, an Actor in Drag
Straightens Out', Movie Review: 'Stage Beauty', *New York*

Times, 8 October 2004, http://www.nytimes.com/2004/10/08/movies/08STAG.html?_r=0 10.18.2013

78 Richard Burt, 'Backstage Pass[ing]: *Stage Beauty, Othello* and the Make-Up of Race', *Screening Shakespeare,* 53–71; see 54.

79 http://bufvc.ac.uk/shakespeare/index.php/title/av67261, 16 October 2013.

80 http://www.aardvark.co.za/search/directory-search.php?scarch=cat&category=44

81 Jiminez; Naresh Kumar Deoshi, 'THE OMKARA MOVIE REVIEW: A brilliant adaptation, but an OK movie', http://www.apunkachoice.com/titles/omk/omkara/mid_755/reviews-editor/, 17 October 2013; Taran Adarsh, 'Omkara', *Bollywood Hungama,* 28 July 2006, http://www.bollywoodhungama.com/moviemicro/criticreview/id/201587, 17 October 2013. The film was the second Indian rendition of the play, the first being *Saptapadi* or 'The Seven Steps', in 1961. See Jiminez.

82 Michael Crabb, 'Alberta Ballet's Othello', *Dance Magazine,* http://www.dancemagazine.com/reviews/November-2007/Alberta-Ballets-Othello, 16 October 2013.

83 Denise Duguay, 'Da Vinci vs. Othello: A Tale of Two Dramas on CBC', *Gazette,* 13 June 2008, http://blogs.montrealgazette.com/2008/06/13/da-vinci-vs-othello-a-tale-of-two-dramas-on-cbc/, 17 October 2013.

84 'JARUM HALUS: Malaysian Othello, Trailer Now Online', http://twitchfilm.com/2007/12/jarum-halus-malaysian-othello-trailer-now-online.html, 16 October 2013; Jiminez; 'Film Review – JARUM HALUS', http://archive.is/wsHLB, 17 October 2013. See Jimenez.

85 Scott R. Ireland, '*Othello's Passion: A Kabuki Play by Karen Sunde, Shozo Sato*', Review, *Theatre Journal* 59.3 (2007): 495–7.

86 Chungfang Fei and William Sun, 'Othello and Beijing Opera: Appropriation as a Two Way Street', *Tulane Drama Review* 50.1 (2006): 120–3.

87 *Shakespeare in Asia: Contemporary Performance* ed. Dennis Kennedy and Yong Li Lan (Cambridge: Cambridge University Press, 2010).

88 Dan Bacalzo, 'Othello', *Theatre Mania*, 27 September 2009, http://www.theatermania.com/new-york-city-theater/reviews/09-2009/othello_21466.html, 17 October 2013.

89 Elaine Sciolino, '"Desdemona" Talks Back to "Othello"', *The New York Times*, 25 October 2011, http://www.nytimes.com/2011/10/26/arts/music/toni-morrisons-desdemona-and-peter-sellarss-othello.html, 17 October 2013.

90 Sciolino.

91 Rebecca Ascher-Walsh and Jess Cagle, 'Othello Goes Bollywood', *India Currents* 25.3 (2011): 46.

92 K. B. Nair, 'Terence Lewis Graces MAD Bollywood Dance Show', *India Journal*, 30 June 2011, http://www.indiajournal.com/archives/7570, 17 October 2013.

93 Ascher-Walsh and Cagle.

94 'Othello-Review', *The Observer*, 27 April 2013, http://www.theguardian.com/culture/2013/apr/28/othello-adrian-lester-national-review

95 Hedy Weiss, '"Othello: The Remix" Beats It Out of the Box', http://voices.suntimes.com/arts-entertainment/the-daily-sizzle/yo-billy-shakes-turn/

96 Burt (55). Burt makes this assertion to frame his analysis (cited earlier) of *Stage Beauty*. For the latter assertion that there is no authentic Shakespeare left any more, see 67–8.

97 Kathleen Glenister Roberts, *Alterity and Narrative: Stories and the Negotiations of Western Identities* (Albany: State University of New York Press, 2007), 191–200; also see 93–116 for a discussion of *Othello* in its parallels to modern history.

98 Burnett and Wray, 'Introduction', *Screening Shakespeare*, 5.

99 *Alternative Shakespeares*, Vol. 3, ed. Diana Henderson (London: Routledge, 2008).

Chapter 4

1 Margo Hendricks, 'Surveying "Race" in Shakespeare', in Catherine M. S. Alexander and Stanley Wells, eds, *Shakespeare*

and Race (Cambridge: Cambridge University Press, 2000), 1–23; see 20.

2   See, for a comprehensive survey of such work as it pertains to *Othello*, the previous chapters of this book.

3   A. C. Bradley, *Shakespearean Tragedy*, 2nd edn (London: Macmillan, 1905), 187.

4   G. K. Hunter, 'Elizabethans and Foreigners', in Alexander and Wells, eds, *Shakespeare and Race*, 37–63; see 56.

5   William Shakespeare, *Othello*, ed. E. A. J. Honigmann (Walton-on-Thames: Thomas Nelson, 1997), Introduction, 2. *Othello* is cited throughout from this edition.

6   Honigmann, Introduction, 29, with typographical error silently corrected.

7   Dympna Callaghan, '"Othello was a White Man": Properties of Race on Shakespeare's Stage', in *Alternative Shakespeares*, Vol. 2, ed. Terence Hawkes (London: Routledge, 1996), 192–215; see 193.

8   Imtiaz Habib, *Black Lives in the English Archives* (Aldershot: Ashgate, 2007), 12.

9   Duncan Salkeld, 'Black Lucy and the 'Curtizans' of Shakespeare's London', *Signatures* 2 (2000): 1.1–10, online at http://web.archive.org/web/20120209010831/http://www.chiuni.ac.uk/info/documents/signature_pdfs/Signatures_Vol2.pdf; Gustav Ungerer, 'The Presence of Africans in Elizabethan England and the Performance of *Titus Andronicus* at Burley-on-the-Hill, 1595/96', *Medieval and Renaissance Drama in England* 21 (2008): 19–55; Gustav Ungerer, 'Recovering a Black African's Voice in an English Lawsuit: Jacques Francis and the Salvage Operations of the Mary Rose and the Sancta Maria and Sanctus Edwardus, 1545–ca 1550', *Medieval and Renaissance Drama in England* 17 (2005): 255–71; Justin Champion, 'Elizabethan Subjects', a five-part Radio 4 series broadcast in March 2003; Miranda Kaufmann's Oxford D Phil thesis (2011) contains a number of new primary citations and awaits full publication; see also Guildhall Library, 'Black and Asian People Discovered in Records Held by the Manuscripts Section', http://www.history.ac.uk/gh/baentries.htm. All references to websites are implicitly dated January 2014.

10 Miranda Kaufmann, 'Caspar van Senden, Sir Thomas Sherley and the "Blackamoor" Project', *Historical Research* 81.212 (May 2008): 366–71.

11 For a more detailed review of the legal precedents, see Miranda Kaufmann, 'English Common Law, Slavery and', in Eric Martone, ed., *Encyclopedia of Blacks in European History and Culture* (Westport, CT: Greenwood, 2008), I: 200–3. On early English slaving, and the connections with *Othello*, see Robert Hornback, 'Emblems of Folly in the First *Othello*: Renaissance Blackface, Moor's Coat, and "Muckender"', *Comparative Drama* 35.1 (2001): 69–99.

12 William Harrison, *The Description of England*, quoted in Michael Neill, *Putting History to the Question: Power, Politics, and Society in English Renaissance Drama* (New York: Columbia University Press, 2000), 13.

13 Ungerer, 'Recovering a Black African's Voice', 264.

14 Kaufmann, 'English Common Law, Slavery and', 200–3.

15 For historical documentation, including Petrarch's evocative description of the slave-boats arriving at St Mark's, see Sally McKee, 'Domestic Slavery in Renaissance Italy', *Slavery and Abolition*, 29.3 (2008): 305–26.

16 *The Merchant of Venice*, 4.1.88–102, cited from John Drakakis, ed., *The Merchant of Venice*, 3rd edn (London: Bloomsbury, 2010). For recent discussion see Amanda Bailey, 'Shylock and the Slaves: Owing and Owning in *The Merchant of Venice*', *Shakespeare Quarterly* 62.1 (2011): 1–24.

17 Note also Iago's later casual allusions to slavery, discussed below.

18 My account here is somewhat at odds with Camille Wells Slights' 'Slaves and Subjects in *Othello*', *Shakespeare Quarterly* 48.4 (1997): 377–90. Slights' account of subjecthood in the play is compelling, but her stress is on the later English colonial toleration of slavery rather than on the contemporary rejections of the idea.

19 Habib, *Black Lives*, 184 and 189–90.

20 On the problems of historicizing racism see Meredith Anne Skura, 'Reading Othello's Skin: Contexts and Pretexts',

Philological Quarterly 87 (2008): 299-334. Skura argues – in a way that the current essay hopes to build on – that 'Othello is a play about prejudice, not race' (320).

21 Habib, *Black Lives*, 168.

22 Richard Brome, *The English Moor*, ed. Matthew Steggle, in Richard A. Cave, gen. ed., *Richard Brome Online* (2010). Online at http://www.hrionline.ac.uk/brome/. Revolving as it does around race, jealousy and a double time-scheme, *The English Moor* is also interesting as a little-discussed contemporary witness to *Othello*'s early reception.

23 Henry Jackson is about the only named individual: see Gāmini Salgādo, *Eyewitnesses of Shakespeare* (1975), 30.

24 Imtiaz Habib and Duncan Salkeld, 'The Resonables of Boroughside, Southwark: an Elizabethan black family near the Rose Theatre/Alienating laughter in *The Merchant of Venice*: a reply to Imtiaz Habib', *Shakespeare* (forthcoming). Online at http://www.tandfonline.com/doi/abs/10.1080/17450918.20 13.766633#.VKhK7yvF-So, and 'Alienating Laughter in *The Merchant of Venice*: A Reply to Imtiaz Habib', *Shakespeare* (2014). Roslyn L. Knutson was among the first scholars to draw attention to the records of the Resonables: 'A Caliban in St. Mildred Poultry', in *Shakespeare and Cultural Traditions: The Selected Proceedings of the International Shakespeare Association World Congress Tokyo 1991*, eds Tetsuo Kishi et al. (Newark: University of Delaware Press, 1994), 110–26.

25 Habib, 'The Resonables', 2.

26 Steve Rappaport, *Worlds within Worlds: Structures of Life in Sixteenth-Century London* (Cambridge: Cambridge University Press, 2002), 57, citing a complaint of 1595. This useful record reinforces the suppositions of Habib and Salkeld, and I owe it to the work of Kelechie Ezie, and to Miranda Kaufmann who drew my attention to that work.

27 Habib, 'The Resonables', 3.

28 Habib, 'The Resonables', 6.

29 Salkeld, 'Alienating Laughter', 20.

30 See Charles Nicholl, *The Lodger: Shakespeare on Silver Street* (London: Penguin, 2007), esp. 162–6. Nicholl quotes, for instance, Aufidius's description of Coriolanus: 'Breaking

his oath and resolution, like / A twist of rotten silk ...'
(*Coriolanus*, 5.2.96–7).

31 Salkeld, 'Alienating Laughter', 20.

32 For instance, Edward Blackman and Rose Banester, married
on 13 May 1612 at Saint Andrew By The Wardrobe: 'England
Marriages, 1538–1973', index, *FamilySearch* (https://
familysearch.org/pal:/MM9.1.1/NVJH-JHH). An 'Edmund s.
of Reasonable, blackmor' was buried at St Olave's in 1592, but
this is not necessarily the same sibling as our Edward: Habib,
Black Lives, 317.

33 Habib, *Black Lives*, 244, 316; Salkeld, 'Alienating Laughter', 14.

34 Coleridge, cited by Honigmann, Introduction 33.

35 Madhavi Menon, 'Of Cause', *English Studies* 94.3 (2013):
278–90.

36 On the 1595 report see Matthew Dimmock, *New Turkes:
Dramatizing Islam and the Ottomans in Early Modern
England* (Aldershot: Ashgate, 2005), 188–9. On the slipperiness
of identities, see Daniel Vitkus, *Turning Turk: English Theater
and the Multicultural Mediterranean, 1570–1630* (New York:
Palgrave Macmillan, 2003), especially Chapter 4 on *Othello*.

37 Habib, 'The Resonables', 9; G. E. Bentley, *The Jacobean and
Caroline Stage*, 7 vols (Oxford: Clarendon Press, 1942–68), 2:
541–3.

38 Edwin Nungezer, *A Dictionary of Actors* (1929; New York:
AMS Press, 1971), 49; Bentley, *JCS*, 2: 380.

39 Bentley, *JCS*, 2: 458, 459. Additionally, Habib proposes that
'Jehan Sehais', an English actor mentioned at Paris in 1598,
has a Persian-sounding name (*Black Lives*, 255): but this is
surely merely an effect of the record in question being in French
(Nungezer, *Dictionary of Actors*, 314).

40 Daphne Knott, 'John Accomy', *Hertfordshire Memories*, http://
www.hertsmemories.org.uk/page_id__594_path__0p3p101p.
aspx; Ann N. King, ed., *Muster Books for North and East
Hertfordshire, 1580–1605* (Cambridge: Hertfordshire Record
Society, 1996), xviii, 154. Thanks are due to Daphne Knott for
help in the writing of this piece, and for sharing the research
originally carried out by Dr Jill Barber.

41 For the whole family history see William Minet, 'The Capells at
    Rayne, 1486–1622', *Transactions of the Essex Archaeological
    Society* n.s. 9 (1906): 243–72.

42 'Henry Capell (II)', in P. W. Hasler, ed., *The
    House of Commons* (1981), online at http://www.
    historyofparliamentonline.org/volume/1558-1603/member/
    capell-henry-ii-1579-1622

43 Reproduced, for instance, in Ronald Hutton, 'Capel, Arthur,
    first Baron Capel of Hadham (1604–1649)', *Oxford DNB*.

44 See Virginia F. Stern, *Gabriel Harvey: His Life, Marginalia, and
    Library* (Oxford: Clarendon Press, 1979).

45 'Henry Capell (I)', in P. W. Hasler, ed., *The House of Commons*
    (1981), online at http://www.historyofparliamentonline.org/
    volume/1558-1603/member/capell-henry-i-1588; Jason Scott-
    Warren, 'Harvey, Gabriel (1552/3–1631)', *Oxford DNB*.

46 Dedication to 'The right Worshipfull Sir Arthur Capell, &
    his noble Sons': Camden, *Annales*, trans. Abraham Darcie
    (London: Benjamin Fisher, 1625), n.sig.; William Perkins,
    Lectures vpon the three first chapters of the Reuelation
    (London: Cuthbert Burbie, 1604), ¶3r.

47 James Shapiro, *1599: A Year in the Life of William
    Shakespeare* (London: Faber and Faber, 2006), 79–80.

48 W. I. Zeitler, 'The Date of Spenser's Death', *Modern Language
    Notes* 43.5 (May 1928): 322–4; but note that Zeitler's
    judgement is founded partly on the fact that he can't find a
    Henry Capell of an appropriate age, when in fact Henry Capell
    (II) fulfils that requirement perfectly.

49 J. and J. A. Venn, eds, *Alumni Cantabrigienses Part I: From
    the Earliest Times to 1751*, 4 vols (Cambridge: Cambridge
    University Press, 1924), 1: 290.

50 For the Lincoln's Inn entry, see *The records of the honorable
    society of Lincoln's Inn* (Lincoln's Inn: n.p., 1896), 1: 122; for
    the other details, the *History of Parliament* biography.

51 For the debate about Othello's Christianity, and the widespread
    belief that he is identified as a Christian convert, see
    Honigmann, Introduction, 22–3.

52 Barber's notes, citing HALS ref: DP43/1/1.

53 'England Marriages, 1538–1973', index, *FamilySearch* (https://familysearch.org/pal:/MM9.1.1/NVPW-6QL), Willyam May and Peronell Wright, 28 January 1580; William is listed in 1583 among the 'Chief inhabitantes and householders' of the village: see King, ed., *Muster Books*, 10.

54 *Othello*, 1.2.66, 70–1; Barber's notes, citing HALS ref: DP43/1/1.

55 Minet, 'The Capells at Rayne'.

56 In 1580, a 'Temperance Swain' had been baptized in Campton, about 30 miles north of Hertford, and she could possibly be John's wife in 1614, although both geography and chronology are a little awkward.

57 'African Caribbean People in Hertfordshire, 1570–1830', http://www.hertsmemories.org.uk/page_id__174_path__0p3p101p.aspx; for the history of the parish, see Graham Irwin, *A History of Brickendon* (2004), online edition at http://www.compassion-in-business.co.uk/brickendon

58 'England Births and Christenings, 1538–1975', index, *FamilySearch* (https://familysearch.org/pal:/MM9.1.1/J74N-Z58), Penelope, 20 March 1614. The 1631 record is in HALS: Hertford Borough Records, Vol. 25, f.7.

59 'England Marriages, 1538–1973', index, *FamilySearch* (https://familysearch.org/pal:/MM9.1.1/N28Z-Z47), Richard Clarke and Dambrose Ochymy, 4 February 1632.

60 Habib, 'The Resonables', 3.

61 Habib, *Black Lives*, 68; for Elizabeth's black servant, Thomasen, recorded in 1577, see *Black Lives*, 72.

62 Habib, *Black Lives*, 75.

63 Habib, *Black Lives*, 76.

64 Salkeld, 'Alienating Laughter', 14.

65 Reproduced in Maureen M. Meikle and Helen Payne, 'Anne (1574–1619)', *Oxford DNB*. Discussed by Miranda Kaufmann in a blog post: 'The Other Man in Red', *Miranda Kaufmann*, http://www.mirandakaufmann.com/3/post/2013/08/the-other-man-in-red.html

66 Habib, *Black Lives*, 147–9.

67 Habib, *Black Lives*, 325.

68 For servants attending the theatre, see Andrew Gurr, *Playgoing in Shakespeare's England*, 3rd edn (Cambridge: Cambridge University Press, 2004), 233, 238, 272 (in the retinue of their masters); 57, 77, 79, 250 (apparently without their masters).

69 Karen Newman, '"And Wash the Ethiop White": Femininity and the Monstrous in *Othello*', in Jean Howard and Marion F. O'Connor, eds, *Shakespeare Reproduced: The Text in History and Ideology* (New York: Methuen, 1987), 143–62; see 144.

70 For two competing discussions of the play in terms of service, see Mark Thornton Burnett, *Masters and Servants in English Renaissance Drama and Culture: Authority and Obedience* (London: Macmillan, 1997); Michael Neill, '*Servant Obedience and Master Sins*: Shakespeare and the Bonds of Service', in *Putting History to the Question*, 33–48; for a reading in terms of slavery, see Slights, 'Slaves and Subjects in *Othello*'. The reading offered here is to some extent at odds with all three of these.

71 *Othello*, 5.2.337; 'slave' is used of Cassio (3.3.445); Roderigo (5.1.62); Othello, arguably (5.2.274); and Iago (4.2.134; 5.2.241, 288, 330).

Chapter 5

1 See, for instance, Robert B. Heilman, 'Dr. Iago and His Potions', *The Virginia Quarterly Review* 28 (1952): 568–84; James A. S. McPeek, 'The "Arts Inhibited" and the Meaning of *Othello*', *Studies in English* 1 (1955): 129–47; David Kaula, 'Othello Possessed: Notes on Shakespeare's Use of Magic and Witchcraft', *Shakespeare Studies* 2 (1966): 112–32.

2 See Barbara Rosen, ed., *Witchcraft in England, 1558–1616* (Amherst: University of Massachusetts Press, 1991). Rosen reprints *Newes from Scotland* (190–203); see 198.

3 See Rosen, 196–8.

4 Laura Apps and Andrew Gow, *Male Witches in Early Modern*

Europe (Manchester: Manchester University Press, 2003), 13, 25–6, 45.

5 Apps and Gow, 104, 107, 110, 126.

6 E. J. Kent, 'Masculinity and Male Witches in Old and New England, 1593–1680', *History Workshop Journal* 60 (autumn 2005): 69–92; 71.

7 Marion Gibson, *Early Modern Witches: Witchcraft Cases in Contemporary Writing* (New York: Routledge, 2000).

8 Gibson, 178, 291.

9 Gibson, 50. See R. A. Foakes, ed., *Coleridge's Criticism of Shakespeare: A Selection* (London: Athlone, 1989), 113.

10 Gibson, 51.

11 Gibson, 53, 61, 63–4.

12 All references to *Othello* are to the Arden text, ed. E. A. J. Honigmann (London: Bloomsbury, Arden Shakespeare, 2007).

13 Gibson, 125, 139.

14 Gibson, 149.

15 See, for example, Gibson, 182–5, 189, 192–3, 199, 206–17, 239–42, 247, 255, 276, 281–2, 286–7 and 291–5).

16 See, for example, Gibson 184, 192, 193, 207, 214, 281–2 and 286.

17 Gibson, 276, 294–5.

18 See, for instance, Alison Rowlands, ed., *Witchcraft and Masculinities in Early Modern Europe* (New York: Palgrave Macmillan, 2009); Rolf Schulte, *Man as Witch: Male Witches in Central Europe* (New York: Palgrave Macmillan 2009); and especially Malcolm Gaskill, 'The Devil in the Shape of a Man: Witchcraft, Conflict, and Belief in Jacobean England', *Historical Research* 71.175 (1998): 142–71. See also Erika Anne Gasser, 'Manhood, Witchcraft, and Possession in Old and New England' (PhD dissertation, University of Michigan, 2007); and David Davis, 'Regarding Men: The Insufficiency of the Current Early Modern Witchcraft Paradigm', *Eras Journal* (Monash University), http://www.arts.monash.edu.au/publications/eras/edition-7/davisarticle.php (accessed 11 January 2014).

19 Rosen 55, 58.

20 [King James VI of Scotland], *Daemonologie In Forme of a Dialogie Diuided into three Bookes*. By James RX, printed by Robert Walde-graue, printer to the Kings Majestie. [Edinburgh] An. 1597.

21 King James, *Daemonologie*, xi, 2, 44, 49, 51, 63.

22 King James, *Daemonologie*, 63.

23 King James, *Daemonologie*, 8.

24 King James, *Daemonologie*, 35–7.

25 *Othello*, ed. Alvin Kernan in *Four Great Tragedies*, eds Kernan et al. (New York: Signet, 1998), 18; *Othello*, ed. Michael Neill (Oxford: Oxford University Press, 2006), 222; *Othello*, ed. Norman Sanders (Cambridge: Cambridge University Press, 2003), 83; *Four Tragedies: Hamlet, Othello, King Lear, Macbeth*, ed. David Bevington and David Scott Kastan (New York: Bantam Dell, 2005), 338; *Othello*, eds. Barbara A. Mowat and Paul Werstine (New York: Washington Square, 1993), 36; *Complete Pelican Shakespeare*, eds. Stephen Orgel and A. R. Braunmuller (New York: Penguin, 2002), 1407; *Othello*, ed. Russ McDonald (New York: Penguin, 2001); *CliffsComplete Othello*, ed. Kate Maurer (New York: Wiley, 2000), 47.

26 Edward Pechter, *Othello and Interpretive Traditions* (Iowa City: University of Iowa Press, 1999), 75.

27 King James, *Daemonologie*, 78–9.

28 King James, *Daemonologie*, 32–4.

29 King James, *Daemonologie*, 4.

30 King James, *Daemonologie*, 4.

31 See note in Ridley's 1958 Arden edition (London: Methuen, 1958), for 2.3.304–5.

32 King James, *Daemonologie*, 45.

33 For this and other such statistics, see Marvin Spevack, *The Harvard Concordance to Shakespeare* (Cambridge: Harvard University Press, 1969).

34 King James, *Daemonologie*, 37.

35 King James, *Daemonologie*, 23.

36 King James, *Daemonologie*, 47.

37 King James, *Daemonologie*, 44.

38 Honigmann, ed., *Othello*, 327n.

39 King James, *Daemonologie*, xi.

40 King James, *Daemonologie*, 9.

Chapter 6

1 I am grateful to Lena Cowen Orlin who organized the Shakespeare Association of America seminar (2012) to which I contributed an early version of the current article, and I would also like to thank the seminar members who commented on my paper.

2 Emrys Jones, '"Othello", "Lepanto" and the Cyprus Wars', *Shakespeare Survey* 21 (1968): 47. Other critics have also seen the play as a tribute, even if for considerably different reasons. See, for example, Eric Griffin, 'Unsainting James: Or, *Othello* and the "Spanish Spirits" of Shakespeare's Globe', *Representations* 62 (1998): 83: 'the play might have been considered an appropriate occasional piece of James's 1613 wedding of state'. Griffin bases his conclusion on a somewhat strained idea of faith, and, curiously, a mistaken impression regarding 'the triumph of the Holy Catholic League in the War of Cyprus' (83).

3 *Othello*, ed. E. A. J. Honigmann (Walton-on-Thames: Thomas Nelson, 1997), 2.1.22. Further references to the play are in the text.

4 In her abstract for the SAA seminar mentioned above, Joanna Montgomery Byles made similar observations about the Ottoman occupation of Cyprus and asked why Shakespeare depicted the Turkish raid as unsuccessful. Shakespeare and his audience might well have shared the understandable misconception that the naval triumph at Lepanto had freed the island.

5 Battista Giraldi Cinthio, *Hecatommithi, overo Cento Novelle* (Venice, 1608; first published 1565), Part 1, decade 3, story 7,

315: 'Et non passò molto, che il Moro, per haver messa mano
alla spada il Capo di Squadra, nella guardia, contra un soldato,
& datagli ferite, lo privò del grado: la qual cosa fù gravissima
a Disdemona. E molte volte haveva tentato di rappacificare il
Marito con lui'. ('And not much time passed before the Moor
deprived the Corporal of his rank for having put his hand to
his sword against a soldier while on guard duty and given him
a wound: which was very serious to Disdemona. And many
times she had tried to reconcile her husband with him.') I have
regulated *u* and *v*. Translations are mine.

6   By pleading for a soldier whose crime is so serious, Desdemona
makes herself particularly vulnerable to Iago's insinuations.

7   Cinthio, 319.

8   Robert Appelbaum, 'War and Peace in *The Lepanto*', in Peter
Herman, ed., *Reading Monarchs Writing: The Poetry of Henry
VIII, Mary Stuart, Elizabeth I, and James VI/I* (Tempe, AZ:
MRTS, 2002), 199; see 180.

9   Appelbaum, 199.

10 Jones, 50.

11 James I, *His Maiesties Lepanto, or Heroicall Song* (London,
1603), B1r, no line numbers. This edition was published to
coincide with James's accession to the throne. As Jane Rickard
notes, 'the *Lepanto* ... was published in Edinburgh in [James's]
second collection as a separate edition, and republished in
London in 1603. It was also translated into French in 1591,
into Dutch in 1593, and into Latin in 1604.' She argues that,
by adding a preface to the original, unpublished text of the
mid-1580s, James sought to change his representation of
himself as equally a poet and a king and 'to emphasize that
he is writing as a King'. See Jane Rickard, 'From England to
Scotland: The Poetic Strategies of James VI and I', *Renaissance
Forum* 7 (winter 2004), Π.2: 7–8: online journal: http://www.
hull.ac.uk/renforum/v7/rickard.htm#top. See also Peter Herman,
*Royal Poetrie: Monarchic Verse and the Political Imaginary in
Early Modern England* (Ithaca, NY: Cornell University Press,
2010), esp. 171–4 where Herman offers a subtle reading of the
Lepanto as a poem that 'splits itself neatly down the middle in
its valuation of the anti-Turkish forces' religion' (173).

12 Andrew Wheatcroft, *Infidels: A History of the Conflict Between Christendom and Islam* (New York: Random House, 2005), 18.

13 Wheatcroft, 18.

14 Paul A. Jorgensen, Review of *Shakespeare Survey*, ed. Kenneth Muir, *Shakespeare Quarterly* 23 (1972): 268. Jones points out that Richard Knolles in 1603 dedicated the *Generall Historie of the Turkes* to King James (Jones, 48).

15 Richard Knolles, *The Generall Historie of the Turkes from the first beginning of that Nation to the rising of the Othoman Familie: with all the notable expeditions of the Christian Princes against them* (London, 1610; 2nd edn), author's induction, no page numbers. I have silently regularized *v* and *u* in this text.

16 Knolles, 847.

17 Giovanni Canevari, *In Mustafam*, in *The Battle of Lepanto*, ed. and trans. by Elizabeth R. Wright, Sarah Spence and Andrew Lemons (Cambridge: I Tatti Renaissance Library, Harvard University Press, 2014), pp. 44–7. The quotation is taken from lines 1–4, and the translation is on the facing page. All further citations will be in the text.

18 Daniel J. Vitkus, 'Turning Turk in *Othello*: The Conversion and Damnation of the Moor', *Shakespeare Quarterly* 48 (1997), 169–70.

19 Ibid., Canevari, xiv.

20 Cinthio, 313; cf. Geoffrey Bullough's translation in Honigmann, 371.

21 Knolles, 855.

22 Cinthio, 313; cf. Bullough in Honigmann, 371.

23 Knolles, 855.

24 William Malim, *The true Report of all the successe of Famagosta* (London, 1572), 9.

25 Malim, 13. See also 14–15 for Malim's account of Bragadino's further humiliations: he was made 'to carrye two baskets of earth' and 'enforced also to kisse the ground' as often as the 'unfaythfull tyrant *Mustafa*' passed him; he

was 'placed in a chaire ...was winched up in that chaire, and fastened unto the Maineyarde of a Galley, and hoysted up with a Crane, to shew him to all the Christian soldiers and slaves ... he being afterward let down, and brought to the market place, the tormentors tooke of hys clothes from hym, and tacked hym unto the Pillary, whereas he was most cruelly fleyed quicke'.

26 George Gascoigne, *A Hundreth Sundrie Flowres*, ed. G. W. Pigman III (Oxford: Clarendon Press, 2000). The 'devise of a masque' is Flowre, 71, pp. 301–12. Further references will be to line numbers and will appear in the text. Cf. p. 657 for Pigman's remark on Hakluyt.

27 Robert Ralston Cawley, 'George Gascoigne and the Siege of Famagusta', *MLN* 43 (1928), 297.

28 'And for further proofe, he shewed his hat, / This token whiche the *Mountacutes* do beare always, for that / They covet to be known from *Capels* where they passe, / For ancient grutch which long ago tween those two houses was' (261–4). Like Shakespeare, Gascoigne would have known of the families from Arthur Brooke's *Romeus and Juliet* as well as from William Painter.

29 Tempests, storms and shipwrecks are ubiquitous in early modern drama, so it's probably absurd even to suggest that Shakespeare needed Gascoigne to give him the idea of a tempest in connection with Cyprus. Nevertheless, it's an interesting coincidence.

30 Cf. *Royal Poetrie*, 172. Peter Herman discusses a similar 'balancing' in regard to religious affiliations: 'the *Lepanto* exemplifies James's sometimes clumsy, sometimes adept strategy throughout his Scottish reign of balancing Catholic interests against those of the Protestants'.

31 See Peter Moore, 'Shakespeare's Iago and Santiago Matamoros', *N&Q* 43 (1996): 162–3. Cf. William Woodson, 'Iago's Name in Holinshed and the Lost English Source for *Othello*', *N&Q* 25 (1978): 146–7: Woodson strongly suggests that Shakespeare derived Iago's name and age from Holinshed's passage on King Iago or Lago, 'who dyed without issue, when hee had raigned eyght and twentie yeeres'. His argument is

meant to dismiss M. R. Ridley's postulation of a lost ur-text, and does not engage the question of Santiago.

32 Laurie Maguire, *Shakespeare's Names* (Oxford: Oxford University Press, 2007), 48.

33 G. N. Murphy, 'A Note on Iago's Name', *Literature and Society* (1964), 43; see 41.

34 Wheatcroft, 31.

Chapter 7

1 John Ford, *Love's Sacrifice*, ed. A. T. Moore (Manchester: Manchester University Press, 1,627), I.i. 243–372. All further quotations from the play will be taken from this edition and reference will be given in the text.

2 William Shakespeare, *Othello*, ed. E. A. J. Honigmann (London: Thomas Nelson and Sons, 1997), 2.1.189, 5.2.345 and 5.2.141.

3 Clare Carroll, ed., *Othello and the Tragedy of Mariam* (London: Longman, 2002).

4 Elizabeth Cary, *The Tragedie of Mariam, the Faire Queene of Iewry* (London: Thomas Creede for Richard Hawkins, 1613), sig. F3r.

5 Lisa Hopkins, 'Pocahontas and *The Winter's Tale*', *Shakespeare* 1.2 (December 2005): 121–35.

6 Lisa Hopkins, 'Black but Beautiful: *Othello* and the Cult of the Black Madonna', in *Marian Moments in Early Modern Drama*, ed. Regina Buccola and Lisa Hopkins (Ashgate, 2007), 75–86; see 80.

7 Caroline P. Murphy, *Isabella de' Medici: The Glorious Life and Tragic End of a Renaissance Princess* (London: Faber and Faber, 2008), 326.

8 Sara Eaton, 'Beatrice-Joanna and the Rhetoric of Love in *The Changeling*', *Theatre Journal* 36.3 (October 1984): 371–82; see 381.

9 Kim F. Hall, *Things of Darkness: Economies of Race and*

Gender in Early Modern England (Ithaca, NY: Cornell University Press, 1995).

10 Dympna Callaghan, '"Othello was a White Man": Properties of Race on Shakespeare's Stage', in *Alternative Shakespeares*, Vol. 2, ed. Terence Hawkes (London: Routledge, 1996), 198 and 202.

11 See, for instance, Gary Younge, 'Is it cos I is black?', *The Guardian*, Wednesday 12 January 2000. Online: http://www.guardian.co.uk/world/2000/jan/12/race

12 See, for instance, G. F. Sensabaugh, 'John Ford and Platonic Love in the Court', *Studies in Philology* 36.2 (April, 1939): 206–26.

13 William Shakespeare, *Cymbeline*, ed. J. M. Nosworthy (London: Arden, 2007), V.i.1–5.

14 'Knowing their Loves: Knowledge, Ignorance and Blindness in *'Tis Pity She's a Whore*', *Renaissance Forum* 3.1 (spring 1998), http://www.hull.ac.uk/renforum/v3no1/hopkins.htm

15 John Ford, *The Lady's Trial*, ed. Lisa Hopkins (Manchester: Manchester University Press, 2012), 5.2.142–3.

16 See Lisa Hopkins, 'The Representation of Narrative: What Happens in *Othello*', *Journal X* 1.2 (Spring 1997): 159–74; see 168.

17 See, for instance, Lina Perkins Wilder, *Shakespeare's Memory Theatre: Recollection, Properties and Character* (Cambridge: Cambridge University Press, 2010), 142, and Richard Wilson, 'Dyed in Mummy: *Othello* and the Mulberries', in *Performances of the Sacred in Late Medieval and Early Modern England*, ed. Susanne Rupp and Tobias Döring (Amsterdam: Rodopi, 2005), 135–53; see 147.

Chapter 8

1 For complete bibliographical information about works cited in this article, see the list of resources at the conclusion.

SELECT
BIBLIOGRAPHY

Adamson, Jane. *Othello as Tragedy: Some Problems of Judgment and Feeling*. Cambridge: Cambridge University Press, 1980.

Altman, Joel B. *The Improbability of Othello: Rhetorical Anthropology and Shakespearean Selfhood*. Chicago: University of Chicago Press, 2010.

Aspects of Othello: Articles Reprinted from Shakespeare Survey. Ed. Kenneth Muir. Cambridge: Cambridge University Press, 1977.

Barthelemy, Anthony Gerard, ed. *Critical Essays on Shakespeare's Othello*. New York: Hall, 1994.

Benson, Sean. *Shakespeare, Othello, and Domestic Tragedy*. London: Continuum, 2012.

Bradley, A. C. *Shakespearean Tragedy: Lectures on Hamlet, Othello, King Lear, Macbeth*. London: Macmillan, 1905.

Calderwood, James L. *The Properties of Othello*. Amherst: University of Massachusetts Press, 1989.

Campbell, Lily Bess. *Shakespeare's Tragic Heroes: Slaves of Passion*. Cambridge: Cambridge University Press, 1930.

Carlisle, Carol Jones. *Shakespeare from the Greenroom: Actors' Criticism of Four Major Tragedies*. Chapel Hill: University of North Carolina Press, 1969.

Dean, Leonard F., ed. *A Casebook on Othello*. New York: Crowell, 1961.

Draper, John W. *The Othello of Shakespeare's Audience*. New York: Octagon, 1966.

Elliott, George Roy. *Flaming Minister: A Study of Othello as Tragedy of Love and Hate*. Durham, NC: Duke University Press, 1953.

Elliott, Martin. *Shakespeare's Invention of Othello: A Study in Early Modern English*. New York: St Martin's, 1988.

Erickson, Peter and Maurice Hunt, eds. *Approaches to Teaching*

Shakespeare's Othello. New York: Modern Language
  Association of America, 2005.
Granville-Barker, Harley. *Preface to Othello*. Princeton: Princeton
  University Press, 1958.
Hadfield, Andrew, ed. *William Shakespeare's Othello: A
  Sourcebook*. London: Routledge, 2002.
Hall, Joan Lord. *Othello: A Guide to the Play*. Westport, CT:
  Greenwood, 1999.
Hampton-Reeves, Stuart. *Othello*. The Shakespeare Handbooks.
  New York: Palgrave Macmillan, 2011.
Hankey, Julie, ed. *Othello*. 1987. 2nd edn. Shakespeare in
  Production. Cambridge: Cambridge University Press, 2005.
Heilman, Robert B. *Magic in the Web: Action and Magic in
  Othello*. Lexington: University of Kentucky Press, 1956.
Honigmann, E. A. J. *The Texts of Othello and Shakespearian
  Revision*. London: Routledge, 1996.
Johnson, Vernon Elso, ed. *Race in William Shakespeare's Othello*.
  Farmington Hills, MI: Greenhaven, 2012.
Jones, James Earl. *Othello*. London: Faber, 2003.
Kaul, Mythili, ed. *Othello: New Essays by Black Writers*.
  Washington, DC: Howard University Press, 1997.
Kolin, Philip C., ed. *Othello: New Critical Essays*. New York:
  Routledge, 2002.
MacLiammóir, Micheál. *Put Money in Thy Purse: The Filming of
  Orson Welles' Othello*. 2nd edn. London: Methuen, 1976.
Mikesell, Margaret Lael and Virginia Mason Vaughan. *Othello: An
  Annotated Bibliography*. New York: Garland, 1990.
Nardo, Don, ed. *Readings on Othello*. San Diego: Greenhaven,
  2000.
Nostbakken, Faith. *Understanding Othello: A Student Casebook
  to Issues, Sources, and Historical Documents*. Westport, CT:
  Greenwood, 2000.
Orlin, Lena Cowen, ed. *Othello*. New Casebooks. New York:
  Palgrave Macmillan, 2004.
Pechter, Edward. *Othello and Interpretive Traditions*. Iowa City:
  University of Iowa Press, 1999.
Potter, Lois. *Othello*. Shakespeare in Performance. Manchester:
  Manchester University Press, 2002.
Potter, Nicholas, ed. *William Shakespeare: Othello*. Columbia
  Critical Guides. New York: Columbia University Press, 2000.

Potter, Nick. *Othello: Character Studies*. London: Continuum, 2008.

Rosenberg, Marvin. *The Masks of Othello: The Search for the Identity of Othello, Iago, and Desdemona by Three Centuries of Actors and Critics*. Berkeley: University of California Press, 1961.

Snyder, Susan, ed. *Othello: Critical Essays*. New York: Garland, 1988.

Stanislavsky, Konstantin. *Stanislavsky Produces Othello*. Trans. Helen Nowak. London: Bles, 1948.

Swindall, Lindsey R. *The Politics of Paul Robeson's Othello*. Jackson: University Press of Mississippi, 2011.

Vaughan, Virginia Mason. *Othello: A Contextual History*. Cambridge: Cambridge University Press, 1994.

Vaughan, Virginia Mason and Kent Cartwright, eds. *New Perspectives on Othello*. London: Associated University Presses, 1991.

Wain, John, ed. *Shakespeare: Othello – A Casebook*. London: Macmillan, 1971.

INDEX

Lightning Source UK Ltd.
Milton Keynes UK
UKOW05f0616300916

284084UK00013B/228/P